Poverty, Riches and Social Citizenship

Hartley Dean
Reader in Social Policy
Department of Social Studies
University of Luton

with

Margaret Melrose
Researcher
Department of Social Studies
University of Luton

Foreword by Ruth Lister

Consultant Editor: Jo Campling

First published in Great Britain 1999 by
MACMILLAN PRESS LTD
Houndmills, Basingstoke, Hampshire RG21 6XS and London
Companies and representatives throughout the world

A catalogue record for this book is available from the British Library.

ISBN 0–333–71455–5 hardcover
ISBN 0–333–76498–6 paperback

First published in the United States of America 1999 by
ST. MARTIN'S PRESS, INC.,
Scholarly and Reference Division,
175 Fifth Avenue, New York, N.Y. 10010

ISBN 0–312–21684–X

Library of Congress Cataloging-in-Publication Data
Dean, Hartley, 1949–
Poverty, riches and social citizenship / Hartley Dean with
Margaret Melrose.
p.   cm.
Includes bibliographical references (p.   ) and index.
ISBN 0–312–21684–X
1. Income distribution—Great Britain.   2. Welfare state.
3. Public welfare—Great Britain.   4. Citizenship—Great Britain.
5. Marginality, Social—Great Britain.   6. Social values—Great
Britain.   I. Melrose, Margaret.   II. Title.
HC260.I5D4   1998
339.2'0941—dc21   98–7075
                                                                  CIP

This book is printed on paper suitable for recycling and made from fully managed and
sustained forest sources.

10   9   8   7   6   5   4   3   2   1
08   07   06   05   04   03   02   01   00   99

Printed and bound in Great Britain by
Antony Rowe Ltd, Chippenham, Wiltshire

Also by Hartley Dean

DEPENDENCY CULTURE: The Explosion of a Myth
(*with P. Taylor-Gooby*)

ETHICS AND SOCIAL POLICY RESEARCH (*editor*)

PARENTS' DUTIES, CHILDREN'S DEBTS: The Limits of Policy
Intervention (*editor*)

SOCIAL SECURITY AND SOCIAL CONTROLS

WELFARE, LAW AND CITIZENSHIP

Contents

List of Figures

List of Tables

Foreword

Citizenship has reemerged as a pivotal academic and political concept in recent years both in the UK and more widely. Politically, in the UK, notions of citizenship underpin, either explicitly or implicitly, many of New Labour's pronouncements. The academic literature on citizenship is burgeoning. Much of this literature has been a mixture of the theoretical and the normative. It has rarely been grounded in empirical work that investigates the range of popular understandings of citizenship.

Herein lies the value of Hartley Dean and Margaret Melrose's new work. It combines the theoretical and the empirical, thereby helping to move on our thinking not only about citizenship but also about how understandings of citizenship relate to the experience and perception of poverty and wealth. The empirical work is located in a wide-ranging theoretical discussion and, in turn, informs further theorising. As the authors acknowledge, much of this theorising is inevitably tentative and speculative, given the 'exploratory' nature of their study. Moreover, the findings are often complex, reflecting sometimes contradictory sets of responses. They thus lend themselves to more than one interpretation.

The discussion of perceptions of poverty and riches takes us back to Runciman's path-breaking study of relative deprivation and it attempts to update his analysis in the context of the more acute inequalities of the 1990s. It highlights how the fear of poverty seems to outweigh the aspiration to wealth and how comfort, security and possibly a bit of fun can be more important ambitions than riches as such. The mixture of complacency and anxiety that the researchers detected among the members of 'comfortable England' could be seen as giving more support to Will Hutton's thesis of the 30:30:40 society, in which the middle group are marked by insecurity, than to J.K. Galbraith's notion of the 'contented majority'.

The findings on citizenship are salutary to those of us who incessantly debate its meaning and significance: for most of the study's respondents the word itself meant nothing and had little or no significance! Nevertheless, when questioned about the substance of citizenship and their perceptions of the 'good' and 'bad' citizen, some interesting insights emerged. Among these were the importance attached to social citizenship. Most of the respondents disagreed with the neo-liberal thesis that social rights are categorically different from civil and political rights and therefore do not constitute rights of citizenship. Instead, they believed that rights to health care, education and social security are or should be the same kind of rights as those to the vote or free speech. There was also, particularly among women, a conception of the 'good citizen' as someone who looks after others. This is in tune with much recent feminist theorising about citizenship which has made the case for the recognition of care work to citizenship, thereby challenging the centrality accorded to paid work in the construction of citizenship obligations. Interestingly, paid work did not seem to figure in the respondents' conceptions of citizenship.

The recognition of the value of care is one element in contemporary feminist attempts to refashion citizenship on more inclusive lines. Another key challenge is the accommodation of diversity and difference into what is an essentially universalist concept, albeit an imperfect and exclusive expression of universalism. The authors explore this from the perspectives of gender and ethnicity/'race'. They suggest that women and minority ethnic groups face the options of assimilation to dominant white masculine paradigms or ghettoisation in the private sphere or ethnic community. These represent 'equality' and 'difference' strategies, neither of which offers, on its own, a satisfactory path to a more genuinely inclusive model and practice of citizenship. There is, though, they suggest a third option: the renegotiation of 'the basis of their citizenship by insisting on changes in publicly defined assumptions and universal values'. This is an example of how we need to transcend the dichotomous thinking that places an obstacle in the way of more creative thinking about how to forge a more inclusive model of citizenship.

This leads the authors to a more normative discussion of how social citizenship should be seen as a strategic terrain upon which to take forward struggles for both social redistribution to challenge the persistence of poverty and inequality and cultural freedoms that give recognition to diverse identities and voices. Here they draw upon Nancy Fraser's attempt to reconcile what she calls a 'politics of redistribution' and a 'politics of recognition'. Indeed, the whole approach taken in the book can be seen as just such an attempt to address both material and cultural/identity issues in taking forward the theorisation of poverty, riches and citizenship.

Ruth Lister
Professor of Social Policy, Loughborough University and author
of Citizenship: Feminist Perspectives (Macmillan, 1997).

Introduction

In Britain, by the 1990s, the gap between rich and poor had become greater than at any time since the modern welfare state ushered in the age of 'social citizenship'. There is at present a considerable volume of up-to-date academic literature on poverty and inequality (for example, Alcock 1993; Barclay 1995; Hills 1995; Oppenheim and Harker 1996; Becker 1997; Gordon and Pantazis 1997), and a vigorous intellectual debate about the nature of citizenship (for example, Roche 1992; Twine 1994; Lister 1997). There are, however, three things which make this particular book distinctive: the perspectives from which we examine the issues; the way in which our inquiry develops the work of other commentators; and a unique theoretical approach. As such the book will be of interest to students, teachers and researchers in social policy, sociology and related subjects, but also to anybody who has ever wondered how it is that, while social inequality is so stark, political commitment to tackle it is so ambivalent.

From What Perspective?

We share with many social policy academics an overriding concern about poverty and how to abolish it. This book, however, deliberately concerns itself with the rich as well as the poor and, most importantly, with the perceptions of those 'ordinary' citizens who are neither rich nor poor. Outside the world of academia and those who study or comment on the development of social policy, people tend not to talk very much or very openly about the issues of poverty and riches, or the significance of social citizenship for human welfare. We have therefore set out to explore popular rather than expert discourses and values. It is through everyday experiences and beliefs that poverty and riches have their impact and through which citizenship and welfare achieve their importance.

Building on Past Research

This book has grown, not only out of original research on the part of the authors, but also a body of past research. First, we have sought to follow in the steps of Runciman's classic investigation,

Relative Deprivation and Social Justice (1966), although that was carried out over 30 years ago when the size and significance of the divide between rich and poor was not so great and the future of the welfare state was less under threat. Second, we have drawn on such sources as the British Social Attitudes surveys, although here we have been concerned to develop deeper qualitative insights into the way that people regard issues of citizenship and welfare than is possible through public opinion surveys alone. Third, we have been concerned critically to explore the apparent contradictions between the findings of those commentators who suggest that contemporary Britain is shaped by the complacency of a comfortable majority (for example, Galbraith 1992) and those who suggest, in different ways, that it is shaped by chronic anxiety (for example; Pahl 1995; Hutton 1996).

A New Contribution to Theory

The argument developed throughout the book has two novel elements. First, it introduces models or taxonomies through which to define, on the one hand, the competing traditions that inform theories and discourses of citizenship and, on the other, the contradictory moral repertoires which inform popular discourses and values. The importance of this approach is that it helps to make sense of the dynamics of political trends and of the contradictory tendencies and potential within popular perceptions and beliefs. Secondly, the book explores the sense in which social citizenship represents an intermediary sphere of action which can confront both the structural or class determinants of poverty and riches, and the manner in which they are constituted at the level of social and cultural experience and individual identity. The importance of this approach is that it provides the possibility of a strategy which combines concerns with equality with concerns about difference.

Plan of the Book

Our opening chapter attempts to convey the sheer scale of the gap between the poor and the rich, before introducing the work of Runciman and others on relative deprivation, and the more recent debate about changes in the fundamental nature of capitalist society. The chapter concludes by introducing the first stage in our theoretical argument concerning the classification of popular discourses.

The next two chapters are concerned with poverty and riches; with the extent to which people worry about becoming poor; the vicarious fun they obtain from observing or imagining the lives of the rich; the store they place on being comfortable and of having security against the risks of everyday life. Chapter 2 focuses on the way in which poverty is socially constituted as a spectre which haunts us all, and Chapter 3 upon riches as a spectacle whose allure, though pervasive, is not as strong as the fear of poverty.

The next three chapters are concerned with citizenship, with the limited sense of obligation and belonging which people obtain from often highly restricted conceptions of citizenship, and how such conceptions may be insufficient to allay the immanent anxieties associated with the imperatives of contemporary lifestyles. Chapter 4 introduces a discussion of the various concepts of citizenship, of their associated moral repertoires and of social attitudes to welfare. Chapter 5 explores the extent to which the current transitions affecting the nature of the welfare state are experienced and how they relate to people's expectations. Chapter 6 is concerned with differential experiences of citizenship on the part of women and minority ethnic groups.

The final chapter presents both a synopsis of the principal arguments and a concluding discussion. Readers wishing to follow the theoretical argument advanced in the book, without focusing on the evidence that sustained its development, may wish to concentrate on Chapters 1, 4 and 7. It is suggested however that, in order properly to evaluate the argument, the text needs to be read as a whole. Technical details of the specific study that informed the writing of the book – including a summary of key 'headline' findings – are presented separately as an Appendix.

Acknowledgements

The authors would like first to express their gratitude to the Economic and Social Research Council, which funded the research on which this book is substantially based (under Award Ref: R000236264); Whitbread plc, who generously assisted with the construction of the interview sample for that research; the numerous informal and community contacts who also contributed to the construction of the sample; Louise Hoile for administrative support; and to the 76 people from different backgrounds and widely differing levels of income and wealth who gave so generously of their time to make that research possible.

We should also extend our thanks to Jo Campling for her assistance and support and to the various colleagues who have read and helpfully commented on early drafts of some or all the chapters, including Alison Assiter, Tony Fitzpatrick, Martin Powell and Peter Taylor-Gooby. None the less, responsibility for errors of fact and interpretation and for the views expressed in this book rest with the authors – and primarily with Hartley Dean who, as the principal author, would like to extend his personal thanks to Margaret Melrose for her conscientious and insightful assistance.

1 Of Poverty and Riches

> The rich man in his castle,
>   The poor man at his gate,
> God made them high and lowly,
>   And ordered their estate.

This trite homily, from a nineteenth century English hymn, has been held up as a classic manifestation of the outdated theodicy that once justified or mitigated the sufferings of landless labourers and the urban proletariat (Walter 1979: 19–20). Though quaintly atavistic, the words themselves and the sentiment they express remain pertinent. They announce a view that attributes the distinction between rich and poor, if not to fate, then to some inevitable ordinance or structure: a view that dwells on the spectacles of wealth and poverty (the grand castle and the public beggar) and so obscures the everyday nature and variety of the pleasures, expectations and injustices experienced, not only by rich and poor *men*, but by invisible women and children and by the anonymous majority that lays claim to be neither rich nor poor.

The terms 'rich' and 'poor' are functions of social inequality. A widely endorsed view within contemporary social policy is that poverty is 'the unacceptable face of inequality' (Alcock 1993: 255). Though 'wealth' is not usually said to be unacceptable in the same way as poverty, Tawney (1913) once remarked that 'What thoughtful rich people call the problem of poverty, thoughtful poor people call with equal justice a problem of riches'. Inequality does not necessarily imply the existence of poverty or riches. It is the result of the processes by which material resources are distributed to and between individual members of society; both income (the *flow* of resources) and wealth (the *stock* of resources) (see, for example, Spicker 1988: 112). Rich and poor are essentially moral categories which are employed in the discourses we apply to the process of social distribution.

The ordering of the income and wealth which constitute the 'estates' of the rich and poor may seldom now be attributed to God. Later in this book, we shall discuss the different 'moral repertoires' on which people do draw to define the nature of their membership

1

in society and the justice of the social distribution of resources. For now, however, we shall briefly outline the different ways in which people might apprehend or explain the persistence of poverty and riches. Where people regard the *extent* of inequality as 'unacceptable', it is possible that this is still seen by some as a matter of fortune or fate. Others (including left-leaning political commentators, the poverty lobby and many social policy academics) see it as a matter of social injustice; as the result of relations of class, status or power in society; and as a consequence of social divisions based on gender, ethnicity, disability or age. There are, however, people who do not necessarily regard inequality as unacceptable (the classic case for the functionality of inequality is put by Davis and Moore 1945); who may think or 'feel' that most, if not all, inequality is justifiable on the basis of individual merit or desert. Others consider that it is right that competence, effort and achievement should be rewarded with riches, while incompetence, sloth and failure should be punished by poverty. It is possible that some may still believe that the respective statuses of the poor and rich are rightly and properly ascribed by birth or breeding.

Defining poverty and riches is therefore ideologically controversial. What this chapter will do is first to discuss recent evidence concerning the gap between the rich and poor, before moving on to introduce the concepts of deprivation and privilege; concepts which have been developed in ways which to some extent sidestep the moral considerations outlined above. We shall then turn to the critical concept of social class and recent arguments that the nature of class and social divisions is changing. In the light of that discussion we shall outline a theoretical model which we plan to develop further in the course of the book in order to help understand the different ways in which people understand poverty and riches.

THE GAP BETWEEN RICH AND POOR

During the last quarter of the twentieth century the gap between the richest and the poorest members of society increased, not only in the UK, but throughout the world.

It is a trend which has been particularly marked in the UK, where the income share of the poorest tenth of the population fell from 4.2 per cent of national income in 1961 to 3.0 per cent in 1991,

Figure 1.1 Changing income inequality in the UK
(Gini-coefficient for equivalent net incomes of individuals, after housing
costs, with three year average smoothing, from 1961 to 1991)

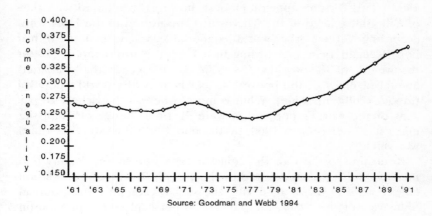

Source: Goodman and Webb 1994

while that of the richest tenth rose from 2 per cent to 25 per cent
(Goodman and Webb 1994: 66). Applying an index of inequality –
the Gini coefficient, which uses a scale from 0 (complete equality)
to 1 (complete inequality) – it may be seen from Figure 1.1 that
the change in income inequality (after incomes are adjusted for
household size and inflation) had been on a general downward trend
until the end of the 1970s, but that it rose rapidly during the 1980s.

In the 1980s income inequality increased faster in the UK than in
any other developed country except New Zealand (Barclay 1995: 14).
At the time of writing, the latest official government statistics (DSS
1996a) show that the gap between the rich and poor has at last stopped
widening: they show none the less that, although aver-age real
incomes in the UK rose by 40 per cent between 1979 and 1993–95,
for the richest tenth of the population they rose by 65 per cent,
while for the poorest tenth they actually fell by 13 per cent.

Changes in the distribution of marketable wealth as opposed to
income appear to be less marked. Though inequalities had been
declining since the 1960s (and indeed throughout the twentieth
century – see Scott 1994), they flattened out in the 1980s. None
the less, the distribution of wealth remains far more unequal than
the distribution of income. In 1992, the richest tenth of wealth holders
owned nearly 50 per cent of all individual wealth (Barclay 1995:
31). Evidence from the *Sunday Times'* survey of Britain's richest

500 people shows that the very richest in the population are getting richer, with the top ten places going to billionnaires, the richest of them being reputed to own £3000m (*Sunday Times*, 6 April 1997). This fortune appears modest, however, compared with that of Bill Gates, head of the Microsoft Corporation in the USA who, according to the Forbes world league table, was valued at $18 billion (Keegan 1996). According to a United Nations report (1996) the wealth of the world's 358 billionaires exceeds the combined annual incomes of the poorest 45 per cent of the world's population (2.3 billion people). What is more, whereas the richest 20 per cent of the world's population were 30 times better off than the poorest 20 per cent in 1960, by the mid 1990s they were 61 times wealthier.

Returning to the UK, the concern expressed by the *Inquiry into Income and Wealth* sponsored by the Joseph Rowntree Foundation (Barclay 1995) was that, during the social, economic and political upheavals of the 1980s, the poorest 30 per cent of the population had simply failed to share in economic growth. Even the OECD (cited by Balls 1996) has acknowledged that, whereas the UK and the USA in the 1980s and '90s had faster growth in wage inequality than any other OECD country, there was no evidence of wealth 'trickling down' to benefit the poor as a result. Evidence from the EU (reported in *The Guardian*, 28 April 1997 and *Poverty*, No. 97, Summer 1997) shows that in 1993 the extent of poverty in the UK (defined as the proportion of households having less than half national average income) relative to other EU members was worsening: with 23 per cent of households at or beneath the EU poverty line, the UK was in tenth place out of twelve countries. The proportion of children living in households with less than half average national income, at 32 per cent, was higher than in any other EU country. A wider study, using an income inequality measure (allowing for the effects of taxes and social security benefits) and based on some 20 countries, put the UK in third worst place, after Russia and the USA (Bradshaw and Chen 1997). Data is available which, again using the Gini coefficient (see above), makes it possible to compare changes in income inequality in ten quite different countries. The outcome, summarised in Figure 1.2, confirms that inequality has been increasing especially fast in the UK.

The reasons for this are complex. At a national level it is clear that economic restructuring, demographic and social change, and changes in welfare and fiscal policy have all played a part (Barclay

Figure 1.2 Changing income inequality in ten countries
(Gini-coefficient for equivalent net incomes drawn from Luxembourg
Income Survey data sets circa 1980, 1985 and 1990)

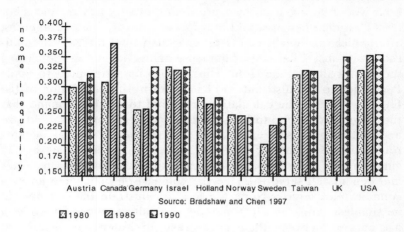

Source: Bradshaw and Chen 1997

1995; Hills 1995; George and Howards 1991). By the end of the
twentieth century the UK was experiencing higher levels of unemployment, wider pay differentials, greater fluidity in family and
household arrangements, and less redistributive tax and social security systems than during the immediate post-war period. Situat-
ing these changes in a global context, the last quarter of the twentieth
century has witnessed the spread of New Right thinking in the First
World, the collapse of communism in the Second World, and the
dominance of monetarist policy prescriptions by the IMF and the
World Bank in the Third World. The result, it has been argued, is
the ascendancy or reassertion of a classical or neo-liberal version
of the capitalist project and the global permeation and tolerance
of the patterns of inequality upon which that project depends (Taylor-
Gooby 1994a; Jordan 1996).

Our purpose in this chapter, however, is not to debate the extent of inequality, but to give readers some sense of its scale. Perhaps the best way to conceptualise the sheer size of the gap betwen
the poorest and the richest in the UK is to deploy a device first
suggested by the Dutch economist Jan Pen (1971). Pen suggested
that, if we could imagine how tall people would be if their height
was proportionate to their incomes and what it would be like if
the entire population then paraded past us in order of size, this
would give a dramatic visual illustration of how income is distributed.

Pen reckoned that, if the entire British population were transformed and paraded in this way so that people on average incomes were of average height and the parade lasted for an hour, most of that hour would be taken up by a procession of very tiny people. People of average height would not appear until the last 12 minutes, after which the height of the processants would increase dramatically, with just a handful of immense giants passing in the closing seconds of the parade. John Hills (1995) has attempted to apply Pen's idea to the distribution of incomes in the population of the UK in 1990–91. The calculations required to do this demand that the income attributed to individuals be adjusted for household size and that account is taken of taxes paid and social security benefits received: the economic consequences of living alone or having children and the effects, for example, of housing tenure on taxes and benefits all serve to make the comparison of income levels a complicated exercise. None the less, to illustrate the outcome in its simplest terms, in Hills' parade, a childless couple of working age earning between them an average equivalent net income of £254 per week would each have measured about 5 ft 8 in (173 cm); a pensioner couple on a state pension would each have measured 2 ft 1 in (63 cm); an 'empty nester' middle aged couple with a combined gross income of £36 600 per annum would each have measured 11 ft 11 in (363 cm). At the beginning of the parade some people would be invisible, because they effectively had negative incomes, and the giants at the end of the parade would have been up to 4 miles (over 6 km) tall!

In an industrialised liberal democracy such as the UK, at the end of the twentieth century the gap between the poorest and the richest citizens is quite staggering (and is as great as it is, for example, in Nigeria – see UN 1996).

DEPRIVATION AND PRIVILEGE

Examining the extent of inequality does not tell us what constitutes poverty or riches. It has been said that poverty, like beauty, 'lies in the eye of the beholder' (Orshansky 1969: 37), and the same could be said of riches. There have been attempts by right wing politicians in the UK to deny the existence of poverty. Successive Secretaries of State with responsibility for social security have claimed that economic progress has put an end to poverty (Moore 1989;

Lilley 1996). It has been argued that poverty is a concept artificially perpetuated by left-leaning academics and the poverty lobby and that, given the adequacy of water and food supplies and the living standards achieved even by those on the lowest incomes in the UK, measures to tackle poverty are appropriate only in the 'underdeveloped' countries of the Third World. In 'developed' countries, what is more, poverty is not only relative, it is dynamic: people may move out as well as in to poverty in the course of time. Poverty rates calculated on the basis of life-time incomes have been shown in the USA and the UK to be half those calculated on the basis of annual incomes (Walker 1995).

Such arguments reflect a fierce debate about the definition of poverty. Although this book is concerned more with popular discourses and understandings of poverty and wealth than with those of experts or politicians, it is important briefly to revisit controversies about definition. The issues date back to seminal inquiries into poverty and wealth conducted in the late Victorian era (Rowntree 1901; Booth 1902; Chiozza-Money 1905). These commentators applied more or less arbitrary thresholds by which to distinguish poor from rich and it is sometimes assumed that they were defining the 'absolute' standards below or above which they believed poverty and riches to occur. In fact, the essential preoccupation which informed those studies was with proving or disproving the existence of avoidable poverty or undeserved riches: they sought explanations in the *behavioural* characteristics of the rich and poor. Booth and Rowntree each quantified and demonstrated the existence of extensive urban poverty. Booth, however, distinguished the poverty of 'loafers', the 'vicious and semi-criminal' and 'feckless' casual earners from the 'ordinary poverty' of those in regular or unavoidably intermittent work whose means in spite of their efforts were 'barely sufficient for decent independent life'. Rowntree similarly distinguished between 'primary' poverty attributable to a lack of resources sufficient for bare 'physical efficiency' and 'secondary' poverty which was attributable, not to want, but to waste or lack of knowledge. Chiozza-Money sought to distinguish between those whose wealth rendered them 'comfortable' and those whose resources would permit the indulgences of the 'rich'. He demonstrated that, at the turn of the twentieth century in Britain, just over a third of all household income went to the 'rich', who, by his definition, made up just under 3 per cent of the population. This 'error of distribution' he attributed in substantial part to the distorting and

Figure 1.3   Depths of poverty (after George and Howards 1991)

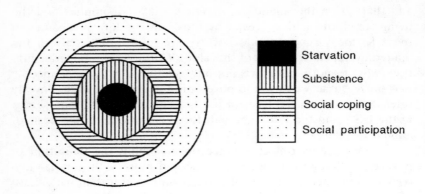

unmeritocratic effects of family property and inheritance as opposed to the legitimate wealth of successful industrialists and entrepreneurs. Poverty or riches alike may be regarded as either deserved or undeserved.

In the 1960s and '70s, both in the UK and the USA (Abel-Smith and Townsend 1965; Harrington 1962), renewed concerns were expressed about poverty. The approaches which were subsequently developed drew a distinction between 'absolute' measures of poverty (such as Rowntree's measure of mere 'physical efficiency') and 'relative' measures which take account of changing living standards and which assume that the explanation of poverty and riches is to be found in the *structural* characteristics of society, rather than the behavioural characteristics of those who experience poverty. Peter Townsend's authoritative definition of relative poverty held that people experience poverty 'when they lack the resources to obtain the types of diet, participate in the activities and have the living conditions and amenities which are customary, or are at least widely encouraged or approved, in the societies to which they belong' (1979: 31). George and Howards (1991) insist that this expansive definition of poverty is not necessarily inconsistent with narrower definitions. They chart a continuum of four possible definitions of poverty which do not conflict but complement each other. The depth of poverty, they say can be assessed in a composite manner by applying consecutively criteria based on starvation, subsistence, social coping and social participation standards (see Figure 1.3). While in counties like Britain we may claim to ensure that people do not starve and that they are guaranteed the means of subsistence, we do not necessarily ensure that everybody can cope by the standards of our own society or that they can be full participants in the economic, cultural and political life of society.

While poverty in Britain may not be as 'deep' as in sub-Saharan Africa or on the Indian sub-continent, it remains by Townsend's definition both severe and extensive. In a major study, conducted in 1969, Townsend sought to define a poverty line. His argument was that 'as the resources for any individual or family diminish, there is a point at which there occurs a sudden withdrawal from participation in the customs and activities sanctioned by the culture' (1979: 57). To locate the point at which this withdrawal occurs, Townsend constructed an elaborate index of relative deprivation based on people's capacity to attain various different aspects of every day social activity.

The methods Townsend used and his search for a definitive point at which lack of income results disproportionately in relative deprivation proved controversial (Piachaud 1981; Mack and Lansley 1985), but the concept of relative deprivation remains important. Writers such as Lister (1990a) and Scott (1994) have sought to make explicit what is implicit in Townsend's work, that poverty may be understood as an exclusion from the public sphere of citizenship. Increasingly, the notion of 'poverty' has been superseded in European debates by the broader term 'social exclusion' (Room 1995). Scott takes the idea of exclusion a stage further by suggesting that relative privilege as much as relative deprivation entails a kind of exclusion. Scott argues that it is possible to study privilege in a way that is analagous to that in which Townsend studied deprivation:

> Privilege arises at a particular point in the distribution of resources, which can be termed the 'wealth line'. It may be hypothesised that the wealth line marks a point in the distribution of resources at which the possibility of enjoying special benefits and advantages of a private sort escalates disproportionately to any increase in resources. The wealth line, like the poverty line, is a threshold point at which exclusionary mechanisms come into operation. (Scott 1994: 152)

The poverty and wealth lines may be conceived as the very boundaries of our citizenship (see Figure 1.4). The concept of citizenship and

Figure 1.4 Deprivation, privilege and citizenship
A visual presentation of Scott's (1994) model

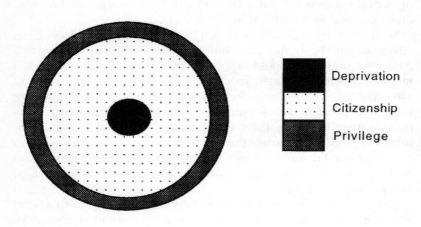

institutionalised notions of 'membership' of the public world of society are issues to which we shall return in Chapter 4. For now, however, we should like to emphasise a particular aspect of Scott's thesis, for which he relies on the common etymological roots of the words 'deprivation' and 'privilege'. Both words originate from the Latin word *privatus*, from which the modern English word 'private' is derived (*ibid*: 150). Private is the opposite of public: it refers to a state of exclusion – whether it be enforced or voluntary – from that which is public. To be deprived is to be dispossessed from those things which other members of the public enjoy. To be privileged is to be secluded or immune from the ordinary course of public life. Whether or not the boundaries which delineate the extremes of deprivation and privilege in Figure 1.4 are susceptible to quantitative definition, the conceptual meaning or symbolic relevance of such boundaries to social actors ought to be capable of empirical investigation at a qualitative level.

In fact the concept of 'relative deprivation' had been explored empirically, in a study in 1962, by Runciman (1966). Runciman's concern was not poverty or riches, but social justice. His study sought sociological explanations of the ways in which patterns of social inequality are tolerated and a normative critique of inequality based on a contractarian theory of social justice (cf. Rawls 1972). Runciman's study is important for us, not for his theory of social justice, but because it represented a seminal attempt to explore relative deprivation as an intersubjective phenomenon. The notion of relative deprivation and the related concept of 'reference groups' had been appropriated by sociology from psychology in the 1950s (see Merton 1957).

Put simply, the argument is that people may identify and/or compare themselves with a variety of different social reference groups. Depending on their choice of reference groups, people may feel varying degrees of relative deprivation; for example, because they resent the disadvantages to which their own group is subject, or because they aspire to membership of another. One of the classic studies cited by Runciman (1966: 23) related to the effects of a tornado in Arkansas, USA, where it had been observed that householders resident quite close to the epicentre of the tornado and those resident at the very periphery of the disaster area felt less deprived than those who had been living in the intermediate zones. Those who had been very close to the households that had been hardest hit felt themselves lucky to have escaped death or serious injury, while those on the periphery felt themselves lucky to have escaped serious damage to their property: the intermediate residents, however, were less likely to be aware of the devastation suffered at the epicentre and were more likely to contrast their situation unfavourably with those at or beyond the periphery who had suffered little or no loss. The extent to which people *feel* deprived does not necessarily correlate directly with any objective measure of the extent to which they *are* deprived.

Reflecting the preoccupations of sociology in Britain in the early 1960s, Runciman sought to explore the extent to which people assigned themselves to classes which might not coincide with objective classifications based on occupational status, income or political interests. He went further, however, by also exploring the extent to which people felt relatively deprived in relation to other reference groups. His findings indicated that 'comparative reference groups were limited in scope' and that 'relative deprivation is low in both magnitude and frequency even among those who are close to the bottom of the hierarchy of economic class' (1966: 192). Runciman goes so far as to assert that the choices of comparative reference groups particularly by manual workers was, not only restricted, but 'even illogical'. To paraphrase, the extent of inequality in Britain in the 1960s was sustainable because people's perceptions of their own relative deprivation or privilege was moderated by their limited awareness of other people's circumstances and the scope of inequality.

This important finding must be considered in the light of three factors. First, the extent of social inequality, as has been shown above, is even greater now than in the 1960s. Second, the dynamics of class and social divisions and the nature of our understanding of social diversity have radically changed since the 1960s: these changes will be discussed below. Third, there are certain theoretical limitations to Runciman's approach and these we shall address briefly here.

Runciman acknowledges that the 'most difficult question of all' is 'how far a person's reference group should be seen as the cause or the effect of his [*sic*] other aspirations and attitudes' (1966: 15). The concept of reference groups remains intractably psychologistic and to explain how people determine their choice of reference group Runciman tends to resort to further psychological concepts (such as 'salience') rather than to reflect on the ways in which reference groups may themselves be socially constructed. To the extent that different reference groups are available for individuals to 'choose' from, they are not *a priori* options. They are neither naturally nor purposively created, but derive and sustain themselves from an historically specific social relational context in which the individual is already implicated as a contributing actor and creator of meanings. In fairness, the elaboration of notions of social construction was only beginning at the time of Runciman's study (e.g. Berger and Luckman 1967).

Runciman seeks to characterise individuals with reference to an ideal type taxonomy. This we present – in an adapted form – in Figure 1.5. Reference group theory distinguishes between relative deprivation which stems from a person's dissatisfaction with the reference group to which s/he belongs and relative deprivation which stems from dissatisfaction with inequalities between different reference groups. If this is accepted there are four types of person: 'orthodox' people who do not experience relative deprivation and are satisfied with their lot – however rich or poor they might be; 'egoists' who are dissatisfied with their present reference group and aspire to achieve the advantages enjoyed by another; 'fraternalists' who identify strongly with their own reference group but resent the disadvantages to which that group is subject; people who are doubly relatively deprived because they are dissatisfied both with the position of their group and their membership of it (1966: 32–34).

Figure 1.5 Relative deprivation and Runciman's taxonomy of individual 'types'

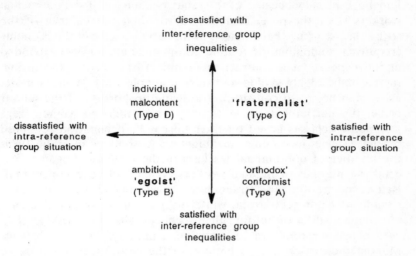

The taxonomy is inherently unsatisfactory and Runciman himself only makes use of the distinction between 'egoistic' characteristics (which he contends to be suggestive of middle class propensities) and 'fraternalistic' characteristics (which he contends to be suggestive of working class propensities). The reasons for our interest in this flawed taxonomy (and for the particular orientation of the axes in Figure 1.5) will become clear later in this chapter. The taxonomy, we suggest, is capable of taking on meaning if one considers each of the quadrants in Figure 1.5, not as a type of individual personality, but as a socially constructed tradition or set of discursive repertoires or strategies on which individuals may in certain circumstances draw. It is possible to analyse and define the ways in which people contend with inequality on an everyday basis: acquiescence; selfishness; solidaristic resistance; individualistic resistance. This is a theme to which we shall shortly return.

FROM CLASS SOCIETY TO RISK SOCIETY

British society in the 1960s, like most industrialised western societies, was conventionally conceptualised in terms of a cleavage between a working class principally composed of manual workers and a 'middle class' composed of non-manual workers, although the boundary between these classes was even then seen to be potentially problematic, especially because of the relative affluence of skilled manual workers (Goldthorpe *et al* 1969). Since then the balance of the social class structure has changed as the service sector of the economy (requiring predominantly routine non-manual employees) expanded at the expense of a contracting manufacturing centre (requiring, increasingly, highly skilled and flexible employees). What is more, as women began to constitute a growing proportion of the labour force, the patriarchal convention by which married women were assigned to classes based on their husband's occupation rendered official statistics increasingly meaningless. At some point in the 1980s the number of non-manual workers in the economy began to exceed the number of manual workers. What had been conceptualised as the 'middle class' fragmented or was revealed as containing significantly different strata, while the growth of structural unemployment made it more difficult to conceptualise the working class as a single stratum (for an excellent summary, see Sarre 1989). Marxist theorists began to emphasise the contradictory nature of occupational class locations (Wright 1985), while Weberian theorists posited the emergence of a new and relatively powerful 'service class' composed of executives and managers (Goldthorpe 1980).

Other theorists have questioned the importance of class divisions, emphasising that other social divisions – such as those of gender and 'race' – are and have always been at least as significant in determining patterns of substantive inequality. This is an argument which has been advanced from a Weberian position on the one hand, and from feminist and anti-racist positions on the other. Parkin (1979) has sought to develop the concept of 'social closure': the idea that groups in society manoeuvre to exclude other groups from benefits and privileges or to usurp the benefits and privileges enjoyed by others. Williams (1989) has emphasised the ways in which ideologies of family and nation are implicated in the social distribution of resources and the particular disadvantages experienced by women and minority ethnic groups. She has also pointed to the ways in which recent social and economic upheavals render diversity and difference within society more visible (Williams 1992).

As the class basis of inequality has become increasingly obscured, new ideas have emerged about where the fault lines in society might lie. Some of these ideas are informed by changes in patterns of consumption, others by changes in processes of production. From a predominantly Weberian perspective, writers like Saunders (1984; 1990) have argued that changes in the mode of consumption have generated classes based on status rather than economic location. He has claimed that the decisive social divisions (including those which predict voting behaviour) tend to stem from consumption location and, in particular, whether people satisfy their requirements for housing, transport, education, health care and so forth privately, or from the public sector. From what is sometimes termed a post-Marxist perspective, a very different view has been advanced which suggests that the 'new times' in which we live are characterised by a shift from Fordist to post-Fordist modes of production and distribution (Hall and Jacques 1989; Burrows and Loader 1994). These commentators argue that new technologies, management processes and marketing techniques have resulted, on the one hand, in a fissure between a secure 'core' within the labour market and a vulnerable 'periphery', and on the other in an explosion in the diversity of lifestyles. The economic journalist Will Hutton (1996), has recently portrayed Britain, not in conventional class terms, but as a '30/30/40' society in which, he claims, 30 per cent of the population are 'disadvantaged' in terms of employment prospects and life-styles, 30 per cent are 'insecure' and the remaining 40 per cent are 'privileged'.

Therefore, while the gap between the richest and poorest can be demonstrated quite clearly, there is considerable disagreement and uncertainty about how to conceptualise the distribution of resources and the extent of deprivation and privilege within the compass of that gap. It is a paradox that, as inequality has increased, traditional conceptions of class have been challenged. The most extreme way in which the top and bottom class locations have been characterised has been in terms of an 'underclass' and an 'overclass'. The term 'underclass' has been employed on both the right and the left of the political spectrum to define or, more usually, to symbolise, either those who are alleged by their behaviour to have excluded themselves from the realms of ordinary society, or those whom society itself has excluded or oppressed. One of the present authors has already argued at some length that the underclass concept is so theoretically flawed and empirically imprecise as to be valueless (Dean and Taylor-Gooby 1992; Mann 1994). Equally, while it is possible to posit the existence of an overclass – a rich elite which uses its economic wealth to isolate itself from society in exclusive fortified communities or settlements while continuing to exercise power over the lives of others – the value of the term by itself is limited. None the less, a recent contribution to the debate by Jordan (1996) provides an interesting reformulation of the ideas of underclass and overclass. Drawing on Hirst (1994), Jordan distinguishes between 'communities of fate' and 'communities of choice'. The former are those ghetto communities which are entrapped by a particular set of social-ecological circumstances (cf. Wilson 1987) and may define themselves through a retaliatory 'culture of resistance'. The latter are those communities which have the freedom and the power to 'vote with their feet' and establish themselves without regard for the social-ecological consequences (the replacement of community housing with exclusive luxury residential developments in London's Dockland is, perhaps, a good example).

Jordan's central thesis – elements of which we shall call into question in Chapter 2 – is that our society is composed of overlapping multi-layered social formations which are differentiated in increasingly complex ways.

> The processes by which such collectivities have formed include coercion and subordination (for instance, of women and slaves in households, or of subjects in polities), technological forms of inclusion and exclusion (as in all kinds of 'clubs', including nation states) and self-selection ('voting with the feet', as in residential segregation). Most group interactions involve elements of all three of these processes. The common future of all kinds of collectivities is that members benefit from restrained competition among themselves, and mobilize for more effective competition with other social formations. (1996: 41)

The concept of 'collectivities' employed here is at the same time more concrete and more dynamic than that of Runciman's concept of reference groups. It is a model of social organisation which, while purporting to be of universal application, is appropriate to a society in which the calculation and management of risk is a central preoccupation. To an extent, therefore, the model chimes with what Beck (1992) has defined as the 'risk society'. Beck contends that the process of modernisation which dissolved feudal society replaced the myths of religion with new myths based on science. What is now occurring is a new process of 'reflexive modernisation' which is dissolving industrial society by making transparent the 'collective self-injury' to which scientifically informed processes of global economic growth subject us. The social and ecological hazards of wealth production (such as inequality, pollution and the depletion of natural resources) are less easily managed or justified as mere side-effects. In place of the statuses ascribed by fate in mediaeval society, and overlapping with the positions accorded by class in industrial society, we are are now subject to a fate or position that is risk-determined. The implication of Beck's argument is that 'we no longer live in a class society, but a risk society' (Offe 1996: 33).

Beck's ideas are linked to an essentially normative ecological project, but they do cast light on the ambiguity of class as an organisational category and, for example, the rise of new social movements. Research in Britain in the 1980s by Marshall *et al* (1988) suggested that people do still locate themselves in terms of class; that society is still 'shaped predominantly by class rather than other forms of social change' (*ibid*: 183). It was acknowledged none the less that 'awareness of class is not a function of class location' (*ibid*: 184) and, regardless of class identity it seems, people tend to be individualistic, instrumentalist and pragmatic in a way which led Marshall *et al* to conclude – rather dramatically – that 'contemporary British society lacks a moral order, and. . . . its cohesion is rooted more in resignation and routine than consensus and approval' (*ibid*: 143). Whatever has happened to class, it can be said that perceptions of the risks of living in a highly unequal society and the context in which people are able to apprehend and negotiate those risks clearly do seem to be changing.

NEGOTIATING INEQUALITY: THE FOUNDATIONS OF A NEW TAXONOMY

Poverty and riches are a part of the context in which we live out our lives, but how do we identify who is poor and who is rich? How do we know whether or not we are ourselves poor or rich? How might we contend with the risk that we may become poor or rich? These are questions which this book will attempt to answer but, in order to do so, it is necessary to develop a rather more effective theoretical model or taxonomy of the different ways in which people might respond than that used by Runciman (see Figure 1.5 above). To do this we shall first call, rather briefly, on the work of two very different theorists: Anthony Giddens and Mary Douglas.

There are parallels between the work of Giddens (1990; 1991) and that of Beck whom we have just discussed. These two writers have more recently together developed the concept of 'reflexive modernization' (Beck, Giddens and Lash 1994). Giddens' original formulation of the concept was closely linked to a discussion of the conditions for ontological security under conditions of 'late modernity'. He was concerned with the impact of social processes: with the reflexivity which is required of individuals under conditions of modernity in order that they might place trust in abstract technical and administrative systems and maintain social relations across increasingly indefinite spans of time and space; with the anxiety that is entailed in the maintenance of self-identity and ontological security in a society that is full of 'social hazards' (Beck 1992) and increasingly characterised by economic and environmental risk and uncertainty.

In another context, the present authors (Dean and Melrose 1997) have sought to articulate Giddens' particular concepts of reflexivity and ontological security with the concepts of 'grid' and 'group' in the work of the anthropologist Mary Douglas (1978) (and one of us more recently has sought to develop this line of thinking further – see Dean, forthcoming). Douglas is best known for developing a cultural typology model based on two intersecting dimensions which she defines as 'grid' and 'group'. The concept of grid relates to the extent to which systems of classification in society are shared or private, to which a society employs common rituals as a means to negotiate social reality, to which (borrowing from Bernstein) codes of discourse are restricted or elaborated. A grid-bound person, therefore, will characteristically draw on received myths and established traditions, whereas a person less constrained by grid might draw on more radical or independently contrived interpretations of the world

The concept of group relates to the extent to which individuals in society are controlled by other people's pressure or to which they are able to exert pressure on others, to which people are integrated through group social relations or alienated from them. A group-bound person, therefore, will characteristically share reciprocal loyalties with members of the community of organisation in which s/he lives or works, whereas a less group constrained person may live or work relatively autonomously of communities or organisations (or be a leader of one). There is, it must be said, an ambiguity or tension in Douglas' framework between explanations for differences between groups within societies and explanations for differences between different kinds of society or different historical phases.

There is a sense, however, in which, where Douglas is describing the ways in which some individuals, groups or societies may depend less on ritual and more on elaborated communicative codes, Giddens would speak of reflexivity; a reflexivity which, in Runciman's terms, might increase the propensity of individuals to feel relatively deprived because of inter-reference group inequalities. The globalised nature of late modernity entails a weakening of grid determinants and constraints, a discarding of received certainties and renders social structures and injustices more transparent. Where Douglas is describing the ways in which some individuals, groups or societies are less bounded by collective power and more alienated, Giddens would speak of loss of ontological security; a loss which, in Runciman's terms, might increase the propensity for individuals to feel relatively deprived because of their intra-reference group situation. The recent re-ordering of social ties and structures entails a weakening of group controls and loyalties and renders individual inequalities and differences more transparent.

It cannot be said that Giddens' ideas map exactly onto those of Douglas. Giddens' analysis is culturally specific in that he seeks to provide an account of a very particular form of impersonal globalised modernity inhabited by 'clever people' (1994: 7); people who are necessarily well informed and who believe the world to be knowable. Douglas' analysis is more generic in its historical applicability and, unlike Giddens', it does not underestimate the endurability, richness and complexity of social tradition. None the less, by incorporating Douglas' and Giddens' respective theoretical distinctions as intersecting dimensions or continua, it is possible to construct the schematic taxonomy which we now set out in Figure 1.6. The taxonomy supersedes the notions of grid and reflexivity by articulating them with a more general concept of *voice*, by which we refer to the forms in which discourses are exhibited. It supersedes the notions of group and ontological security (or its converse, anxiety) by articulating them with the realm of *ideology*, through which substantive experience is apprehended. Although there is a certain correspondence between Figures 1.5 and 1.6, the model presented in the latter is, we believe, superior because it is based, not on the characterisation of individual personalities, but on the kinds of discourses which people might employ in response to the risk of social

Figure 1.6	A taxonomy of discourses surrounding the risk of social inequality under conditions of 'late modernity'

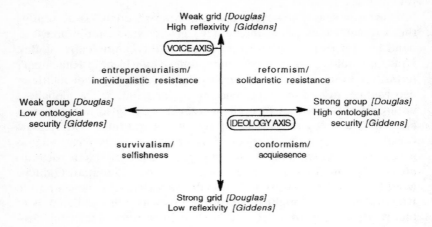

inequality under conditions of what Giddens would call 'late modernity'.

In the chapters which follow we shall critically investigate the validity of this taxonomy as an heuristic device. It is not necessarily the case that any of us as individuals will respond consistently over time in terms of merely one of the quadrants on this diagrammatic representation. What this speculative model is intended to provide is a framework within which to consider the ways that people think about poverty and riches and the different kinds of socially constructed discourses upon which they draw. The vertical axis in this taxonomy contrasts reflexive with mythologising voices. It is only partly concerned with how articulate, perceptive or communicative people are or how consistently they eschew popular myths and prejudices. It is also concerned with the balance between the extent to which their accounts of inequality represent received wisdom on the one hand, and to which their accounts contain elements which they have reworked for themselves. The horizontal axis in this taxonomy is essentially concerned to contrast autonomistic with deterministic ideologies; with the extent to which risk is experienced as being individually or collectively borne. It is concerned with the balance between the extent to which people's accounts of inequality are informed by notions of free agency or individual desert on the one hand, or notions of social or natural determination on the other.

What is defined in the top left-hand quadrant as entrepreurialism is constituted through a discourse that is both autonomistic and reflexive; in which the individual must embrace the complexity of the social order and negotiate it on the basis of calculative self-interest and principles of *utility*. What is defined in the bottom left-hand quadrant as survivalism is constituted through a discourse that is autonomistic, but mythologising; in which the individual must negotiate a hostile social order to her/his own advantage, but in accordance with self-evident maxims or familiar principles of *authority*. What is defined in the top right-hand quadrant as reformism is constituted through a discourse that is both deterministic and reflexive; in which the individual must recognise the complexity of the social order and negotiate it critically in accordance with some collectivist principle of *justice*. What is defined in the bottom right-hand quadrant as conformism is constituted through a discourse that is deterministic, but mythologising; in which the individual must negotiate the social order on the basis of a paramount need to belong within that order and a principle of *cohesion*.

The voices and ideologies on which people draw in every day life are furnished from a variety of sources, but we know comparatively little about the sources which specifically construct or inform people's attitudes to poverty and riches. Runciman's work demonstrated that, in the 1960s, different groups in society had limited awareness and perceptions of each other, but might it be the case that all groups in society share the same or similarly constructed perceptions of the poverty and riches which lie at the very extremities of society? The work of Golding and Middleton (1982) in the 1980s demonstrated that the press and broadcasting media represent important sources of the images which people have of poverty. Bearing in mind that minority ethnic groups are proportionately over-represented within the poorest fifth of the UK population (Amin and Oppenheim 1992; Hills 1995; DSS 1996) it is known, for example, that the attitudes which white people have about black people will vary significantly depending on whether their knowledge of other ethnic communities is 'situationally based' or 'media relayed' (Hartman and Husband 1974). What we do not know is how the poorest 10–30 per cent of the population regard the richest 10–30 per cent or *vice versa*. Writers such as Anderson (1983) contend that diverse national communities are sustained in the imagination of their members, not because any one of them will ever meet or know more than a handful of her/his fellow citizens, but because s/he can maintain 'complete confidence in their steady, anonymous, simultaneous activity' (1983: 31). Anderson points to newspapers as just one of the mechanisms for providing imaginary links between the members of a national community. Later in this book, therefore, we shall be considering the relationship which contemporary news media output may have with popular attitudes to poverty and riches.

However, we do not suppose that popular voices and ideologies are the instant constructions of the press and broadcasting media and when, in Chapter 5, we turn to discuss concepts of citizenship we shall be seeking to trace the historical and philosophical roots of the moral repertoires which underpin the different voices and ideologies through which we address the subjects of poverty and riches.

CONCLUSION

In this chapter we have firstly shown that there is by any standards a substantial gap between the richest and the poorest in British society. In the closing years of the twentieth century the gap between rich and poor grew all around the world, but it grew especially quickly in the UK.

Secondly, we have shown how discussions about the definition of poverty and riches have resulted in concepts of deprivation and privilege; concepts which relate to the ways in which the poor and the rich are excluded or exclude themselves from society. However, seminal research in Britain in the 1960s suggested that, in spite of inequality, people may not then have felt themselves to be deprived or privileged because they had limited perceptions of their own material position in relation to that of others.

Thirdly, we have discussed the ways in which the class structures which applied in Britain in the 1960s have unravelled or, at least, become more complex. In this context we have discussed new thinking which has emphasised the importance of other kinds of social division and which suggests that the complexion of society is changing; that society appears to be characterised less by relations between classes with distinctive interests in the production of wealth, and rather more by global relations of risk in which everybody may be vulnerable – albeit in different ways and to different extents – to the consequences of poverty and riches.

Finally, we have discussed the different ways in which people's understanding of poverty and riches may be socially constructed. We have presented a theoretical model through which to interpret the different voices and ideologies which constitute the discourses that surround the risk of social inequality; the discourses through which poverty and riches are popularly defined and understood.

The aim of the research which gave rise to this book was to explore prevailing beliefs and popular discourses relating to the nature, extent and 'risk' of poverty and riches. We shall be presenting evidence which suggests that people seem to fear poverty rather more than they revere wealth. We shall be arguing that, for most people, their citizenship provides, at best, an ambiguous framework within which to endure worry, anticipate fun, and go in search of comfort. We shall suggest that the moral categories of poverty and riches, as currently socially constructed, furnish for the new millennium a disciplinary discourse of fear and desire that is no less potent than any promulgated by the hymn writers of the nineteenth century.

2 The Spectre of Poverty

No, I don't worry about [the gap between the rich and poor] because I have the confidence that I will always be able to earn enough money to not feel poor.

[Professional woman in her early thirties]

I think it worries anybody [the prospect of being poor]. You know, if you don't know where your next meal's coming from or you can't pay your bills.

[Middle-aged self-employed man]

This chapter will discuss two competing interpretations of the contemporary meaning of poverty. One is illustrated by the first of the above quotations (taken from interviews conducted in the course of the authors' research). It is a view authoritatively reflected in the recent writings of J.K. Galbraith, who argues that societies like the USA and Britain are dominated by the self-regarding interests of a contented electoral majority that is indifferent to poverty: in this scenario poverty is a source of concern 'only when there is a threat or possible threat to present well-being and future prospect – when government and the seemingly less deserving intrude or threaten to intrude their needs or demands' (1992: 17). The other interpretation is illustrated by the second quotation. It is a view reflected by Will Hutton, who argues that profound insecurity in the labour market and the weakening of welfare structures in Britain are leading to 'an increase in anxiety, dread of the future and communal breakdown' (1996: 197): in this scenario, worry about the threat or the prospect of poverty is something which haunts people perhaps at every level within late capitalist society.

There is in Britain a long tradition of both journalistic and scholarly writing which has documented the lives of people living in poverty. There is the sometimes impassioned work of campaigning journalists such as Mayhew (1867) Orwell (1937) and Campbell (1984); there is descriptive work reaching back into the nineteenth century by investigators such as Booth and Rowntree whom we discussed in Chapter 1; there is the rigorous analytical work of sociologists such as Townsend (1979); and there is more recent work – much of it based on academic studies commissioned by charities – such as that by Cohen *et al* (1992), Kempson (1996) and Gordon and Pantazis (1997). However, very little has been written about the meaning which poverty has for society as a whole, including those who are not in poverty.

In this chapter we shall firstly present an argument about the socially constructed nature of poverty as a concept having relevance and disciplinary potential for *all* members of society. We shall then critically examine recent suggestions that poverty is to be researched and understood primarily in terms of processes of social exclusion and argue that the poverty which constitutes such exclusion may be as much symbolic as it is objective. Research which examines the impact of exclusion *solely* in terms of the fears and experiences of the poor may in one sense be looking, if not in the wrong place, then in the wrong direction. Finally, the chapter will review existing data about social attitudes to poverty and will present new evidence concerning the meaning of poverty for people with widely differing levels of income and wealth. One commentator has recently called for an approach which examines poverty, not in terms of the dependency of the poor, but in terms of the 'social reactions'. . . . 'which label the poor as "different"' (Becker 1997: 159). Here, we do just that.

POVERTY AS A SOCIAL CONSTRUCTION

In Chapter 1 we discussed a range of different definitions and explanations of poverty and demonstrated the extent to which poverty is a contested concept. While people may not agree about the nature or severity of the condition that constitutes poverty or whether anybody in a late capitalist society may be said to be in such a state, it is significant in itself that the concept continues to be debated and that poverty survives as a preoccupation within everyday discourse.

For those on the political left who both acknowledge and deplore the existence of poverty in advanced Western countries, its persistence in the midst of affluence is 'one of the wonders of the modern world' (Seabrook 1985: 12). Poverty is necessary to capitalism and, in Britain, it is 'only by extraordinary ingenuity' (Kincaid 1975: 219) that the tax and social security systems of the modern welfare state have failed to reduce inequality and prevent poverty. If the creators of the welfare state had indeed believed in a 'strategy of equality' (see Le Grand 1982), not only has the implementation of that strategy fallen short, its impact has in some respects sustained and promoted inequality, benefiting the middle classes at the expense of the poor (but see Powell 1995). Even right wing commentators, to the extent that they are willing to acknowledge poverty as a contemporary social problem, blame it in part on poor people themselves, but also on the perverse behavioural incentives allegedly created by an overweaning welfare state (for example, Murray 1984).

It has been argued elsewhere that the welfare state in general and the social security system in particular are indeed implicated in the perpetuation of poverty under late capitalism (Dean 1991: ch. 4), though not necessarily in the ways conventionally described by critics of the left and right. Poverty is inseparable from the logic of the practices that are directed to relieving or preventing it. Poverty is not so much defined as constituted through the language by which its nature and its existence are contested. In feudal times, poverty was an ascribed, unalterable and in a sense, therefore, unproblematic status into which most of the population was born (George 1973: 3). There was even virtue in poverty (Lis and Soly 1979). It is modernity itself that has constituted poverty as a social problem. Through a variety of discourses – popular and political, professional and academic – poverty is constructed as an issue of social concern, as the subject of technical knowledge, and as an object of political regulation and control (see, for example, Manning 1985).

It may be argued that, just as the modern prison manifestly fails to reduce criminality, so modern social security systems fail to reduce poverty. Criminal justice reformers point to the dismal record of Western prison systems since the nineteenth century, which appear neither to deter crime nor to reform offenders. In spite of these protestations Foucault (1977) has argued that such systems have not failed. On the contrary, they have 'succeeded extremely well in producing delinquency, a specific type, a politically or economically less dangerous . . . form of illegality; in producing delinquents, in an apparently marginal, but in fact centrally supervised milieu' (*ibid*: 277). We might similarly contend that first the Poor Laws, and subsequently the modern social security system, have not failed. They have succeeded in creating poverty as a manageable and less explosive form of social deprivation; in defining 'the poor' as an apparently excluded minority, but in fact a closely regulated section of the population (see Dean 1991; Squires 1990).

The Foucauldian concept of the 'disciplinary society' and associated relational theories of power provide a quite different way of conceptualising poverty from those discussed in Chapter 1. Essential however to the insight which this approach offers is that the disciplinary mechanisms associated with poverty bear not only on 'the poor', but on society as a whole. The key to the process is the refined 'partitioning' of populations and a technique which Foucault characterises as 'binary division and branding' (1977: 199). The multitude of distinctions which public policy makes explicit – between the abnormal and the normal, the dangerous and the harmless, the mad and the sane, the criminal and the decent, the poor and the respectable – determines the identity, the status, the location, and the conduct of each and every individual subject. Whatever her or his substantive needs, every citizen of a welfare state is uniquely identified by her or his personal case records and/or social insurance number, and each is individually endowed with formal rights to various kinds of conditionally defined benefit. The edifice of the administrative state presents itself to those who do not depend on it as well as those who must engage with its workings. The possibility or propensity for poverty is perpetually and constitutionally present for those who are not poor as well as those who might be. The spectre of poverty will not be eliminated so long as mechanisms for the relief or prevention of poverty remain in place, nor so long as such mechanisms make poverty an object of definition and regulation.

This is the sense in which poverty is a socially constructed phenomenon: it is a symbolic presence as well as a contested concept. This is illustrated by the diverse images which people have of poverty and 'the poor'. Earlier research with social security claimants (see Dean 1992), together with anecdotal evidence obtained in the course of teaching and tutorial discussions and more recent research by the writers (see below), demonstrate the extraordinary variety of imagery and discursive expression which people employ when they speak of poverty. Although the categories used are neither exhaustive nor mutually exclusive, a taxonomy of the most commonly employed images or discourses is set out in Figure 2.1. People may of course employ several types of imagery or discourse and their own circumstances and experiences will affect the combinations of images and discourses on which they draw.

Figure 2.1 Popular images/discourses of poverty

Nature of imagery or association	Types of discursive expression	Examples
DISTANT (poverty as a remote phenomenon)	• temporally distant	Outmoded imagery drawn from the past, such as from Victorian or Dickensian times, or from the Depression of the 1930s.
	• spatially distant	Catastrophic imagery drawn from overseas, such as of famines or natural disasters in the Third World.
	• socially distant	Social-exclusionary imagery drawn from circumstances or environments endured by 'others', such as homelesness, slums, council housing estates, unemployment, welfare dependency.
PEJORATIVE (poverty as an immanent phenomenon)	• blame-laden	Images of personal failure: of scrounging, laziness, overfecundity, fecklessness, degradation, lack of cleanliness.
	• danger-laden	Threatening images: of individuals or groups who are violent, aggressive, contaminating or infectious; *or* of poverty as an affliction which might strike one down.
EXTERIOR (poverty effected from outside the person)	• structurally informed	Association of poverty with class disadvantage and/or failures of public policy; imagery which draws on such expressions as 'bottom of the pile', 'underprivileged', 'underclass'; *or* which equates poverty with being 'ordinary' or 'working class'.
	• morally informed	Association of poverty with social injustice or distress; imagery which draws on references to starvation, hunger, raggedness, indignity, insecurity, inability to cope.
INTERIOR (poverty affected from inside the person)	• state of mind	Association of poverty with the way people think about themselves or with personal phases or crises.
	• matter of will	Association of poverty with 'giving up', 'letting go', self-indulgence or self-pity.
	• sense of shame	Association of poverty with a personal pedicament or burden which is concealed or kept secret from the outside world.

Of the sample of British social security claimants interviewed for the research referred to above (all of whom, by authoritatively accepted definitions, could be said to have been in poverty), around two thirds denied that they were poor and, of those who admitted their poverty, nearly half were reluctant to do so. Even for 'the poor', poverty is something which is believed by and large to affect other people. Lone parents struggling to survive on means-tested benefits would say such things as 'I'm not really, really, really poor . . . there's always people worse off than myself' (see Dean 1992: 84).

Poverty is either apprehended as a *distant* phenomenon – as something which existed in the past or which may happen in other places or to other kinds of people – or it is apprehended in *pejorative* terms as something blameworthy, threatening or unspeakable: certainly, it is not something that many people will readily admit to.

There tends also to be a curious detachment about the terms in which the existence of poverty is acknowledged. Popular discourse does on occasions share with expert commentators understandings of poverty which relate it to *exterior* factors, such as social class or structural influences; or else it expresses a sense of moral or charitable concern about the injustice or the awfulness of poverty. On the other hand, when the existence of poverty is related to factors which are *interior* to the individual, it may be associated – even by people surviving on very limited resources – as something quite intangible; as a state of mind or failure of will which can potentially be overcome, or even as a sense of shame that is not necessarily justifiable.

Edwin Chadwick, architect of the Victorian Poor Law, had (wishfully) envisaged that the reformed workhouse would be regarded, not – like poverty itself – as an 'object of wholesome horror' (see Spicker 1984), but as a place of strict hygiene, good order and tight discipline; as a *corrective* to poverty. The coercive disciplinary regime of the nineteenth century Poor Law has given way to the more sophisticated sanctions and constraints of the modern social security system (see Dean 1991: ch. 3); yet, for many, poverty survives as that 'object of wholesome horror' which – though its presence can touch or taint those who are subject to the social security system – is the symbolic manifestation of that which lies just beyond the system's bounds.

It is important none the less that we should not overdramatise the power of a word. There clearly are at least some people for whom 'poverty' does not conjure up horrific associations, because for them, it seems, poverty comes from just being 'ordinary'. However, ordinariness in an increasingly polarised society can be a frustrating, capricious and unjust condition. For example, one of the few claimants interviewed in the abovementioned research to admit that he was poor was a young unemployed man who believed the only way not to be poor was to attain the altogether unachievable status of a rock star or similar celebrity. If there ever was virtue in poverty, there is certainly none now.

SOCIAL POLARISATION AND EXCLUSION

In Chapter 1 we discussed the breathtaking gap between the rich and poor in Britain at the end of the twentieth century. The process by which the size of that gap has tended to increase is often referred to as 'social polarisation'. There is a sophisticated new vocabulary developing around the subject of poverty: a vocabulary which avoids the controversial and image-laden discourse of poverty by concentrating on the effects of polarisation and, particularly, on the idea of 'social exclusion'. Social exclusion is a term which, on the one hand, has resonance with Peter Townsend's influential concept of social deprivation (see pp. 8–9 above), but on the other, has been absorbed into technical European Union policy debates about the social consequences of economic and labour market processes (see Room 1995).

An important attempt to outline a new paradigm for research on inequality, social exclusion and poverty has recently been offered by Williams and Pillinger (1996). Williams and Pillinger helpfully define social polarisation and exclusion as processes that are located, as it were, in the middle range, between the the structural dynamics of inequality at the macro-level and the condition or state of poverty at the micro-level. Poverty is the *concern* of social policy research; inequality is the *frame* in which such research is conducted; but the proper *focus* is the relational dynamics of social exclusion and the effects of social polarisation. The questions, in other words, are: firstly, just how is access by individuals, households and groups to resources and opportunities to protect themselves from poverty weakened? and secondly,

> how far does the process of social exclusion . . . exert a dilating pressure on society as a whole, first, by *widening the gap* between the quality of life enjoyed by those who are 'comfortable' and the quality of life of the poor and, second, by excluding *more* numbers of people from access to a 'comfortable' quality of life? (1996: 25)

Williams and Pillinger's objective is to promote work on poverty that is more securely connected to new theories of social divisions, social change and social movements. To this end, they believe, the meaning and dynamics of poverty are best understood in relation to: agency (the subjectivity of social actors); the social distribution and meaning of risk, opportunity and resources; the discourses which provide the context of policy intervention; and the global dynamics of both social and economic change.

It is refreshing that this approach centrally acknowledges issues of subjectivity and the constitutive significance of discourse while articulating these with concern for structural dynamics. However, the articulation remains in some respects problematic. Williams and Pillinger are right when they allude to the 'dilating pressure' of social exclusion as something which bears on society as a whole. It is disappointing, therefore, that the new research paradigm they propose would seem, for example, to be concerned with risks and uncertainties which are experienced *by the poor* and with 'testing how far and in what ways the concept of reflexivity pertains to those who are poor' (*ibid*: 37). This is a contention which does not sit easily with an acknowledgement that poverty and 'the poor' themselves are socially constructed: that they are as much discursive as real phenomena. Poverty – as distinct from objective need – has no meaning without some understanding of what constitutes a 'comfortable' quality of life, and social exclusion has no meaning without knowledge of the delimiting social body or entity from which exclusion occurs or is threatened. If we are serious about exploring the meaning of poverty and exclusion, we must explore how those meanings are created for those who *deny* they are poor and for those who would *practise* exclusion.

There are dangers with concepts such as social exclusion. Ruth Levitas has argued that the way the concept is currently being used 'actually obscures the questions of material inequality it was originally intended to illuminate' (1996: 7). She points to a number of publications and reports, including European Union White Papers (EC 1994a and 1994b) and reports of the Labour Party's Commission on Social Justice (Borrie 1994) and the Joseph Rowntree Foundation Inquiry into Income and Wealth (Barclay 1995; Hills 1995). These documents rely in different ways on the concept of social exclusion, and to varying degrees, according to Levitas, they all fail adequately to address the question of the *unpaid* work that is necessary to the maintenance of social life (and which is performed largely by women), and of *low paid* work (resulting from global economic competition and restructuring). In the discourse of these documents, the opposite of exclusion is not inclusion, but integration. The exclusion with which such discourse is concerned is primarily exclusion from labour market processes and the wage relation, and the consequence that is feared is a failure of social cohesion as a prerequisite of effective market conditions: 'Under cover of a concern with "social exclusion", and a rhetoric of solidarity, society dissolves into market relations' (*ibid*: 12). The documents assume a consensual, functionalist model of society and ignore the exploitative nature of capitalism. Levitas calls this a 'punk Durkheimianism' in which the language of efficiency and deregulation reflecting the ascendancy of New Right ideology is juxtaposed with semi-sociological discourses of solidarity and integration drawn from older political traditions.

Levitas is similarly critical of Will Hutton (1996, and see discussion on p. 15 above). His critique of social inequality in contemporary Britain recognises a fissure (as does the Rowntree study) between the 30 per cent of the population who are broadly excluded and the 70 per cent who are comfortable, but also a fissure *within* the comfortable majority between the 30 per cent who are insecure and the 40 per cent who are privileged. The problem for Levitas, however, is that Hutton's critique, though perceptive, is of the pathological or abnormal form which capitalism is supposed to have assumed and not of the fundamental nature of capitalist social relations in which effective power over the social distribution of life chances rests in the hands of a very tiny and elusive minority.

> The 'real' society is not that constituted by the (unequal) 70 per cent, to which the poor are marginal or from which they are excluded. The real society is that made up by the whole 100 per cent, in which poverty is endemic. (1996: 19)

A corollary to this argument might be that, to understand the impact of poverty, we need similarly to look, not at the minority (however defined) who constitute 'the poor', nor even as Hutton suggests at the 'bottom' 60 per cent of society, but at the whole 100 per cent for whom poverty is a (however distant) threat or presence.

While Williams and Pillinger call for a 'new paradigm' through which to articulate experiences of poverty with the concept of social exclusion, and Levitas warns that the concept of social exclusion embodies a 'new Durkheimian hegemony', Bill Jordan (1996) has recently advanced a new theory of poverty and social exclusion. It is a theory which purports to account for the global degenerative polarisation of human society – at the level of economies, nation states and even households – in terms of a fragmentation or 'narrowing of mutualities'.

Jordan starts from the worthy premise that we should look upon people in poverty as social actors and not as victims. To this end, however, he assumes that we are all actors within inherently exclusive social formations and he draws upon a novel and provocative interpretation of public choice theory and, in particular, club theory. In conditions of scarcity all human beings both co-operate and compete. 'Clubs' or voluntary associations, whether they exist at a trans-national, community or individual level, invoke exclusion and regulation in order to maximise benefits (by maintaining a collective competitive advantage against other clubs) and minimise disbenefits (such as congestion or free-riding). The trend to privatisation and deregulation in public policy has favoured the development of often powerful voluntary associations on the one hand and a reduction in the accountability of centralised state power on the other. The behaviour of voluntary associations and antagonisms between them can be both counterproductive and wasteful; they can drive up social costs and they can fuel ever more repressive policies towards marginalised groups, such as refugees, unemployed people, lone parents and 'underclass' groups. Excluded groups may adopt strategies which circumvent their exclusion, but invite further repression.

While it is difficult to do justice to the complexity of Jordan's thesis in the compass of a few sentences, the essence of his argument seems to be that social exclusion results from failed and counterproductive strategies on the part of the excluded. He calls for policies that will accommodate the strategies of the poor within a democratic community, but his bid to cast the poor as rational calculative actors appears to have resulted in a form of collective rather than individual victim blaming. Empirical evidence for his theory is in short supply and is contradicted by other research findings (Dean and Taylor-Gooby 1992; Dean and Melrose 1997) which suggest that 'the poor' – even those who adopt such strategies as social security fraud to circumvent their exclusion – are not behaving as members of separate or distinctive 'clubs', but retain by and large the same values, aspirations and prejudices as the rest of society. Jordan's theory provides interesting new insights, but it fails to account for wider relations of power and for the hegemonic force of disciplinary discourses which permeate society as a whole (and, in this respect, it sits uncomfortably with other elements of Jordan's work).

It is necessary and important to consider the manner in which social polarisation leads to social exclusion, but poverty as a discursive construction may have its greatest impact on those who are or aspire to be socially included.

SOCIAL ATTITUDES TO POVERTY

Large scale social attitude surveys tell us something about poverty's hold on the social imagination. The British Social Attitudes (BSA) survey, for example, demonstrates that people do not by and large find the increasing gap between the highest and lowest incomes in society acceptable (see Spencer 1996 and Table 2.1 below). Attitudes to 'poverty', however, are a little more ambiguous, although a distinct and growing majority is prepared to acknowledge the existence of poverty in Britain (see Taylor-Gooby 1990; 1995 and Table 2.2).

The most significant variations within public opinion would seem to relate to explanations for the causes of poverty (see Table 2.3). There is a persistent minority within the population which attributes poverty (or 'living in need') to laziness or lack of willpower on the

Table 2.1 Perceptions of the gap between high and low incomes

	1983 %	1989 %	1995 %
Percentage agreeing that the gap is:			
(a) too large	72	80	87
(b) about right	22	15	8
(c) too small	3	3	2

Source: British Social Attitudes survey

Table 2.2 Perceptions as to the existence of poverty

	1986 %	1989 %	1994 %
Percentage agreeing that 'there is quite a lot of real poverty in Britain today':	55	63	69

Source: British Social Attitudes survey

Table 2.3 Perceptions of the causes of poverty

	1983 %	1986 %	1989 %	1994 %
Percentage agreeing that 'there are people who live in need because:				
(a) they have been unlucky	13	11	11	16
(b) of laziness or lack of will-power	22	19	19	15
(c) of injustice in our society	32	25	29	29
(d) its an inevitable part of modern life	25	37	34	32

Sources: Breadline Britain survey for 1983; British Social Attitudes survey for 1986, 1989 and 1994

part of the poor. There is evidence from the past that the size of this minority has been greater in the UK than in other European countries (see EUROSTAT 1977), and more recent evidence that Britons generally are less inclined than other Europeans to attribute poverty to social injustice (Golding 1995). Within Britain, there are striking differences between Conservative and Labour Party supporters on this issue, with the former – regardless of income – being much more likely than the latter to attribute poverty to the failings of the poor (Taylor-Gooby 1990). It must be stressed, however, that a clear majority of the population do *not* blame poverty on the victims of poverty but attribute it either to bad luck, to social injustice, or else they regard it as an inevitable feature of modern life.

It would seem therefore that, while some do deny the existence of poverty and others will lay the blame for poverty on the poor themselves, most people accept that poverty is, if not in our midst, then on our door-step; that it is, if not inescapable, an endemic side-effect of our particular social arrangements. It is extremely difficult, however, for social attitude surveys based on pre-formulated questions to capture what it is that poverty means to people. The BSA has periodically attempted to do this by asking respondents to say whether they agree with three different definitions of poverty

Table 2.4   Popular definitions of poverty

	1986 %	1989 %	1994 %
Percentage agreeing that someone in Britain is in poverty if they have:			
(a) enough to buy the things they really need, but not enough to buy the things most people take for granted (a relative definition)	25	25	28
(b) enough to eat and live, but not enough to buy other things they need (a breadline definition)	55	60	60
(c) not enough to eat and live without getting into debt (a sub-minimal definition)	95	95	90

Source: British Social Attitudes survey

(see Table 2.4). Almost everybody is inclined to agree with the most stringent of the definitions offered, a sub-minimal definition by which people are in poverty if they are forced to choose between starvation and debt. A majority of the population accept an absolute or 'breadline' definition of poverty, by which people are in poverty if they have no more than enough for basic subsistence needs. However, only about a quarter of the population accept a relative definition of poverty by which people are in poverty if, while having enough to meet basic subsistence needs, they do not have enough to share in normally prevailing living standards.

The popular preference therefore is for 'hard-nosed' definitions of poverty, a finding which has customarily been construed as evidence of people's prejudices and hostility towards 'the poor'. All but a quarter of the population accept – as Right wing politicians have urged (see Chapter 1 above) – that the concept of relative poverty is a sham. None the less, in the context of the widespread acknowledgement of poverty's existence, the finding can also be construed as evidence for the intensity of people's fear of poverty. The fact that getting on for two thirds of the population believe in the presence of poverty demonstrates that it is perceived as a significant concern. Though people may reject the more 'generous', relative conception of poverty in favour of more 'rigorous', absolute conceptions, this does not mean they are complacent about poverty. On the contrary, it suggests that poverty is much to be feared.

AN OBJECT OF WHOLESOME HORROR

It is to get a clearer picture of people's perceptions of poverty that the authors have undertaken their own qualitative research, based on in-depth interviews, not exclusively with people dependent on social security benefits, but with a sample of 76 people with widely differing income levels. In the remainder of this chapter we shall discuss some of our findings. Details of the study, the sample and of the methods used are contained in the Appendix to this book. The key findings to be discussed in this chapter are summarised in Table A.4a on p. 180.

The Meaning of Poverty

When asked what being poor means, without prompting them with options from which they might choose, half our respondents replied in terms of 'breadline' or 'sub-minimal' concepts. They defined poverty as not being able to feed oneself, or of not being able to afford basic things like food, warmth and/or shelter. Fewer than a tenth of the sample thought of being poor in relative terms, in terms of not being able to do the sort of things that other people take for granted. Allowing for the fact that some respondents combined 'absolute' and 'relative' definitions in their replies, this picture is broadly consistent with that provided by BSA data. However, other people gave different kinds of answer. A small number said that being poor meant having no choice. Others gave such replies as 'being at the bottom of the social ladder', 'being less respected', and, tellingly, 'not having sufficient assets or income to avoid being frightened'.

None the less, it was the 'hard-nosed' definitions which predominated and, if anything, slightly more so among women, among younger respondents, among those with lower to middle incomes, and among those whom we identified as drawing on survivalist and conformist (that is, less reflexive) discourses (see Figures 1.6 and A.1 and the discussions on pp. 18–21 and 177–8). Possibly, it is those who are objectively more at risk of poverty or, alternatively, who are more inclined to 'mythologising' discourses that are also more likely to conceptualise poverty in narrow terms; to distance themselves from poverty by defining it as an especially dire or extreme state of affairs. Those who are more removed from poverty and/or who are more inclined to reflexive discourses, are perhaps more

likely to countenance wide definitions; not only 'relative' definitions, but the kind of definition (particularly favoured by respondents whom we identified as drawing on entrepreneurial discourse)
which regards poverty as a denial of choice; as exclusion from the
freedom of the market place.

In giving their definitions of poverty respondents had already
disclosed an array of imagery, but they were also separately asked
what mental picture or image they had of poverty. About a third
of the sample responded with more than one image. Of those
who responded with a single image, a substantial proportion
alluded to what we have defined in Figure 2.1 as 'socially distant'
imagery, with references particularly to homelessness and homeless people, but also to council housing estates and to various
kinds of welfare dependency (that is, to unemployed people, lone-
parents and pensioners). Other responses included instances of
spatially distant imagery ('compared to Africa, no-one is poor in
Britain') and instances which, for example, elided 'pejorative' with
what we have called 'interior' imagery ('people who don't respect
themselves').

Respondents whom we had identified as drawing on entrepreneurial and reformist (that is, reflexive) discourses, those in 'higher'
occupational groups and, particularly, those who were readers of
broadsheet rather than tabloid newspapers, were most likely to
express multiple or complex images of poverty. Of the single images cited, the starkest – that of homelessness – was most likely to
be mentioned by people who had higher incomes. Arguably, the
more remote people are from destitution, the more dramatic is
the imagery they choose. Those with fewer resources and an objectively greater risk of poverty seem to be more likely to choose
imagery that is further down the hierarchy of horror. Although this
is only tentatively suggested by our data, it is consistent with the
possibility that those who are themselves closer to poverty tend to
have narrower definitions of it and to think about it in more pragmatic or less speculative ways.

Respondents were prompted to speculate about the disadvantages of being poor; about whether poor people receive less respect than others; and about whether poor people enjoy fewer rights
than others. All three questions required respondents to think more
substantively about the meanings they attached to poverty. A majority of respondents identified the disadvanges which the poor might

face in terms of externally or stucturally imposed disadvantages; in terms of a lack of opportunity or an inability to do the things which other people take for granted, such as going out for an evening. In the case of respondents who had elected for a narrow or 'absolute' definition of poverty, there is something of a paradox here; when invited to think about the constraints of being poor, people are more likely to construe the disadvantages in 'relative' terms. Only a minority of respondents interpreted the question by referring to the inherent personal shortcomings or disabilities to which they attributed poverty; to the lack of self-confidence and skills which poor people had that prevented them from competing effectively in the labour market.

Men, younger people, those in higher income groups and in 'higher' occupational groups were marginally more likely than others to refer to the opportunity constraints of poverty. In the case of men and younger people this may reflect a greater volatility of opinion compared with women and older people, whose opinions tend, it has been observed, to be more consistent and pragmatic (cf. Dean and Melrose 1996 and see Chapter 6 in this book). In the case of the people who are better off, this apparent tendency is again consistent with the proposition that people who are closer to poverty are perhaps less inclined to speculate about its nature.

When thinking about the disadvantages of poverty a small proportion of respondents specifically referred to a belief that poor people command less respect than others. It seemed that women, those in the 'Middle England' income band (that is, having between one and one and a half times national disposable income – see Table A.3, p. 176) and those in 'lower' occupational classes could be particularly inclined to express this view, as were respondents whom we had identified as subscribing to survivalist and conformist (less reflexive) discourses (as also, incidentally, were the readers of tabloid as opposed to broadsheet newspapers). The loss of respect which some people fear to be associated with poverty may refer to a threatened loss of self-identity arising from the disruption of household arrangements, or of affective or customary status patterns. In the event, when the proposition that poor people get less respect than others was put *explicitly* to respondents, a substantial majority agreed. Although the differences between respondents in the broad income bands used in Table A.3 were not that great, it was noticeable that those on the *very* highest incomes (more than twice average) were the most likely to agree, while those on the *very* lowest incomes (less than half average) were least likely to do so. People with very high incomes are perhaps most likely to imagine that poverty must be accompanied by disgrace, while those on poverty level incomes are perhaps least likely to acknowledge that their 'respectability' and self-identity are at risk.

Asked whether poor people have fewer rights than others, a majority of respondents agreed, although a substantial minority disagreed. Those who agreed often made clear that this was not as it should be, saying for example 'I don't think they have much of a voice, that's the problem', or 'Well, they're not supposed to have [fewer rights] legally, are they, but I think they do because they haven't got the money to have full rights'. Men were more inclined than women to respond in the direction which the question led them. Once again, those on the highest incomes were more inclined than those on the lowest incomes to agree. Those on very low incomes may be reluctant to acknowledge the significance of the issue, precisely because they tend to deny they are in poverty. For those on very high incomes, on the other hand, a loss of rights may symbolise a peculiarly horrific kind of deprivation of which they are for some reason acutely aware.

The Threat of Poverty

Only six respondents in our sample admitted they were poor, a similar proportion to that which claimed to be permanently poor in the 1990 *Breadline Britain* survey (Gordon and Pantazis 1997: 31). However, 12 members of the sample had disposable incomes of less than half the national average and could, by the most widely accepted definition, be defined as 'poor'. The poorest member of the sample was in part-time employment and was entitled to receive (but was not claiming) family credit. We have already remarked that people on low incomes are often reluctant to acknowledge the status of 'poverty'. What we were able to do in this research was to ask those who do not admit to poverty, including many who manifestly were not in poverty, whether they would be worried about being poor. The results were striking.

A substantial majority of respondents said they did worry about being poor. Understandably, older people (over 35) were slightly more likely than younger people to say so, probably because the

Figure 2.2 Fear of poverty

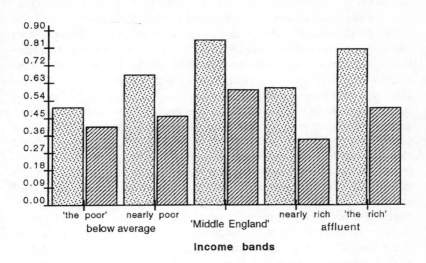

 proportion of those responding worried about being poor

proportion of those responding believing they are at risk of poverty

risks of poverty during retirement were more immediate for them. The extraordinary finding, however, was that those on the highest incomes were *more* likely to be worried about being poor than those on the lowest incomes. Those respondents whom we had identified as drawing on survivalist and conformist discourses were marginally less likely to worry than the more reflexive respondents.

The pattern of the data was quite complex (see Figure 2.2). The proportion of respondents in what we have called the 'Middle England' income band who were worried about poverty was similar to that of those in the very top band. Curiously, however, the proportion of respondents in the second-to-top income band (the 'nearly rich' – see Table A.3, p. 176) being worried about poverty was closer to that of respondents in the second-to-bottom income band (the 'nearly poor') than it was to that of those in the middle band. Put another way, it seemed that people in our 'Middle England' income range were more likely to be worried about poverty than those in the bands on either side of them.

We observed in Chapter 1 how Runciman (1966) drew on classic social psychological evidence relating to the attitudes of tornado victims: those who had been, not at, but close to the epicentre of the tornado and those who had been, not outside, but close to its periphery tended to feel less aggrieved than those in the intermediate zone. The analogy is far from perfect but it illustrates that relative proximity to *boundaries* – whether they be inner boundaries or outer boundaries – may result in a convergence of opinion or perception. In some instances the correlation between income and attitudes to poverty does not necessarily take the form of a simple or uniform gradient. There can be convergence between those close to the top and those close to the bottom of the income distribution, or at least a divergence between them and those in the middle. One of the arguments which is developed in the course of this book is that there are not only differences but similarities between the boundary between 'ordinary citizenship' and poverty on the one hand and that between 'ordinary citizenship' and riches on the other. The influence of those boundaries – even if their definition is disputed and their locations are elusive – may be real enough.

Clearly, much of what we suggest needs to be more rigorously tested. There are limits to the inferences which may be drawn from an exploratory qualitative study in which both the sample size and the differences in response rates are comparatively small. It remains the case, however, that in this particular study:

- those who were 'in poverty' (though they may not have acknowledged it), were least likely to worry about being poor;
- both the group we have called 'Middle England' and the *very* affluent (we might call them 'rich') were the most worried about being poor (the latter, possibly, because its members felt they had the most to lose);
- people in the groups with incomes which were just above 'the poor' and just below 'the rich' worried less than 'Middle England' – in the case of the former, perhaps, because they compared their circumstances with and felt more secure than 'the poor' and, in the case of the latter, perhaps, because they compared their circumstances with and felt more secure than 'Middle England'.

It also appeared that those in 'higher' occupational groups and the readers of broadsheet newspapers were more likely to worry about being poor than were those in 'lower' occupational groups and the readers of tabloid newspapers. Those whom we identified as drawing on reformist discourse were more likely than those from the other groupings to say they worried about poverty.

Those respondents who said they were worried, were asked why. Some did not offer direct replies, qualifying their original answers by saying such things as, 'its not something I would lie awake at night worrying about'. Of those who did reply, just over half said they worried about changes to their lifestyles; they feared a reduction to the standard of living to which they were accustomed. We also asked respondents to say, less speculatively, whether they actually thought there *was* a risk they might be poor. Of those who addressed the question, around half said there was and a third said no: others concluded they did not know or that they would prefer not to think about that possibility. Although the paradox was not quite so clear (see Figure 2.2), people on the highest incomes and those on middle incomes appeared to be rather more likely than those with the lowest incomes to say they were at risk. Characteristically, it would seem, broadsheet-reading households with ostensibly comfortable incomes may in fact be those who worry most about the risk of poverty.

To determine where the threat of poverty might be seen as coming from, we asked respondents who or what is to blame for the fact that some people are poor. Half referred to structural or external factors relating, for example, to the effects of government policy or the self-perpetuating nature of class inequality. About a quarter conveyed a fatalistic belief that poverty is an inevitable feature of society and only a small proportion sought to blame poverty on those who were poor. These findings are broadly consistent with the BSA findings discussed above. Women and older people seemed marginally more inclined towards the view that poverty was inevitable. Respondents with less than half average disposable income were in fact more likely than any other group to attribute poverty to structural causes and none of this group attributed poverty to inevitability or fate: for those who, technically speaking, are 'in poverty', it seemed, poverty was regarded more as an unjust imposition than as a matter of bad luck. In contrast, those in the 'nearly poor' income band were the least likely to attribute poverty to structural causes and the most likely to attribute it to inevitability or fate. For some within this group, it seems, it was only good luck that kept them from poverty. None of the respondents from more affluent income groups blamed poverty on the poor themselves.

Those whom we had identified as drawing predominantly on reformist discourses were (as is to be expected) the most likely to attribute poverty to structural causes, but those whom we have identified as drawing on entrepreneurial discourses were (in spite of their general preference for autonomistic explanations) more likely than others to regard poverty as a matter of fate. All but one of the respondents who attributed poverty to the failings of the poor were among those whom we had identified as drawing on survivalist and conformist (that is, less reflexive) discourses and none came from the higher income groups. The majority which does not attribute poverty to the failings of the poor must by implication acknowledge that there are factors leading to poverty over which there can be little or no individual control. One way of interpreting our evidence is to conclude that affluence and reflexivity certainly do not remove, and may even heighten, people's awareness of poverty as a threat.

Fate, Injustice or Desert?

The assimilation of neo-liberal thinking across the Western world in the last quarter of the twentieth century might have been expected to focus the popular imagination on meritocratic principles and to have strengthened the notion that the poor and the rich merely get what they deserve. None the less, notions which draw on other moral repertoires – in which poverty is seen on the one hand as a matter of fate or, on the other, as a consequence of social injustice – have clearly survived within contemporary discourse.

We shall see in Chapter 3 that, although a rather different pattern of replies obtained when we asked our respondents to what they attributed the fact that some people are rich, it was still only a very small number of respondents who attributed riches to individual attributes, enterprise or skill. When required to reflect on the causes of either poverty or riches, people tend not to speak in terms of individual desert, but resort to discourses of fate on the one hand or to discourses of injustice on the other: poverty and riches are – albeit in rather different ways – a matter of bad or good luck, or they are determined by outside forces. There is ostensibly little support for the idea that our rights of citizenship guarantee equality of opportunity. Comparatively few people believe that we live in a meritocracy or claim that the prevailing disparities of income and wealth can be explained by differences in aptitude or achievement. However, we cannot conclude that people are rejecting the autonomistic values necessary to sustain an individualist-meritocratic paradigm of citizenship. Such a conclusion is contradicted by other findings.

In particular, a closer but more holistic analysis of the underlying formulations, concepts and ideas represented within the discourses of our respondents (see Figure A.2 and pp. 177–8) disclosed a deeper dimension. Paying attention, not to the answers respondents gave to specific questions, but to the discourses on which they drew throughout the course of their interviews, it could be seen that the use of discourses which attributed the co-existence of poverty and riches to either fate or social injustice did indeed predominate over the use of discourses which attributed them to individual desert. None the less, the latter were still much in evidence: more so than the analysis outlined above might suggest. Instances of non-meritocratic discourses might include explanations framed in terms of luck, naturally or socially bestowed advantages or afflictions, or systemic injustice. Discourses of individual desert might include explanations framed in terms of merit, personal success or failure, or individual determination, weakness or state of mind.

Those respondents whom we had identified as drawing generally on more autonomistic (that is, entrepreneurial and survivalist) discourses might be expected to favour meritocratic explanations. This was only narrowly the case among those identified with survivalist discourse, while those identified with entrepreneurial discourse (which is more relexive) drew in fact on non-autonomistic explanatory discourses more often than autonomistic ones (even though they drew on the former less often than any other group). As may be seen from the profile illustrated in Figure 2.3, respondents from lower income groups were more likely than those from higher income groups to favour non-autonomistic explanatory discourses, while autonomistic/pro-meritocratic discourses were used most often by respondents from the 'Middle England' income band. In other words, discourses appropriate to an individualist meritocracy – and to the acceptance of inequality on meritocratic grounds – may not be ascendant, but they are very much current within the prevailing body of popular discourse.

Figure 2.3   The incidence of explanatory discourses relating to social
inequality

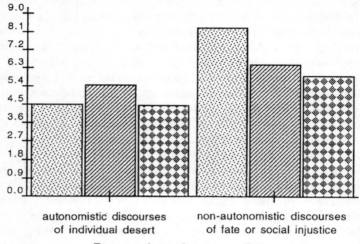

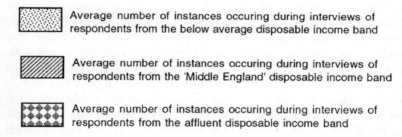

Popular Fears and the News Media

Many people are ideologically disposed to believe that they can by
their own efforts control their destinies, or they might simply hope
that their personal achievements will suffice to avoid poverty and
secure some measure of wealth. However, experience and the evidence that is around them may demonstrate that this is not something of which they can feel assured. One of the factors shaping
people's everyday experience and one of the principal sources of
evidence by which to assess their own life chances is news media

output. It was for this reason that, during the period of the research discussed above, the authors undertook a news monitoring exercise focused on the home news coverage contained in national daily and Sunday newspapers (see Appendix and, in particular, Tables A.5a and A.5b). One of our findings was that, although the newspapers (and especially tabloid newspapers) contain less coverage of poverty-related issues than of wealth-related issues, it was items about unemployment and job losses which dominated the former and items about extravagent payments to executives and celebrities (including, for example, the very high salaries paid to 'fat cat' bosses of recently privatised national industries) which dominated the latter. The overwhelming impression reflected or conveyed by the news media in the course of 1996 was that people were becoming poor or rich in ways which were unmerited.

To the extent that broadsheet newspapers reflect a more reflexive outlook than that represented by tabloid newspapers, it is significant that, together, the broadsheets carried twice as many news items about unemployment or redundancy, about low pay or poor wages, or about homelessness than did the tabloids. Tabloid newspapers were more likely than broadsheets to carry news items concerning alleged welfare 'scrounging' or benefit fraud, reflecting the persistence of an authoritarian mythology that was perpetuated in parallel with, but in spite of, the more dominant theme, emphasising the instability of employment and the new myth – that 'there is no such thing as a job for life'. In such matters, the differences between tabloids and broadsheets were more noticeable than the differences between right and left wing newspapers. None the less, the overall emphasis was remarkably similar. While the broadsheets fed the anxieties of their more reflexive readers with tales of risk and uncertainty, the tabloids established for their readers a rather more selective diet of doom-laden certainties. Whatever moral or political messages the newspapers conveyed about the importance of individual effort and achievement, the climate they were prone to engender was one in which poverty was both a pervasive presence and an unwarranted risk.

CONCLUSION

If we return to the two views of contemporary poverty characterised at the beginning of this chapter – Galbraith's view that the majority of citizens in liberal Western democracies is comfortably indifferent to poverty and Hutton's view that a growing proportion of that 'comfortable' majority is troubled by insecurity and the prospect of poverty – we would conclude that the evidence favours Hutton over Galbraith. Indeed, the significance of poverty is more far reaching than even Hutton supposes.

We have sought to introduce a different way of thinking about poverty. It is an irony that poverty remains as an important component of popular, political and academic discourse precisely because it is such a deeply contested concept. Poverty has its own socially constructed existence within that discourse and it has an impact which extends far beyond the sections of society which may or may not – according to the disputants – be substantively affected by poverty. The images which people have of poverty are diverse, complex and often powerful. Social policies calculated to relieve or prevent poverty in fact sustain poverty as a definable and manageable phenomenon and as a presence in the lives of everybody.

Recent departures in social policy have sought on the one hand to emphasise *processes* of social exclusion rather than the *condition* of poverty; and on the other to take into account the importance of agency, difference, discourse and change. The problems with such approaches are essentially twofold. First, concepts of social exclusion are themselves 'normalising': they leave unquestioned the efficacy of capitalist social relations from which people are axiomatically excluded if they cannot or do not sustain themselves through paid employment and maintain each other within families. Second, in concentrating on the subjectivity and diversity of the poor and the effects upon them of constitutive discourses and global transformations, it risks falling prey to the assumption that the poor and excluded are constitutionally different from the society which excludes them; that exclusion represents the failure of the strategies of the excluded rather than any divisive disciplinary logic which permeates society as a whole.

We have reviewed evidence which suggests that, if it were nothing else, poverty is a spectre – a socially constituted object of wholesome horror – which bears in complex and diverse ways on most people's consciousness. Most importantly, we have seen that worry about poverty is not related to the objective risks of material deprivation; that comparatively few are immune from such worry; that the spectre of poverty figures strongly in the minds of comfortable 'Middle England' and, perversely, with particular poignancy in the thinking of some of the most affluent members of the population; that belief in poverty as an exterior threat is sustained in the public imagination and continues to outweigh countervailing beliefs in the certitude of individual self-determination.

Poverty is probably as much a part of everyday concerns as it ever was.

3 The Spectacle of Riches

I'd like to be well-off or alright, but not like a millionaire or anything; not rich in that sense.

[Twenty-something woman earning less than £150 per week]

. . . . if you've got it you worry about losing it, and I think, you know, that. . . . I've been used to this lifestyle – what the hell happens to the future when it all disappears?

[Middle-aged executive earning £72,000 per annum]

In Chapter 2 we contrasted differing interpretations of the contemporary meaning of poverty. In this chapter we shall discuss competing perceptions of the meaning of wealth and riches. The first of the above quotations (taken from interviews conducted in the course of the authors' own research) illustrates, once again, an aspect of what Galbraith (1992) has characterised as the 'culture of contentment'. Galbraith has argued that, electorally speaking, American and British society is dominated by a contented majority that is characteristically self-affirming, short-termist, sceptical of state intervention, and tolerant of substantial inequality: 'The plush advantage of the very rich is the price the contented electoral majority pays for being able to retain what is less but what is still very good' (*ibid*: 26). The second quotation illustrates a different view. It is a view consistent with Ray Pahl's recent characterisation of the materially successful social stratum, not as a contented majority, but as the 'anxious class' (1995). Though Pahl stresses that anxiety is not a peculiar symptom of late modernity, but endemic to the human condition, he draws on interviews with a small number of highly 'successful' people to acknowledge, like Giddens (see our discussion at pp. 18–20 above), that 'As the language of class gives way to the language of lifestyle, so solidarity, conflict and action are replaced by self-identity, anxiety and balance for most, but certainly not all, members of society' (*ibid*: 20).

Much more has been written about theories of poverty than about theories of riches and still less about social attitudes to riches. In this chapter, none the less, we shall review such attempts as have been made to advance a theory of riches; we shall discuss socially constructed distinctions between 'comfortable' and 'exclusive' lifestyles and consumption patterns; and we shall revisit certain arguments about needs and desires. The chapter will also present evidence from the authors' own study of the meaning of riches and discuss the differences between that evidence and the findings discussed in the last chapter.

DEFINING RICHES

Scott has observed that such research as has been carried out on wealth (or riches) since the pioneering work of Chiozza-Money has become increasingly sophisticated in the way it has addressed the formidable technical difficulties associated with estimating wealth, but it has failed to advance in terms of the conceptualisation of the phenomenon: 'the wealthy are defined simply as the top X per cent of the population, with little consideration being given to the rationale for using any particular cut-off level.' (1994: 87). Scott himself proceeds to advance a theoretical framework, on which we draw extensively in this book, within which he conceptualises poverty and wealth – or deprivation and privilege – as comparable processes of exclusion from citizenship. This is an important insight. However, Scott neglects the contribution which Townsend has made to a theory of riches.

Although they have perhaps become lost in the midst of his voluminous discussion of poverty, Townsend makes two important points. First, he says:

> Riches are not only inherited or made: to be riches they have to be unavailable to the vast majority of the population. A theory of riches depends not only on theories of acquisition – how much wealth is inherited, accumulated by entrepreneurial effort or earned by the exercise of scarce skills. It depends also on theories of denial of access to wealth – through selective succession, testamentary concentration, limitation of entry to the professions, monopolisation of capital and property or at least severe restriction on the opportunity to acquire land and property. (1979: 365)

He therefore draws attention to the institutional structure of wealth, the class basis of wealth distribution, and the access of the very wealthy, not only to political power and influence, but also to the specialist accountancy, legal and financial expertise necessary actively to defend and promote their resources and interests. Secondly, Townsend suggests,

> The rich are not only favoured by the system, and exploit it. They actively shape its standards and values. They set fashions which become the styles sought after by the mass of the population. (*ibid*: 367)

In this way, the rich are continuously setting the standards by which to judge what it is not to be poor. This tendency Townsend defined as 'the proselytisation of lifestyles' and, by so doing, he prefigured elements of a more recent debate which we shall examine shortly.

For the moment we should return to Townsend's first point. The key to his structural account of riches is the assumed impermeability of the social stratum that constitutes 'the rich'. As a sociological concern this resonates with the kind of social mobility studies conducted by Goldthorpe and others (1980; 1987) and to which we have already briefly referred in Chapter 1. Just as it is difficult to determine how wealthy individuals are (since it depends, for example, on whether they have access to resources held by other family members or whether any assets they personally hold actually generate income or have realisable value) it can be difficult to deduce individuals' social class (depending, for example, on the stage of their careers, the permanence of their employment, and how their own occupation might compare with that of parents or partners). The validity of any attempt to rank people by wealth or class depends on certain broad assumptions about the meaning of wealth and the worth of certain occupations. Pahl is critical of social mobility studies because of the assumptions they make about what constitutes 'upward' and 'downward' mobility and because 'they say nothing about the distribution of motivation to succeed or whether success has a common and universal meaning' (1995: 11). A similar criticism might arguably be made against structural theories of riches and of attempts to define some structural cut-off point above which wealth ensures privilege. Such theory makes assumptions, not only about individual behaviour, but about the kinds of resources which constitute riches, and it says nothing about whether 'being rich' has any common or universally understood meaning.

There is a striking parallel here with a debate on the subject of poverty which took place in the columns of *New Society* in 1981 between Peter Townsend and David Piachaud (reproduced in Townsend 1993). Piachaud likened Townsend's attempt to locate a poverty threshold to a quest for the Holy Grail. The quest could never succeed because it took no account of the diversity of people's preferences and lifestyles and so obscured the nature of the moral and political judgements which are necessary to understand what poverty truly is. If one were – as Scott would urge – to seek a riches threshold, based on the kind of structural account offered by Townsend, the same sort of objection could be raised. While clearly there are individuals who are disproportionately privileged and have the institutional power to protect that privilege at the expense of others, it is as difficult to try and locate a resource threshold above which people are to be objectively defined as rich as it is to locate that below which people may legitimately be defined as poor. To do so, what is more, tells us nothing about the moral and political judgements by which people approve or disapprove of riches or the social meaning of the exclusivisity which constitutes being rich.

CONSUMPTION, LIFESTYLE AND IDENTITY

This brings us back to Townsend's second point about lifestyles. Townsend was construing lifestyle quite narrowly in terms of consumption patterns. In the event, changes which have occurred throughout the Western world since the 1970s have drawn attention to processes of consumption. In part this stems from changing production technologies and the effects of economic globalisation which make it possible, on the one hand, for specialised goods to be produced for a wide variety of niche markets and, on the other, for consumption-based lifestyles to permeate (or to be 'proselytised') around the globe. At one extreme it is increasingly possible – without being hugely wealthy – to order luxury goods to an exclusive customised specification, while at another, the quality of a MacDonalds hamburger or a pair of Levi jeans will be virtually identical wherever in the world one might choose to buy them. Consumption locations and patterns are argued by some commentators to reflect, not only the way in which people meet their needs, but also the basis of their social locations and/or the way in which they realise their identities.

In Chapter 1 we briefly discussed the work of Saunders (1984; 1990) in which he claimed that, in the 1980s, consumption sector cleavages represented a more significant basis of social division than differences based on production location or social-occupational class. The access of some working class households to previously exclusive forms of goods means that class has become a poor guide to 'consumption location'. A more significant social indicator, according to Saunders, is whether people elect to meet their needs for housing, health care, education, transport, leisure and so forth in the private sector or the public sector. The growth in Britain of owner-occupation and the expansion of occupational and private pensions (see, for example, Papadakis and Taylor-Gooby 1987) have certainly resulted in more people accumulating and being dependent upon private as opposed to collective sources of wealth. At the same time, in such areas of provision as housing and pensions, people who remain dependent on public sector provision tend increasingly to be drawn from lower income groups; to be marginalised – or indeed 'poor'. None the less, there are goods of the ilk discussed by Saunders, such as private health care and education, which, in spite of attempts to promote them, remain a relatively exclusive preserve (Taylor-Gooby 1994b). What is more, the extension of car and home ownership and private pension provision means that, as 'positional' goods (Hirsch 1977), these have lost the social value or meaning they once had when they were the exclusive preserve of a minority. At one level, Saunders' thesis is consistent with Townsend's suggestion that elements of the lifestyles of the rich inform the expectations of society as a whole. At another level, however, the thesis fails to explain how some elements of lifestyle are 'proselytised' and others are not, nor how social inequality and the privileges of the rich are sustained (for a more detailed critical discussion of Saunders, see Hamnett 1989).

In Britain towards the end of the twentieth century Conservative governments pursued policies calculated to extend both property and share ownership. Policies which gave local authority tenants the right to buy their homes at discounted prices accelerated a well established trend towards owner-occupation. However, while residential property has become an important form of financial asset for 'middle-wealth owners', for 'the very wealthy' substantial share and land-holdings are far more significant as assets (Hills 1995: 98). The privatisation of nationalised industries through popularly promoted share sell-offs did result in the spread of shareholding.

None the less, the majority of privately owned shares, in spite of privatisation sell-offs, are still highly concentrated (Scott 1994: 110). Wealth and income are related and the gradual long-term trend towards an apparent (but slight) equalisation of asset holdings is off-set by the dramatic increases in income inequality which we have already discussed, including, for example, the spectacular increases in top salaries and associated 'perks' enjoyed by the richest earners. Changing patterns of consumption have not signalled any erosion of the advantages of the rich.

The dominant icon of the capitalist era has evolved 'from satanic mill to shopping mall' (Blackwell and Seabrook 1985). In the process, post-modernist theorists insist, the imperatives of production which characterised industrial society have been superseded by imperatives of consumption. Commodities exist neither as use-values nor exchange-values but as 'signifiers' through which people articulate with the social order and 'negotiate' their individual self-identities (Baudrillard 1970; 1975). We are, so the argument goes, what we buy – or rather what we choose or can afford to buy. Bauman (1987; 1988) uses similar kinds of argument, but suggests that, in our consumption-centred society, the potential for realising the freedom of the sovereign consumer is limited by the existence of state provision. The argument is similar to that of Saunders. People who are not 'seduced' by the free community of independent consumers are 'repressed' by bureaucratised welfare services. However, Bauman's sometimes justifiable pre-occupation with the disciplinary character of state provision for the poor obscures awareness of the hierarchical nature of the rest of consumer society. Alan Warde, for instance, has taken Bauman to task for supposing that there can be 'harmless competition over the construction of self-identities'; for postulating 'difference without power, differentiation without hierarchy' (1994: 229).

Warde, drawing on the writings of Giddens (1991) and Featherstone (1991), caricatures the post-modernist conception of the 'heroic consumer' for whom lifestyle is her or his life project. By her or his calculative hedonism, self-conscious individual preferences and careful shopping, this creature of consumer culture gives ultimate expression to the virtues of the free market. Lifestyle in this sense has become more than Townsend supposed. It has ceased to be a matter of the example set by the rich, but has become a social construction that is paradoxically both differentiating and universalising. Warde himself calls on empirical evidence to show, for example, that while tastes in food since the 1970s in Britain have become more generally diverse and cosmopolitan, class distances in food consumption have not narrowed. His complaint against the notion of the heroic consumer is that 'The very notion of the individual consumer prevents us from appreciating the constraints people face in their consumption practices, as embodied persons rather than ghostly abstractions of economics' (*ibid*: 231).

We have suggested in Chapter 2 that all members of society are to an extent *driven* by the spectre of poverty. Might we similarly suppose that they are *drawn*: not by a spectre of riches, but by the ghostly abstraction of the heroic consumer; by the imperative of self-affirmation through lifestyle?

WASTE, INDULGENCE AND FUN

We wish to argue that people are not drawn directly to emulate the lifestyles of the rich in the way Townsend implies, even if they do have a certain fascination with being rich. The spectoral heroic consumer, we suggest, does not wish to be wasteful or indulgent, but s/he does seek to enliven her/his lifestyle with 'fun'. This is a speculative argument and, to explore it, we must revisit a well trodden discussion regarding the basis of human need and, in particular, the distinction between 'real' and 'imagined' needs.

There is an established theoretical tradition which supposes that the process of capitalist accumulation is driven by the generation of false or imaginary needs (for example, Marcuse 1964; Althusser 1971). What capitalism has accomplished 'has involved the appropriation of human need, and its irretrievable dispersal through a vast proliferation of capitalist commodities which deform and mutilate it; a process which directly reflects the capitalist appropriation and misshaping of human labour' (Seabrook 1985: 12). In thinking about consumption, it is quite commonplace to distinguish between consumption to meet 'basic needs' (however defined) and consumption to meet those new or higher needs which are generated by progress in social living standards in a post-scarcity society: the distinction is fundamental to the distinction discussed in Chapter 1 between absolute and relative poverty. Taylor-Gooby and Dale, however, point to a third type of consumption – 'waste', or 'consumption aimed at displaying social position' (1981: 230). This is the conspicuous consumption of the profligate or the rich. The distinction between ordinary consumption to meet legitimate new needs and 'waste' is as controversial and elusive as the distinction between basic needs and higher needs. It might be argued, once again, that this is a distinction that is as symbolic as it is real. What is at stake is the ideological process by which we negotiate consensus about what is wasteful and what is legitimate; about what is indulgent or ostentatious and what is just 'fun'. A rich person might buy a turbo-Bentley; an 'ordinary' motoring enthusiast might buy an Escort XR3i. Both are spending more than they need to obtain a motor car, but the scale and nature of their extravagence, we suggest, would be popularly perceived as being of a different order. One is being ostentatious. The other is engaging in some (relatively!) harmless fun.

In reality, of course, that consensus about what is wasteful and what is desirable is not negotiated by processes of rational communication. Though it is possible abstractly to envisage circumstances in which human beings would agree upon a distribution of resources which would satisfy real rather than imaginary or ideologically constructed needs (see Habermas 1976; 1986), it has been argued that our capacity to do so is hindered by the way in which our 'desires' are constructed in the realm of the symbolic (Lacan 1977). In grossly unequal contemporary Western societies, the heroic consumer's ideologically constructed desire for riches may be subverted, on the one hand, by contingent demands for 'comfort' falling short of riches and, on the other, by ideal prohibitions against the 'waste' that may be associated with riches: what is left of desire is a quest for security and, perhaps, a little fun. We are left, as Hewitt puts it, 'chasing the fading image of desire: a dot that is forever receding into the distance' (Hewitt 1992: 187).

There is a sense in which the desire for riches and the fear of poverty relate respectively to objects which can both be rather like dots forever receding into the distance. As people approach them, they appear to get further away. Poverty and riches are none the less quite differently constituted, the former being an object of wholesome horror and the latter an object of prurient fascination.

AN OBJECT OF PRURIENT FASCINATION

We therefore turn to evidence from the authors' own research which has investigated people's perceptions of riches through in-depth interviews conducted with 76 people with widely differing income levels (see Appendix A). The key findings to be discussed in this chapter are summarised in Table A.4b on p. 182.

The Meaning of Riches

When asked what being rich means just over half our respondents replied in terms which implied a perceived freedom from constraint. They spoke about being able to do, to buy, or to spend whatever one likes without having to worry or perhaps even to think about money. The freedom these respondents envisaged was sometimes expressed in quite frivolous terms. Being rich would be like being let off the leash: it would be fun. For example, 'I think sometimes I would like to be rich so I can go out; do all the things I've ever dreamt about; going away to faraway islands like blooming Seychelles or somewhere like that'. Only a minority within the sample sought to define riches in relation to some chosen wealth or income threshold. The other respondents (of whom some gave several definitions) offered an array of meanings ranging from references to such factors as 'security' and 'responsibility' on the one hand, to unreflexive comparative judgements – such as, 'someone who has more than me' – on the other.

Perhaps because they themselves already had more occasion to feel constrained, younger people, women and those on lower incomes seemed to be slightly more likely than older people and men and those with middle to higher disposable incomes to equate riches with freedom from constraint. With regard to income, however, the pattern was not a simple one, since respondents with more than twice average disposable income (whom we might call 'the rich' – see Table A.3, p. 176) turned out to be as likely as the very poorest respondents to equate riches with freedom from constraint. It may be that there is a resource threshold above which people acknowledge the freedoms associated with riches much more readily than those who are merely approaching that threshold (see Figure 3.1). Although it was not a decisive pattern, it did appear that the respondents whom we had identified as drawing predominantly on survivalist and conformist (that is, less reflexive) discourses were slightly more likely than those drawing respectively on entrepreneurial and reformist discourses (see Figures 1.6 and A.1 and discussions on pp. 18–21 and 177–8) to equate riches with freedom from constraint. The idea that it would be fun to be rich does perhaps have a certain mythological tenor.

Figure 3.1 Understandings of riches

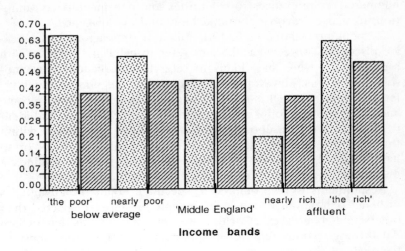

proportion of those responding saying being rich means freedom

proportion of those responding saying advantage of riches is privilege

Asked what kind of mental image or picture they had of riches, respondents gave a variety of replies. About a third of the sample responded with several images. The dominant images – whether expressed on their own or in combination with others – were images of celebrities (famous pop, film and sports stars); images of power and status, particularly of top business people or, less frequently, of royalty or the aristocracy; and images of conspicuous consumption rather than certain kinds of people (of big houses, private swimming pools, expensive cars and unlimited holidays). Personalities associated with power included well-known holders of inherited wealth (the Duke of Westminster), prominent 'fat cat' chairs and directors of top companies (such as Cedric Brown of British Gas), and 'self-made' millionaires. The latter category often included Richard Branson, founder of the Virgin companies group, who, because of his high profile publicity stunts and hot-air ballooning exploits, also tended to figure as a celebrity. Branson represents an ambiguous cultural icon of the late twentieth century and was mentioned at some stage during the interviews by almost a third of our respondents. Although references to images revolving around power and status were prominent, they were out-numbered by references to celebrities and conspicuous consumption; to images revolving around fame and extravagence.

Respondents whom we had identified as drawing on less reflexive discourses were most likely to refer to celebrities. Those with high incomes were least likely to refer to conspicuous consumption. There was, however, a minority within the sample which offered no images of riches and it was respondents from higher income and occupational groups and particularly those whom we had identified as drawing on entrepreneurial discourse that figured within this minority. Possibly, those who are more likely to seek or to have attained riches are less likely to harbour in their minds a distinctive or separable image of what constitutes riches.

Respondents were prompted to speculate about the advantages of being rich, about whether rich people are more respected than others; and about whether rich people enjoy more rights than others. All three questions required respondents to think more substantively about the meanings they attached to riches. Nearly half the sample spoke of the advantages of riches in terms of the privilege and power which rich people were assumed to enjoy. They referred to the social connections of the rich, to the powerful networks to which they belong, and of the resulting ability to fix things or get things done; of the preferential treatment they can expect from officialdom, the police and the courts; of the opportunities and choices which rich people have in relation to health, education, employment and legal services, including the opportunity, in the case of health and education, to opt for private as opposed to state provision. A small group of respondents harped back to the issue of unrestricted consumption and cited this as an advantage of being rich, but a slightly larger group spoke of the security which rich people enjoy. Other respondents (of whom some gave several different answers) offered a wide range of alternative replies: some of these anticipated our question about 'respect', referring to the high esteem in which the rich may be held; other replies dwelt on more trivial advantages, such as the ease with which rich people can get a table in a restaurant or tickets for the theatre.

Although the pattern cannot be regarded as decisive, it did appear that people on lower incomes were somewhat less likely than others to see the advantages of riches in terms of privilege or power and more likely to see them in terms of security. Once again, however, the detailed pattern is complex (see Figure 3.1). Although the likelihood of respondents saying that the advantage of riches is privilege increased with income, there is a 'blip' for respondents with incomes in the 'nearly rich' income band: we can only speculate that those who are close to the riches boundary may feel the need to deny or minimise the privileges which lie beyond that boundary. It also appeared that, of those respondents whom we had identified as drawing on less reflexive discourses, those who at the same time drew on conformist discourses featured prominently among the respondents saying the advantage of riches is privilege, while those drawing on survivalist discourses featured prominently among the respondents saying the advantage of riches is security. The mythology of riches has competing versions, including that which sees riches as a conspiracy of privilege and that which sees riches as an ultimate state of individual security.

When the proposition that rich people get more respect than others was put *explicitly* to respondents, less than a third agreed. A slightly smaller number disagreed and others offered an equivocal reply, saying this would depend on either the source of a person's riches or the way s/he used them. The implication seemed to be that people who had earned their wealth and/or had applied it to charitable or worthwhile purposes may be more deserving of respect than those who had not. Once again, Richard Branson often figured in respondents' discussions as a symbol of what we might with irony describe as the 'deserving rich'! Respondents from lower income groups and with less savings seemed more inclined than others to disagree that the rich attract more respect: those with little wealth might well be expected to deny that more respect should be accorded to the rich. Respondents whom we had identified as drawing on entrepreneurial and reformist (that is, more reflexive) discourses seemed more inclined than others to agree, while those whom we had identified as drawing on survivalist and conformist (that is, less reflexive) discourses (and those who were readers of tabloid newspapers) seemed more inclined than others to disagree. To acknowledge the respectful attention which the rich command is perhaps a reflexive, detached or cynical response, whereas those more inclined to mythologising discourse, precisely because they place an intrinsic value on mutual respect, may be more reluctant to concede any special respect to those who are wealthier than they are.

Asked whether rich people enjoy more rights than others, a majority of respondents agreed. Men were rather more likely to agree than women, but, in view of the leading nature of the question, this may again reflect the tendency on which we have remarked for men's opinions to be especially volatile (Dean and Melrose 1997 and see p. 39 above). Respondents in higher income groups were slightly more likely than those in lower income groups to agree, but it was those in the 'nearly rich' income band that seemed especially inclined to agree, reflecting again a boundary effect: those who are relatively affluent but not quite rich may be especially sensitive to, or resentful of, the things which they see as separating themselves from the rich. It also appeared that those respondents whom we had identified as drawing on reformist and conformist (that is, less autonomistic) discourses were more likely than others to agree, reflecting competing ideological accounts of inequality and differences of opinion between those who feel opposed to substantive inequality and those who value strictly formal equality.

The Attraction of Riches

Only six respondents in our sample acknowledged that they were rich, in spite of the fact that eleven members of the sample had disposable incomes of more than twice the national average and five had declared assets (excluding the value of their own homes and of any pension rights) in excess of £50,000 (and, in a couple of instances, considerably in excess of this figure). The richest member of the sample was identified by the *Sunday Times* as one of the richest 200 people in Britain, and another subsequently featured in several newspapers as one of the 'fat cat' business executives alleged to have been awarded an excessive pay rise. The rich, it would seem, can be reluctant to admit to their status. Some respondents gave qualified replies, saying that they were rich compared to others. A number said they were not 'rich', but 'comfortable': respondents from professional/managerial occupational backgrounds and those whom we had identified as drawing on entrepreneurial discourse featured prominently in this group. Most respondents, however, said unequivocally that they were not rich and these we asked whether they would like to be rich.

Of those responding, more than half said they would like to be rich. It was an answer given particularly by men and by respondents we had identified as drawing on survivalist discourse, reflecting a certain element of bravado or light-heartedness which characterised some of the replies given. Other respondents replied, either that they did not want to be rich, only 'comfortable', or simply that they would not like to be rich. Women, respondents in clerical occupations, and those whom we had identified as drawing on reformist and conformist (that is, less autonomistic) discourses figured prominently in the group that said it would like to be comfortable rather than rich: in other words those groups most at risk of economic insecurity and those more inclined to a deterministic understanding of inequality. Respondents from the 'Middle England' income band figured prominently in the group that did want to be rich, although, interestingly, there were members of higher income groups (including two respondents actually in 'the rich' income band) who said they did not want to be rich.

Those respondents who said they would like to be rich were asked how they thought they might become rich. Some respondents simply dismissed the idea that they would ever become rich or said they didn't know, but, of the respondents who engaged with the question, nearly a third responded in what might be called fatalistic terms, a smaller number in meritocratic terms, and the remainder gave other answers or discussed several ways to get rich, often combining fatalistic and meritocratic ideas. The fatalistic ideas about getting rich were those which referred to good fortune, good luck or the distant prospect of some windfall, such as a win on the National Lottery (an innovation introduced by the Conservative government in 1994 and a phenomenon which – in this and other contexts – loomed large in several interview transcripts). The meritocratic ideas were those which referred to hard work, entrepreurial skill and initiative. Meritocratic thinking was clearly outweighed by a preponderance of fatalistic thinking, especially among women, older respondents, respondents whom we had identified as drawing on survivalist discourse, and the readers of tabloid newspapers; giving some credence to the suggestion by Scott (1994: 159) that contemporary British culture is increasingly fatalistic. Against this view, however, it did seem that, in response to this question, respondents from lower income groups were more likely than others to subscribe to meritocratic ideas: the evidence of course is tenuous but, ironically, the work ethic and belief in individual effort may be strongest among those with the least prospect of obtaining riches.

To explore further what it is that generates the allure of riches, we also asked respondents why some people are rich; what is the cause of riches? Of those who discussed the question, about a quarter referred to such external or structural factors as birth or inheritance or the effects of government social and economic policies; about a third resorted to what might again be characterised as fatalistic discourse, saying that this is just the way that society works, or that it is inevitable; a small number of respondents attributed riches to the personal attributes of the rich, such as their entrepreneurial flair or hard work; and the remaining respondents gave other answers, or more usually combined different sorts of reply. On balance it was fatalistic explanations which predominated.

Respondents from lower income and occupational groups and those whom we had identified as drawing on survivalist discourse featured prominently among those who combined different, sometimes mutually conflicting, replies. The minority which attributed riches to the characteristics of the rich, predictably, all came from amongst those we had identified as drawing on entrepreneurial and survivalist (that is, autonomistic) discourses. This finding, however, should not obscure the fact that, at different moments and to various degrees, autonomistic discourses of individual desert also permeated interviews with other respondents (see p. 45 above). Men and respondents whom we had identified as drawing on reformist discourse featured prominently among those who attributed riches to external or structural factors: the latter was to be expected, but the apparent radicalism of men in this instance is perhaps attributable to more than mere discursive bravado, but a need to justify their own failure to be rich or richer than they are – a need which might not be experienced in quite the same way by women (see discussion in Chapter 6).

The effect of income on the ways in which respondents discussed the causes of riches appeared complex and is summarised in Figure 3.2. Only those on the very lowest incomes were more likely to attribute riches to structural factors than to fate, while respondents in boundary situations – those who were 'nearly poor' or 'nearly rich' – were more likely to attribute riches to fate than to structural factors; to experience an absence of control over their own fortunes.

AN ASYMMETRICAL RELATIONSHIP?

The evidence in this and the preceding chapter demonstrates certain parallels between the feelings which people have about poverty and riches, but also certain asymmetries. Poverty is apprehended

Figure 3.2 Perceived causes of riches

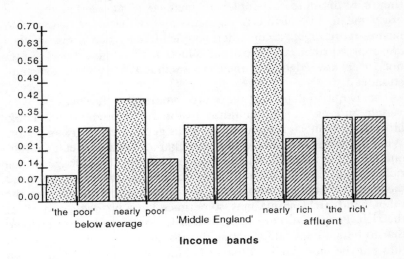

proportion of those responding attributing riches to fate

proportion of those responding attributing riches to structural factors

by many as a descent into an abyss that is to be avoided at all costs. The prospect of riches, however, is not embraced with the same kind of passion or enthusiasm that the descent into poverty is shunned.

Parallels and Divergences

Let us look first at the parallels between the ways in which people apprehend poverty and riches. We have seen that poverty and riches each tend in their way to be regarded as distant phenomena; as things which usually happen to other people. The images which people conjure up tend to relate to people who are unlike themselves or to situations quite different from their own. Poverty is frequently equated with the horrors of homelessness; riches with fame or extravagant lifestyles. The imagined disadvantages of poverty and the advantages of riches are seen by and large in a corresponding light: the former are most often seen in terms of the substantive constraints imposed by poverty, and the latter in terms of the special privileges permitted by riches. Related to this, though they may disapprove, people are inclined to agree that the poor are demeaned by having fewer rights and the rich are favoured by having more rights than other people. Even when arguably they *are* poor or rich, people can be reluctant to admit it; they prefer not to acknowledge that they are excluded from society's mainstream.

This is not to deny that there are important differences between people and, as we shall continue to discuss throughout this book, attitudes are affected by such factors as gender, ethnicity and class. What we have seen in the last two chapters are particular differences relating to disposable income. For example, the images which rich people have of the poor can be more harrowing than those harboured by people who are closer to poverty, although, on the other hand, rich people may sometimes have no images at all of the rich. People who are poor or nearly poor may be less inclined than others to speculate about the disadvantages of poverty, but they may be more inclined than others to think, not about the privileges which being rich would bring, but about the security it would provide. We have observed sometimes quite subtle differences resulting from what we have called boundary effects: people who are 'nearly poor' or 'nearly rich' sometimes see the world differently from either the rich, the poor or those inbetween. We have also seen that certain variations stem intelligibly from the different discursive and ideological repertoires on which people draw.

Intersecting these kinds of variation, however, are some fundamental differences between the way most people regard poverty and the way they regard riches. In certain respects the broad parallels or complementarity between the exclusionary potential of poverty on the one hand and riches on the other break down. People are likely to construe poverty narrowly, as a desperate condition to be strenuously avoided, while construing riches as a kind of freedom which, though it might be pleasant, is not necessarily to be hankered after. People are more likely to worry about becoming poor than they are to desire to be rich: comfort is acknowledged by some to be more important than riches. People are more likely to believe that the poor get less respect than others than they are that the rich get more respect: while poverty is strongly equated with disgrace, the rich are not necessarily to be held in high esteem. Finally, people are more likely to attribute poverty rather than riches to structural causes or external factors and more likely to see riches rather than poverty as a consequence of mere fate. Although we have found that comparatively few people blame poverty on the failings of the poor or attribute riches to the qualities of the rich, the processes which result in poverty and riches are differently understood. People may believe that they are as powerless to prevent their descent into poverty as they are to ensure their elevation to riches, but the mechanisms which might precipitate the former are more transparent and more to be feared, whereas becoming rich can be a matter of mysterious chance.

Comfort and Convention

In the conceptual model offered by Scott (1994), which we discussed in Chapter 1 (see especially Figure 1.4), deprivation or poverty on the one side and privilege or riches on the other lie as it were beyond the bounds of ordinary citizenship or the comfortable conventions of everyday life. The validity of this insight for people's perceptions of poverty and riches is in some measure borne out by the evidence. It is necessary none the less to emphasise two things. First, there are fundamental differences in the way that popular perceptions of deprivation and privilege are socially constructed and sustained. Second, the way that people feel about the boundaries between everyday experience and poverty on the one hand and between everyday experience and riches on the other are qualitatively quite different. These observations flow generally from the evidence discussed above and more particularly from further aspects of the authors' own work.

Though it is by no means a decisive influence on the way that people view the world, one of the factors which helps to shape or to perpetuate their understanding is news media output. During the course of the fieldwork for the research we have been discussing, the authors undertook a news monitoring exercise focused on the home news coverage contained in national daily and Sunday newspapers (see Appendix and, in particular, Table A.5b). We have already observed in Chapter 2 that one of the findings from the exercise was that, in the course of 1996, British newspapers devoted more coverage to news items relating to issues of wealth than they did to items relating to issues of poverty. Riches are deemed more newsworthy than poverty. The fascination of the news media with riches was especially focused on stories about extravagant pay deals, the share-option schemes, 'golden handshakes' and 'golden handcuffs' which characterised the approach in this era to the remuneration of top industrialists and business people. The pejorative expression 'fat cats' had been coined by the media to refer to the beneficiaries of these very substantial remuneration packages (for example, '21% pay rise storm for king of fat cats', *Star*, 2 July 1996; '£10million pay stirs fat cat row', *Guardian*, 29 August 1996). At one level, therefore, the rich did not receive a good press, a factor which both reflects and informs the ambivalence of public opinion.

At another level, however, the prurient fascination of the news media, especially the popular tabloid press, with the lifestyles and experiences of the rich far exceeded the attention given to the lifestyles and experiences of the poor. In the course of 1996 there were seven times more news items about the former than the latter in the tabloids and three times more in the broadsheets. The greater part of this coverage was devoted to spectacular consumption on the part of celebrity figures from the worlds of sport and entertainment, or of royalty or similarly prominent people. However, mixed with the awe in which the consumption of the rich was held was criticism; accounts which deplored the wastefulness of rich people or which called attention to their greed. In a year when the newly established National Lottery, with jackpot prizes of up to £22 million, generated substantial news coverage, there was also a steady stream of stories (four times as many in the tabloids as in the broadsheets) which dwelt upon the effects of sudden wealth on ordinary people, and especially its supposed dangers (for example, 'A big lottery win could test the best of us', *Express*, 5 January 1996; '£11million lotto win wrecked my marriage', *Mirror*, 26 January 1996). Though poverty was self-evidently not a good thing, nor necessarily were riches – in spite of the fact that they attracted so much more attention and excitement than poverty.

To an extent, the view of the world disclosed by a close analysis of news media output conforms with the the view of the world disclosed to us by our respondents when we interviewed them. We were mindful, however, that our respondents were telling us more than was disclosed explicitly in their answers to our questions. Respondents did engage with discourses of deprivation and privilege and most of them conveyed quite strongly their sense of the 'otherness' of poverty and the 'otherness' of riches. However, a holistic reading of the interview transcripts impressed on us the presence of other discourses which were more central. Respondents

Figure 3.3 The incidence of discourses of poverty and riches and the boundaries of ordinary citizenship

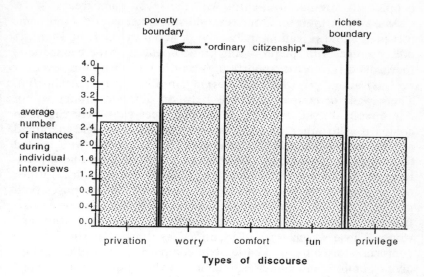

spoke a lot about their desire for comfort or their need to be comfortable; about the value which they placed on security, certainty, sufficiency or contentment. Conversely, respondents spoke a lot about worry; about insecurity, uncertainty and their anxieties. At the same time, respondents often talked about what is best described as 'fun'; they may not always explicitly have used the word and they did not necessarily give voice to personal desires, but they would speak about the attractions of unfettered consumer choice, of luxury, entertainment and escape. Plotting the instances of such discourses within the transcripts generated the simplified profile illustrated in Figure 3.3. The empiricial validity of this profile is open to challenge on several counts, but it is presented here as a means of understanding the boundaries of ordinary citizenship. The illustration is intended to convey the sense we obtained from our respondents that privation and privilege are each in their way a kind of intolerable excess; an excess of worry or an excess of fun. Poverty is envisaged as a state of misery and helplessness that is reached when worry becomes too much. Riches are envisaged as a state of indulgence and the abuse of power that is reached when fun is taken beyond its extremes. Ordinary life – ordinary citizenship – is a preoccupation with comfort. Comfort may be threatened by worry or enhanced by fun, but – provided these are kept within bounds – people will continue to identify with the social mainstream.

As a whole, therefore, our respondents talked more about comfort than about privation and worry, or about privilege and fun. At odds however with the prevailing preoccupations of the newspapers, they talked (given the opportunity) a little bit more (and certainly no less) about privation and worry than about privilege and fun. There were of course variations between different groups within our sample. In the event, gender differences were very slight. In comparison to other groups, respondents whom we had identified as drawing particularly on entrepreneurial discourse, who tended to be especially discursive, none the less talked least about privilege, while those whom we had identified as drawing on reformist and conformist (less autonomistic) discourses talked most about privilege. Similarly, those whom we had identified as drawing particularly on survivalist discourse talked least about privation and worry. Those whom we had identified as drawing particularly on conformist discourse talked least in comparison with other groups about comfort and fun. Respondents in the bottom income band talked more than other groups about both privation *and* privilege, while those from the 'nearly poor' income band talked more than other groups about comfort, but least about fun. In comparison to other income groups, repondents in the topmost income band talked most about worry and fun, while those from the 'nearly rich' income band talked least about privilege. Each of these variations provides a potential flash of insight, but the overall pattern of the profile illustrated in Figure 3.3 was remarkably consistent across all groups and this we believe to be by far the most important finding. Rich and poor alike, it would seem, in common with the majority, aspire to comfort before they aspire to privilege.

CONCLUSION

Galbraith's contented electoral majority is prepared to tolerate inequality; to settle for comfort rather than riches; but it is by no means complacent. Echoing Galbraith, Funken has pointed to the problems which even right-leaning governments experienced across late twentieth century Western Europe in 'meeting the expectations of a fun-loving, egocentric electorate' (1995: 4); but, however much there are those who value unrestricted consumer choice or who aspire to effortless riches (through, for example, the National Lottery), it remains the case, we believe, that the spectre of poverty is a more potent force than the spectacle of riches. Pahl's 'anxious class' may well be driven by anxiety to succeed (or fear of failure) but they are probably driven at least as much by fear of poverty. In a sense, neither Galbraith not Pahl seem quite to capture the sentiments of the Western middle classes, still less those of the general populations of capitalist liberal democracies. It is perhaps the conjunction of comfortable inertia and chronic anxiety which best characterises for all classes the contradictory mood of the late twentieth century.

No doubt people by and large would like to be free from ordinary discipline and prudence – to be 'let off the leash' would be fun – but perhaps they are not quite sure that they would feel comfortable if they no longer had the reassurance of familiar restraints. In extremely unequal societies all members of society are subject both to the repressive presence of poverty and the seductive presence of riches. The disciplinary effect of each presence is differently mediated, but both instil a certain acquiescence to the capitalist order. However, even for those who are neither rich nor poor, the presence and the symbolism of poverty and riches corrodes people's sense of ontological security. Not only is the prospect of poverty unsettling, but so is the capriciousness of riches. The problem with the capitalist order is that neither security nor success can be guaranteed.

4 Of Welfare and Citizenship

> The question is not whether all men will ultimately be equal –
> that they certainly will not – but whether progress may not go
> on steadily, if slowly, till, by occupation at least, every man is a
> gentleman. I hold that it may, and that it will.
>
> (Alfred Marshall, *The Future of the Working Classes*, 1873.
> Cited in T.H. Marshall 1950: 4–5)

We began Chapter 1 with an epigraph to illustrate a particular
nineteenth century view which imagined that the statuses of poverty and riches were natural, proper and unalterable. We begin
this chapter by illustrating a more 'progressive' nineteenth century
view which foretold that the civilising forces of industrialised liberal democracy would ensure the amelioration of class differences
and the possibility, not of social equality, but of equal citizenship.
The symbols in Alfred Marshall's vision are not of beggars and
castles, but of modern factories made congenial by the advance of
technology. It is a view which, precisely because it attributes status
to male occupations within the labour market, once again renders
invisible the lives of women and children. None the less, it is a
view which at least lays claim to encompass the ordinary mass; the
'civilised' working class who are neither rich nor poor.

The hope therefore was that the industrial proletariat or working class would be absorbed into a common citizenship status and
that most people would experience lives which were neither deprived nor privileged. In the event, modern technology did not and
does not now assure congenial employment for all. While the nature of class differences may have changed in the course of the
twentieth century, they have not been ameliorated. The gap between rich and poor, as we have seen, has lately been growing. In
Chapter 1 we discussed the work of Scott (1994) who has suggested
that deprivation and privilege (poverty and riches) remain as conditions which lie, as it were, beyond the pale of ordinary citizenship.
Scott refers to certain 'catastrophic' boundaries in the distribution
of resources (*ibid*: 175). Certainly, the extent of structural inequality

may be said to be catastrophic, although we argue in this book that the boundaries which fence off the rich and poor are essentially symbolic in nature.

We begin this chapter by addressing the concept of citizenship. We shall critically discuss the different conceptual or philosophical traditions which inform notions of citizenship before moving on to describe how the sociologist, T.H. Marshall, built upon the arguments of his (unrelated) namesake, the above mentioned Alfred Marshall, to advance the idea of 'social citizenship'. Social citizenship as a concept has been the cornerstone of much thinking about the nature of social justice and the welfare state. It is a concept which calls us back to issues of morality and we shall discuss the different moral repertoires which may characteristically be called upon in discussions of citizenship. Finally, we shall review some of the latest social attitude data to see what people seem to think about issues of inequality and social justice and the extent to which their values reflect notions of class interest or common citizenship. Are we yet all gentlemen and gentlewomen?

TRADITIONS OF CITIZENSHIP

The concept of citizenship – and of the civilised gentleman – can be traced back to ancient Athens. It was Aristotle (384–322 BC) who contended that 'There are by nature free men and slaves'. For the Athenian elite the concept of liberty associated with citizenship of a city state was a natural and not an ideologically constructed principle. Women did not figure in affairs of state and the state was founded on the exploitation of a social stratum which was regarded in effect as an inferior race. Aristotle's own theory of governance (which differed from that of Plato, his mentor) was sceptical of democracy. Athenean democracy was a form of self-government in which the members of the small and elite citizenry took turns to rule and to be ruled by each other. Aristotle foresaw that, divorced from the constraints of this particular context, the logic of pure democracy could in theory lead to mob rule, because 'as birth, wealth and education are the defining marks of oligarchy, so their opposites, low birth, low incomes, and mechanical occupations are regarded as typical of democracy' (1981: 364). He recognised that 'the democratic idea of justice is in fact numerical equality, not equality based on merit ... the result is that in democracies the poor have more sovereign power than the rich; for they are more numerous' (*ibid*: 362).

The issue of sovereignty is central to notions of citizenship. Modern conceptions of democratic citizenship, for the purposes of the somewhat streamlined argument presented in this chapter, are of two principal types: those which envisage a form of social contract in which sovereign power is negotiated between the citizen and the state; and those which subordinate sovereignty to solidarity and the need for citizens to achieve social integration and mutual cohesion. Some 2000 years after Aristotle, the fundamental normative concepts distilled from the foment of the Enlightenment into the triple slogan of the French Revolution – *liberté, egalité, fraternité* – express, as Hobsbawm once put it, 'a contradiction rather than a combination' (1962: 284). What crudely separates the two traditions of citizenship which we are outlining is that one (the social-contractual) is preoccupied with liberty whereas the other (the social-solidaristic) is more preoccupied with 'fraternity', fellowship, or what we might more properly call solidarity. However, both traditions, as we shall see, are ambiguous on the subject of equality. What is more, as we shall see in Chapter 6, both traditions remain fundamentally problematic so far as both women and minority groups are concerned. We shall examine these traditions in turn.

The Social-Contractual Tradition

The preoccupation of liberal philosophers from the seventeenth century onwards was not with self-government, but with the distinction between state and society (Held 1987). However, the idea of a 'social contract' between the individual citizen and the state has taken many forms, ranging from the essentially authoritarian prescriptions of Hobbes to the essentially libertarian prescriptions of Rousseau. These two thinkers in fact provide a useful illustration of opposing poles within this tradition.

Hobbes' (1651) central contention is that human beings are primarily self-interested and, in a state of nature, social life would amount to a war of all against all. The social contract which he conceptualises entails a surrender of individual sovereignty to a powerful state machine which would, in return, protect and guarantee the liberty of the individual against the predations of others. Rousseau (1762), on the other hand, imagined that in a state of nature human beings are 'noble savages', whose basic instincts – when transposed to a civilised society – will drive them, ideally, to strike a form of social contract that does not surrender sovereignty but retains it for the people. The process of government, according to Rousseau, should entail the articulation of the 'general will' and, at this point, his thinking begins enigmatically to transcend the distinction between contractarian and solidaristic conceptions.

Hobbes, in the gloomy scenario of his own imagination, sought to defend a sphere of civil society in which citizens, 'albeit . . . male citizens with "high standing" and substantial property', would be free from interference by the Leviathan state, although ultimately he failed 'to articulate either the principles or the institutions necessary to delimit state action' (Held 1987: 50–1), or to show how the poor might be protected from the power of the rich. In Rousseau's more optimistic scenario the distinction between state and civil society, between government and 'the people', is abridged. Rousseau is on the one hand anxious that 'no citizen shall be rich enough to buy another and none so poor as to be forced to sell himself', but on the other, he asserts, this does not imply 'that degrees of power and wealth should be absolutely the same for all, but rather that power shall stop short of violence and never be exercised except by virtue of authority and law' (1762: 96). Even for Rousseau, the radical-communitarian, the nature of the authority vested in the state by the general will should at best temper rather than redress the imbalance of power between the poor and the rich.

More recent contributions within this tradition include the theories of social justice advanced by Runciman (1966) (to whom we have already referred in Chapter 1) and, most influentially, Rawls (1972). Rawls' classic theory (which he has himself now partially recanted), like that of Hobbes, was based on a 'thought experiment' or illustrative device in which rational individuals in an imaginary 'original position' (from which they cannot know the material advantages or disadvantages which might befall them) negotiate a constitution for the distribution of 'rights and liberties, opportunities and powers, income and wealth' (1972: 92–3). The social contract which they would negotiate, according to Rawls, would provide for political liberty, for limits to social inequality and for equality of opportunity. The problems with this abstract formulation are first, that the scenario is unrealistic and, without more information about how primary goods would be socially distributed, people might in reality be inclined to gamble against the risk that they will end up poor rather than rich (Plant *et al*: 1980); second that the 'experiment' is predicated on assumptions which endorse the principles of market exchange and a discourse of rights founded on essentially bourgeois legal categories (Campbell 1983, and see pp. 85–7 later in this chapter).

Doyal and Gough (1991) have none the less defended the principles espoused by Rawls as being consistent with a universal theory of human need. Rawls assumed that, in the event of scarcity, the people in his experiment would agree to limit inequality by ensuring that primary goods were distributed equally unless an unequal distribution was to the advantage of the least favoured. This, say Doyal and Gough, would ensure basic need-satisfaction with equal autonomy, although they acknowledge that a more general application of Rawlsian principles runs into difficulty when applied in economic circumstances where poverty and affluence already exist side by side. The problems with all social-contractual theories, we would argue, are thrown into relief by the ways in which they contend with the existence of poverty and riches. The doctrine of contract requires formal parity of status between the parties and, where the initial distribution of power and resources between participants is grossly unequal, any formal contract must be a sham. The discourse of social-contractual citizenship may effectively obscure disparities of income and wealth and differences based on class, gender and ethnicity. At the extremities of the citizenship it constructs, the doctrinal logic of the social-contractual tradition – even in its most humanistic form – becomes strained.

The Social Solidaristic Tradition

While the logic of the social contractual tradition, in its most vulgar Hobbesian version, assumes the common moral nexus of humanity to be a war of all against all, the social solidaristic tradition could be said, in equally dramatic terms, to assume that common moral nexus to be 'the dependency of all upon all' (see Dean 1996: 35). However, the social solidaristic tradition has two very distinct manifestations. The first is an essentially conservative, Christian democratic tradition and the second the essentially reformist, social democratic tradition.

Both traditions have been forged, not so much through abstract reasoning about the nature of citizenship, as through the political struggles through which class conflicts have been institutionalised or accommodated. Michael Mann (1987) provides an analysis of

Figure 4.1 Traditions of citizenship

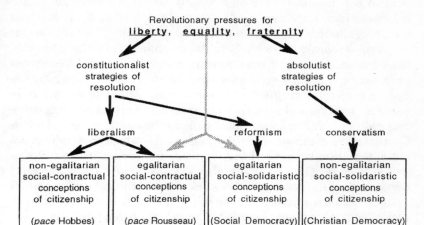

the two distinctive strategies by which the challenges mounted by the new middle class (or bourgeoisie) and the working class (or proletariat) against the *ancien régimes* of feudal Europe were resolved. The first, the absolutist strategy, required that the despotic power of the monarch should be exercised partly through selective tactical repression, but also through 'divide and rule' negotiations with powerful groups in society. It was this kind of strategy which led ultimately to the kind of corporatist, predominantly Catholic, regimes of continental Europe. The second strategy, the constitutionalist strategy, required a much earlier development of civil citizenship and the popular franchise. This kind of strategy led, on the one hand, to the liberal social contractual models of citizenship which we have already discussed, but also to the kind of Fabian and social democratic reformism which informed the development of the British and the Nordic welfare states. A synthesis of Mann's analysis with the ideas developed in this chapter is diagramatically presented in Figure 4.1. This 'ideal-typical' representation does not do full justice to the complexity of the competing ideological influences which have been implicated in the history of modern states, but it does, in particular, help us to distinguish the roots of two rather different conceptions of 'solidarity'.

The first conception of solidarity is that characteristically embodied in the Christian democracy of continental Europe, although

elements of the concept (though *not* the term itself) are also evident in other conservative and conservative-communitarian political discourses, including Anglo-Saxon 'One Nation Toryism'. It is
not an egalitarian conception (see Spicker 1991). 'Solidarity' in this
tradition is consistent with Catholic teaching about the nature of
the common good and mutual responsibility. It stems from commitment to the purposes and collective interests of particular social or corporate groups and communities, rather than society in
general. This kind of solidarity is concerned with social integration
and cohesion, but it is not universalist in nature. Spicker reminds
us 'there are some solidaristic relationships which may inhibit social integration because of the tendency to atomise distinct groups
within society' (1991: 25; see also Levitas 1996). The reciprocity
demanded of the citizen by this kind of solidarity is born of neither
enlightened self-interest, nor altruism. There is a mutually constitutive dynamic to the interdependence of citizen and state: one
cannot exist without the other. The compunction of the individual
citizen to be solidaristic is encapsulated in the Hegelian ideal that
the state is more than the sum of its citizens; that it is 'in fulfilling
his [*sic*] duties as a citizen [that the individual] gains protection
for his person and property, consideration for his particular welfare,
satisfaction of his substantial essence, and the consciousness and
self-awareness of being a member of a whole' (Hegel 1821: 285).

The other conception of solidarity is that characteristically embodied in the social democratic tradition; in the mutualism of the
early utopian socialists; in the trade union and guild socialist movements; and, ultimately, in the Anglo Saxon context, in the Fabian-
ism of the Webbs and such figures as Tawney. Social democratic
political parties have played a significant part in advocating social
reform across Europe and, in Nordic countries, they achieved the
ascendancy necessary to pioneer what has been termed a 'Middle
Way' between capitalism and socialism (Childs 1936) (though one
which is now increasingly fragile – see Gould 1993; 1996). It is,
however, in the Anglo-Saxon variant of the tradition and, specifically, in the writings of Tawney that a very distinctive account of
solidarity, or 'fellowship' may be found (see George and Wilding
1985 and 1994; Deakin and Wright 1995).

Tawney's argument was that political democracy should accommodate, not only a form of governance, but a kind of society in
which 'social institutions ... should be planned, as far as possible,
to emphasise and strengthen, not the class differences which

divide, but the common humanity which unites' (1931: 41). Tawney believed in the moral equality of all human beings. While people's 'natural endowments differ profoundly, it is the mark of a civilised society to aim at eliminating such inequalities as have their source, not in individual differences, but in its own organisation'. The objective was to achieve 'a community of responsible men and women working without fear in comradeship for common ends' (*ibid*: 101). Equality, therefore, was central to 'fellowship'; to the creation of a cohesive, integrated, solidaristic society in which all citizens could participate. Tawney was influential in the mid-twentieth century both generally within the British Left and specifically as a policy adviser to the Labour Party. The moral values which underpinned the reformist project that he represents were derived fundamentally from Christian (Protestant) convictions. However, there is also a broader, albeit unacknowledged resonance, between the moral emphasis of Tawneyism – and that of many other Fabians and social democrats – and the philosophy, not of Marx, but of Kant. This is a point to which we shall return, after we have explored the idea of social citizenship which, although it has attained especial pertinence within the social-democratic tradition, is an important analytical concept that enables us to address the relationship between citizenship and class.

OF GENDER AND NATION

Fiona Williams (1989) has argued that the themes of *work*, *family* and *nation* represent three fundamental organising principles in the development of modern welfare states. These three themes reflect, respectively, social divisions based on class, gender and 'race'. The issue of class and citizenship is central to this chapter and, as indicated, will feature particularly in our discussion of social citizenship. However it is important that we should first consider the relationship between the traditions of citizenship and gender on the one hand, and nation on the other.

Gendered Citizenship

We have remarked several times now on the extent to which, historically, citizenship has been a status conferred on men and not women. In spite of more than a century of piecemeal legal reform by which the impediments to citizenship for women have been eroded, there remain instances in which prevailing legislative arrangements provide for women what amounts to 'second class citizenship'. This is because some rights (for example to certain welfare benefits) may even now be mediated by men (Lister 1990a), or because the nature of rights conferred (for example to child support) subjects women to the possibility of greater state surveillance or control (Smart 1989). What is more, as Lister has remarked, 'a mantle of invisibility cloaks women in much of the more contemporary discourse around citizenship' (1990b: 453).

The philosophers who have articulated the traditions of citizenship which we have outlined were, of course, all men. Liberal seventeenth century social-contractual theorists like Locke believed that women, because of their reproductive capacity, were naturally dependent on men and that their emotional nature rendered them incapable of the 'reasonableness' required for social-contractual citizenship. Similarly, Hegel, whom we have associated with social-solidaristic conceptions of citizenship, justified the subordination of women within the 'natural' realm of the family and their exclusion from the realm of the state in terms of women's 'ethical disposition'. Sydie (1987) has shown how imagined natural differences between men and women have underpinned much Western philosophical thinking.

More fundamentally, perhaps, even in the absence of erroneous assumptions and conscious bias, where the discourse of citizenship theory is concerned with abstract states of mind, feminists have argued that the resulting constructs are inherently masculine; they are theories populated by universal and ahistorical men (for a discussion see Dryzek 1990). From this standpoint, the problem with all citizenship traditions (as distinct from the men who constructed them) is that they fail to address the actual, socially constructed, differences between women and men; they are estranged from particular contexts, situations and relationships. Haraway (1991), for example, would castigate 'master theories' (or 'God-tricks') of the nature we have described because of their totalising character. This critique would apply to all the traditions we have attempted to categorise.

Nation-Based Conceptions of Citizenship

It must also be said that there are normative conceptions of citizenship which do not neatly fit within our categorisation. Most of these tend to be conceptions based on the idea of the nation and nationhood. We wish to argue that such conceptions tend to be nationalistic or racialised variations on the principal categories. This is not to diminish the significance of nation-based conceptions. 'Race' and ethnicity are issues which, historically, have lain at the very heart of definitions of citizenship and social belonging. Colonialism, imperialist struggles, international trading relations and global economic competition between nation-states all have enduring consequences for the way in which understandings of citizenship are contextualised and constructed.

Nation-based conceptions of citizenship may be reflected at one level in exclusionary policies in relation to immigration control and welfare provision, or at another in popular intolerance, xenophobia or racism (Solomos 1989; Miles 1989; 1993). Nation-based conceptions of citizenship may also be reflected in the ways in which the rights and duties of indigenous populations are construed. At one extreme, such political philosophies may appear superficially benign. At the other, they may be transparently odious. As an example of the former, it is possible to point to the social liberalism that characterised the reforming British governments of Lloyd George during the early part of the twentieth century. Here was a political philosophy which was preoccupied with national efficiency, with health and hygiene, and with the well being of the national 'stock'. As an example of the latter, we can point to eugenics and to Fascism. These are philosophies concerned with the close and coercive regulation of populations and the purity of the national stock.

Social liberalism may be said to have defining elements in common with non-egalitarian social-solidaristic conceptions of citizenship. Its underlying objectives reflected an attempt to moderate the impact of economic liberalism (Thane 1982; Peden 1991) and, in many ways, it closely resembles the conservative communitarianism of 'One Nation Toryism'. Eugenics and Fascism, on the other hand, may be regarded as extreme but admittedly highly ambiguous versions of a non-egalitarian social-contractual conception of citizenship. Their underlying objectives, though anti-liberal and in some respects radically conservative (see Goodwin 1987), imply a Hobbesian view of human nature and an impulse towards authoritarian control. In suggesting such associations, we are less concerned with the ideological integrity (or lack of it) of differing political philosophies as with the logic which underpins different understandings of citizenship. *Nation* is a theme which inevitably interpolates and, indeed, is capable of restricting or distorting such logic.

SOCIAL CITIZENSHIP AND CLASS

Citizenship is a status attaching to membership of a community which need not in principle be territorially defined. In theory, at least, citizenship may be highly parochial (as in the Athenian city state); it may be transnational (as in the case of such bodies as the EU); it may in time become global (see, for example, Giddens 1996). Citizenship is a matter of associative principles, whether they be contractarian or solidaristic. The essential point is that status predicated on citizenship, however defined, is logically different from status predicated on class and on processes of domination or struggle.

The Components of Citizenship

Contemporary discussion of citizenship has been profoundly influenced by the insights of the sociologist, T.H. Marshall (1950; 1981). Marshall famously characterised modern *democratic-welfare-capitalist* societies as 'hyphenated societies' (see the diagramatic representation in Figure 4.2). Citizenship in modern Western societies consists of three interdependent components: political democracy; a welfare state; and a market economy. According to Marshall, these three components, to the extent that they embody opposing principles, must exist in equilibrium with each other in order to guarantee full citizenship status.

Corresponding to the three components of citizenship are three different kinds of rights: civil rights, political rights and social rights. Civil rights incorporate the panoply of property rights, legal guarantees and freedoms upon which the development and maintenance of a market economy depends. Without civil rights, capitalist political economies could not have developed and, in England at least, the development of 'modern' civil rights could be said to have been achieved by the eighteenth century. Political rights incorporate, not only the right to vote, but rights of association and constitutional participation; rights which enabled the industrial middle classes finally to break the old aristocracy's hold on power. The extension of the political franchise to the middle classes, and later to most adult males was achieved in England in the course of the nineteenth century (although universal suffrage was not finally achieved in Britain until 1928). Social rights incorporate entitlements to basic standards of education, health and social care, housing and income maintenance. Such rights were developed in the course of the

Figure 4.2 T.H. Marshall's hyphenated society

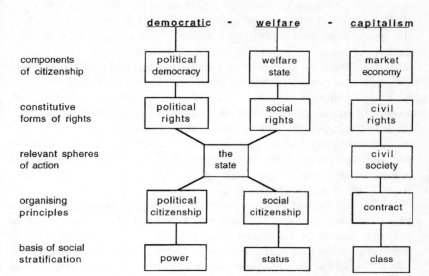

twentieth century and reached their ultimate expression in Britain with the formation of the post-Second World War 'welfare state', which had come into being shortly before Marshall first advanced his theory. Marshall's characterisation of the process by which modern citizenship attained maturity can be criticised for its historical crudity and its ethnocentric orientation (for a discussion of various critiques see, for example, Barbalet 1988). In later writings, what is more, Marshall himself offered an altogether less radical interpretation of citizenship (Rees 1995). None of this has diminished the theoretical importance of the model he initially propounded or the purchase of the idea of 'social citizenship'. The United Nations' Universal Declaration of Human Rights of 1948 had announced that fundamental human rights incorporate not only formal civil and political freedoms, but also substantive social and economic entitlements. Marshall succeeded in translating such rhetoric into sociological analysis.

Central to this theory was the idea that citizenship and class embody opposing principles. Civil rights underwrite the operation of the market economy and are entirely consistent with class inequality. However, in their different ways, political rights and social rights tend to challenge such inequality. The sphere of the state in its democratic and welfare dimensions exists in tension with the sphere of civil society. Political rights provide a basis on which to challenge the distribution of power, but on their own cannot equip the powerless: formal political freedoms may be exploited to perpetuate substantive class inequalities or they may at best enable labour to organise collectively against the interests of capital. Social rights, however, provide a basis on which all citizens ought to be equally able to participate in the spheres of civil and political society; a guarantee that all individuals will be sufficiently educated, healthy and socially and economically secure to compete in the market economy and to play a part in the democratic process. It was the development of social rights, T.H. Marshall claimed, that would realise Alfred Marshall's vision of an equality of status that transcends class difference.

Welfare state reforms therefore wrought fundamental changes in the nature of class differences: 'Equalisation is not so much between classes as between individuals within a population that is now treated for this purpose as though it were one class' (Marshall 1950: 33). In the process, however, one form of stratification would be exchanged for another as differences based on contractual standing within the labour market would be superseded by differences based on citizenship status, social justice and, particularly, educational attainment. Marshall contended that 'in the twentieth century citizenship and the capitalist class system have been at war', but then he adds

> Perhaps the phrase is rather too strong, but it is quite clear that the former has imposed modifications on the latter. But we should not be justified in assuming that although status is a principle which conflicts with contract, the stratified status system which is creeping into citizenship is an alien element in the economic world outside. (1950: 40)

At a theoretical level, Marshall's thesis is distinctively Weberian while, at the normative level, the argument is essentially meritocratic. Quantitative differences of class, he believed, should give way to qualitative differences of status. Inequality of provision was acceptable providing there would be equality of entitlement (Dahrendorf 1996). Citizenship was ultimately compatible with capitalism. That which Marshall defines as 'conflict' represents, not a struggle between competing social classes, but a conflict between abstract principles (Bottomore 1992). The emergence of social citizenship has not dissolved class inequalities or class struggles, but it has furnished a new ideological discourse with regard to the *justice* of riches and poverty.

The Marxist Critique

Marshall's views were shaped by a critical reaction to Marxism and by a belief in the reformist project of the welfare state (see Giddens 1996). Certainly, it is possible to detect three senses in which the Marxist tradition is at odds with Marshall's celebration of democratic-welfare-capitalist citizenship.

First, Marx's conception of social class – though not consistently expressed in his writings – was none the less fundamentally different from that implied by Marshall. The principal emphasis throughout Marxist theory (1848; 1894) is that social classes are distinctively constituted by the mode of production within society. It is not possible for class to be 'ameliorated' other than through a transformation of the mode of production. Even where classes do not exist self-consciously 'for themselves', they may still exist objectively 'in themselves' (1847) and the mere fact that class conflict or resentments may be assuaged through forms of social provision can not of itself create a classless society. The 'dissolution of all classes' and the 'redemption of humanity' would depend, according at least to the early Marx, on the political ascendancy of a particular class, the proletariat.

Second, Marx had expressly criticised what might be called the 'hollowness' of bourgeois citizenship in the nineteenth century; the disparity between the formal legal and political equality it promised and the substantive inequality which characterises capitalist social relations. As Anatole France was later cynically to remark, our citizenship may afford us all 'prince and pauper alike . . . an equal right to sleep under a bridge or eat at the Ritz'. Although Marx himself was far from dismissive of the advances which could be achieved by political reform and constitutional struggle, political emancipation was no substitute for human emancipation (see discussion in Barbalet 1988: 3). Marx dismissed as 'political superstition' the idea that civil society could ultimately be held together or regulated by the state, rather than the other way around. Any form of administrative reform or state action to redress poverty is doomed to fail, as it did when attempted by the ineffectual revolutionary Prussian Convention of the 1840s, of which Marx observed:

In so far as the State admits the existence of social evils, it attributes them to *natural laws* ... England explains pauperism as the consequences of the evil dispositions of the poor, just as the King of Prussia explains it by the unchristian disposition of the rich, and as the Convention explains it by the sceptical, counter-revolutionary outlook of the property owners. Accordingly, England inflicts penalties on the poor, the King of Prussia admonishes the rich, and the Convention beheads property owners. In the last resort, every State seeks the cause in adventitious or intentional defects in the administration, and therefore looks to a reform of the administration for a redress of those evils. ... The contradiction between the aims and good intentions of the administration on the one hand, and its means and resources on the other, cannot be removed by the State without abolishing itself. ... The State is founded upon the contradiction between public and private life, between general and particular interests. The administration must, therefore, limit itself to a formal and negative sphere of activity, because its power ceases at the point where civil life and its work begin. In face of the consequences which spring from the unsocial character of the life of civil society, of private property, trade, industry, of the mutual plundering by the different groups in civil society, *impotence* is the natural law of administration. (1844, cited in Bottomore and Rubel 1963: 222–3)

Third, in Marx's later writings (1867) and in their development, particularly by the Soviet jurist Pashukanis (1978), there is a critique of some of the fundamental categories of citizenship discourse. The argument here is that the bourgeois conception of civil rights and such legal concepts as equity, restitution and entitlement have their origins in the very form of capitalist social exchange. In so far that citizens are constituted as individual juridical subjects they are bearers of rights only in the sense and to the extent that they are also the individual owners of exchangable commodities. In the same way that all socially produced goods, labour itself and even land are reduced under capitalism to commodities, so the individual is reduced to being the bearer of rights and to the abstract fetishised status of citizen. Citizenship in this guise is constructed around the needs or wants of isolated individuals, promoting their own interests in the marketplace. The essential form of civil law, according to Pashukanis, is borrowed or adapted within the sphere of public law to create the fiction of the democratic citizen. Although the

State apparatus is ultimately controlled in the interests of the economically dominant class in society, it is kept formally separate from the sources of economic power and preserves only the appearance of freedom and equality for all.

The original Marxist critique addressed the failures of bourgeois citizenship to remedy poverty, but it did not fully anticipate the development of social citizenship. This task fell to later neo-Marxist commentators and found its expression in what Klein (1993) has mischievously characterised as 'O'Goffe's tale'. O'Goffe's tale is the composite account of the modern capitalist welfare state which has been told by James O'Connor (1973), Ian Gough (1979) and Claus Offe (1984). O'Goffe's tale is loyal to the Marxist tradition to the extent that it regards social citizenship and the welfare state as distinctive products of developing capitalist relations of production, distribution and exchange. It also recognises them as inherently contradictory phenomena.

O'Goffe's tale acknowledges that social citizenship has involved significant achievements for the working class: indeed, it has in part resulted from political struggles by or on behalf of the working class for better living conditions and for protection against the contingencies of sickness, unemployment and old age. In the process, however, capital has benefited, both indirectly from the growth of social consumption, and more directly from reductions in direct labour costs. The development of capitalism actually required investment in 'social capital', so as to provide a skilled, healthy and contented workforce. More fundamentally, social citizenship provided systems of administrative and normative control which were necessary to the viability of the wage labour system: as Offe (1984: 99) argued, 'the owner of labour power first becomes a wage labourer as a citizen of a state'.

According to O'Goffe's tale, the potential of social citizenship is contradictory, not only from the point of view of the working class (to whom it offers freedoms and substantive benefits on the one hand, and controls and discipline on the other), but also from the point of view of capital's own interests. The costs of the social entitlements and of the social expenses involved in maintaining political stability, to the extent that they fall on capital itself, will ultimately prove unsustainable and are bound to lead to fiscal crisis. The ultimate contradiction, once again in Offe's words, is 'that while capitalism cannot coexist *with*, neither can it exist *without* the welfare state' (1982: 11). Social citizenship is part and parcel of class society.

The Limits of Social Citizenship

While the Marxist critique emphasises the distinctive ambiguity of social citizenship in relation to First World capitalism, there are other accounts which emphasise different kinds of limitation. Some of these would seek to limit the extension of social rights; others recognise that social rights have limits of their own.

Numbered among the former are commentators of the political right. Neo-liberal critics like Hayek (1976) give primacy to the civil rights of citizenship. Social rights, they would say, are a dangerous myth. If the rich have obligations to the poor these are moral obligations that have nothing to do with rights. British government ministers in the 1980s (see, for example, Hurd 1989) have argued in favour of a form of 'active citizenship' sustained by voluntary service rather than social citizenship sustained by the payment of taxes. Rather like the King of Prussia in the above quotation from Marx, conservative politicians have enjoined the better off, in the spirit of *noblesse oblige*, to give time and commitment to their communities. Underlying these arguments, paradoxically, is a concern that is shared with the neo-Marxists: while formal civil and political rights are universally affordable, universal rights to substantive social benefits come with a price-tag which may place them out of reach.

A related concern has been expressed by Hirsch (1977). One of the explicit assumptions of the Beveridgean welfare state was that its sustainability would depend on full-employment and continuous economic growth. Hirsch's argument is that the 'reluctant collectivism' which informed the development of the social rights of citizenship exhibited two failings. First, it accepted the erroneous assumption of economic liberalism that the maximisation of individual economic advantage is obtainable by all. Second, it failed to foresee the problem of 'social scarcity'; the reality that, once material scarcity is conquered, a range of goods (such as education) acquire a 'positional' nature (so that their relative value is diminished the more they become universally available). While the principles of economic liberalism were thereby weakened, norms of individual self-interest and advancement were promoted. This amounted to an attempt to 'erect an increasingly explicit social organisation without a supporting social morality' (1977: 12). The only way to achieve a commonly shared sense of social justice, according to Hirsch, will be to accept a restriction on self-advancement and economic growth.

Mirroring this concern with the social limits to growth have been concerns with the physical and environmental limits to growth expressed within the Green movement, the social-ecology wing of which favours an alternative approach to social rights that would support more diverse but sustainable kinds of living (for example, Kemp and Wall 1990).

It is widely held that the welfare state and the basis of social citizenship have undergone something of a crisis since the 1970s (for example, Mishra 1984). T.H. Marshall himself acknowledged that the welfare state had failed to deliver the prosperity and the redistribution of wealth which some had hoped for and that it survived 'in a precarious and somewhat battered condition' (1981: 129). In the event, in Britain the welfare state has proved 'robust', surviving 'an economic hurricane in the mid-1970s and an ideological blizzard in the 1980s' (Le Grand 1990: 350). This is not to say that the welfare state was not in key respects 'reconstructed' (Johnson 1990) or that some of its fundamental principles and assumptions were not re-examined (see, for example, Taylor-Gooby 1991).

The 'ideological blizzard' which social citizenship has weathered included a fierce neo-liberal wind whose impact may be seen in the significant privatisation or 'marketisation' of state welfare provision; but also a penetrating neo-conservative sleet whose chilly authoritarianism has permeated into the recesses of welfare entitlement in the form of new controls and conditions. The concerns reflected by such changes are expressed by commentators like Mead whose concept of 'equal citizenship' required 'that everyone discharge the common obligations, including social ones, like work' (1986: 11). The emphasis of social citizenship shifted from that of rights to duties and, in Britain, this became most evident in such measures as the Child Support Act and the introduction of the Job Seekers' Allowance (see Dean 1996).

Some writers have welcomed this new focus on social duties. Roche (1992), for example, would argue that the emergence of new forms of poverty in the Western world signal, not only a failure, but the 'limit case' of the old model of social citizenship. This opens up for debate such questions as familial, ecological and intergenerational duties and the need to extend social rights into a post-industrial, post-national context. Similarly, Culpitt (1992) believes that the nature of the debate has now been redrawn and that it is possible to rethink the moral and philosophical basis of social obligation in terms of recognition and respect for mutual vulnerability. Within this spirit,

Twine (1994) has sought to reclaim a concept of social citizenship founded in social and environmental interdependence. He argues that 'Arising from our social interdependence, democratic citizenship should be directed to the social development of all. First through provision of social rights and, second, through participation in the recreation of society' (1994: 6).

Against such optimism, it must be recognised that social rights of citizenship remain subordinate to other kinds of rights (see Dean 1996). While civil rights are enforceable through the courts and political rights through the electoral system, social rights are altogether more vulnerable, having no distinctive forum for their expression or realisation. The enforcement of existing social rights is dependent either upon administrative procedures, or upon a court system that is ill equipped to address matters of public policy. The creation or development of social rights is dependent upon the political process, whose centre of gravity reflects (depending on one's perspective) the interests of the dominant economic class and/ or the needs of a comfortable majority. There is a very real sense in which social rights of citizenship are 'boxed in'. Though they may fail to give full expression to social citizenship, neither are they free from the dominance of the civil and political infrastructures that ultimately determine the nature and extent of social inequality.

Moral Repertoires

Bryan Turner has claimed that 'citizenship exists despite, rather than because of capitalist growth' (1986: 141) and he has pointed to a range of other influences – war, patterns of migration, the impact of new social movements – on the development of citizenship. Certainly, it is evident that capitalism does not fashion a distinctive single form of citizenship. We have ourselves outlined above (pp. 73–9) four separate philosophical traditions which have informed the development of citizenship over time. It is possible to link those traditions to four different kinds of discourse bearing upon the control and regulation of human societies. We shall in a moment be making links between the taxonomy of discourses introduced in Chapter 1 and the kinds of 'moral repertoire' that inform the different citizenship traditions. To achieve this, however, we need to make another brief excursion and to weave into our analysis insights from another important theorist, Michel Foucault, whose concern was with the way in which the development of citizenship is associated with new forms of discipline and social control.

According to Foucault (1981), in antiquity the patriarchal family head had power of life and death over children and slaves; in the middle ages the sovereign retained the power of life and death over his subjects; in the modern era, however, 'the ancient right to *take* life or *let* live was replaced by a power to *foster* life or *disallow* it' (*ibid*: 138). From around the seventeenth century onwards the modern political state has been concerned, with ever increasing sophistication, with the *administration* of life and the body. There have been two distinct forms of power over bodies. The first is concerned with the body of the individual, its capabilities, its usefulness and its docility: this form of power is concerned with the refinement of disciplinary procedures and techniques, and with what Foucault calls 'the anatomo-politics of the human body' (*ibid*: 139). The second is concerned with populations of bodies and their propensity for propagation, mortality and morbidity: this form of power is concerned with regulatory controls and a 'bio-politics of the population'.

The substance of social policy and the development of social rights of citizenship have been very much dedicated to 'anatomo-politics', but the form and context of welfare intervention has been determined by movements in the dimension of 'bio-politics'. Drawing both on Foucault and Donzelot (1980), one of the authors has already argued (Dean 1991) that the development of the welfare state in Britain is intelligible in relation to the history of three intersecting discourses. Although we wish now to reconsider that analysis by distinguishing four discourses, those previously identified were:

1. paternalistic/humanitarian/pro-populationist discourse;
2. repressive/'Malthusian'/anti-populationist discourse;
3. utilitarian/philanthropic/'self-help' discourse. (Dean 1991: ch. 3)

Pro-populationist discourse has been evident in such essentially conservative measures as the development in the eighteenth century of the Speenhamland system of relief, which supplemented the wages of labourers in proportion to the size of their families, but also in the introduction of pro-natalist family allowances in 1945. It is a discourse consistent with non-egalitarian social-solidaristic conceptions of citizenship, more characteristic in fact of modern continental European Christian democracy than Anglo-Saxon social policy.

Anti-populationist discourse has been evident in the introduction of puritanical workhouse regimes in the nineteenth century and the punitive work-testing of social security benefits throughout the twentieth century. It is a discourse broadly consistent with non-egalitarian social-contractual conceptions of citizenship and an authoritarian, Hobbesian view of human nature.

The third of the discourses identified is that which has been evident in the development of the detailed case management techniques and legal frameworks which came to characterise the modern welfare state. It is a discourse appropriate to Foucault's category of 'anatomo-politics' and to the development or refinement of administrative and disciplinary techniques in place of coercive and violent methods of social control. It is important to emphasise, however, (more clearly perhaps than in the previous formulation of this argument) that this discourse, which can be traced to the organised middle-class philanthropy of the nineteenth century, had different strands or facets. One such strand is essentially liberal and may be called in aid of a limited welfare state which attends to the failing or dysfunctional components of society: it is a strand which, though it is far more individualistic in its radicalism than Rousseauian or communitarian, is conceptually consistent with a form of egalitarian social-contractual citizenship and a preference for formal or procedural equality. The other strand is essentially Fabian and may be called in aid of a more universal, preventative welfare state which ensures the organic self-regulation of society as a whole: it is a strand that is consistent with egalitarian social-solidaristic conceptions of citizenship, with social-democratic reformism and with support for substantive and unconditional social rights. The argument is diagrammatically illustrated in Figure 4.3.

These discourses need to be located in relation to the actual political struggles which gave birth to different kinds of nation state and the ways in which class conflicts have been historically institutionalised or accommodated. In this respect we can draw upon the distinction elaborated by Mann (1987) which we have also discussed above (see pp. 76–7) between the absolutist and constitutionalist strategies for the containment of class conflict. It is possible to articulate Mann's distinction between absolutist and constitutionalist strategies with Foucault's (1977; 1981) distinction between the coercive power relations which characterised the *ancien régimes* with the disciplinary power relations which characterise modern nation states.

Figure 4.3 Discourses of control and conceptions of citizenship

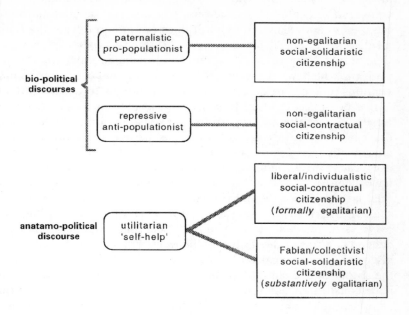

Offe has made the point that state welfare and 'the welfare trans-
action' are regulated by 'moral and political intuitions about rights
and duties, and arguments that activate or invalidate these intuitions'
(1993: 235). He argues that there are different moral repertoires
upon which society may draw in order to validate any particular
pattern of rights and obligations. Offe identifies three such repertoires, corresponding approximately to three of the four philosophical/
discursive traditions which we have identified. The first is the utilitarian moral position (or more accurately, perhaps, an economic
individualist position) which may defend welfare on the basis of a
calculus of second order material benefits (such as economic efficiency) and the avoidance of collective evils (such as epidemics or
social unrest). The second is the conservative (or as Offe calls it
the 'communitarian') moral position which defends welfare on the
basis of a particular set of external preferences and draws on the
principle of solidarity exclusively to protect the welfare of a defined community. The third is 'the Kantian solution' which defends
welfare in terms of a principled commitment to universal and inclusive

rights and obligations: Offe implies that it is moral-universalist idealism – the idea that free will depends on moral choices which transcend self-interest – which underpins social democratic thinking under capitalism. Although it does not amount even to a limited defence of social justice, the fourth moral repertoire to which Offe might have referred is the Hobbesian, moral authoritarian position which would, none the less, countenance welfare interventions in order to deter certain behaviours or to enforce others.

It is possible therefore to construct a taxonomy which characterises the different moral repertoires on which political discourse may draw in relation to issues of social justice and the limits of social citizenship (see Figure 4.4). It is a taxonomy constituted by two axes, each corresponding to the related dimensions or continua that have been discussed above. The horizontal axis encompasses the familiar dimension of individualism *vs.* collectivism (to which we shall shortly return in relation to the work of Rentoul 1989), but overlays this with Foucault's bio-political dimension, schematically defined in terms of the distinction between anti- and pro-populationist discourse. The vertical axis encompasses Mann's distinction between the absolutist and constitutionalist strategic trajectories whose legacies have constituted different approaches to welfare, but overlays this with Foucault's anatomo-political dimension, schematically defined in terms of the distinction between coercive and disciplinary societies.

It must be emphasised that the taxonomy is no more than an heuristic device and one which is specific to the cultural and political traditions of the Western world. When one seeks to locate political parties or individual thinkers on welfare in relation to this model it becomes immediately apparent that their thinking tends to represent a synthesis drawn from more than one of the quadrants illustrated in Figure 4.4. The Beveridge model of welfare, for example, though driven to a certain extent by Kantian morality, was also significantly influenced by elements of both conservatism and utilitarianism (Silburn 1995). Certain major thinkers in the Fabian tradition – from the Webbs (1909) to 'new' Labour's unconventional Minister for Social Security Reform, Frank Field (1996) – have been informed quite clearly by universalist *and* authoritarian notions of morality. To take a different example, the British Conservative Party under the leadership of Margaret Thatcher (see Gamble 1988), although conservative by name, did not correspond at all with the classic continental European mould of Christian Democracy, but exhibited both a radical 'neo-liberal' tendency and

Figure 4.4 A taxonomy of moral repertoires

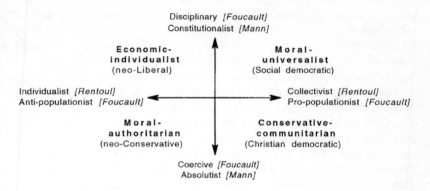

a reactionary moral-authoritarian influence (or what is often, perhaps confusingly, called a 'neo-conservative' tendency, see Roche 1992). Importantly, it may be seen that there is no place in this taxonomy for *radical* communitarian or socialist perspectives or for the influences upon thinking about citizenship which have stemmed, for example, from feminism or greenism. Such perspectives require dimensions not adequately captured by this model. None the less, the model represents a way of classifying and understanding the principal or dominant repertoires upon which people tend to draw in discourses around social citizenship. It represents a direct parallel to the taxonomy illustrated in Figure 1.6, which is concerned with the repertoires on which people draw in discourses about social equality. The taxonomy in Figure 1.6 is concerned with how discourses may reflect the different ways that individuals are bound in to social structures and practices. The taxonomy in Figure 4.4 is concerned with how discourses may reflect the different ways that capitalist societies validate the social distribution of resources and opportunity; with the repertoires which inform discourses of citizenship.

SOCIAL ATTITUDES AND WELFARE CITIZENSHIP

Claus Offe rightly reminds us that 'Structures do not *directly* translate into outcomes and developments; they do so by virtue of the responses, interpretations, memories and expectations, beliefs and preferences of actors who *mediate* the link between structure and outcome' (1996: 159). In the chapters which follow we shall explore how people, depending on their circumstances, do in fact draw upon the moral repertoires outlined above. In the last part of this chapter, however, we shall briefly review evidence from social attitude data relating to people's attitudes to social citizenship and social justice and to how those attitudes change over time.

The principal source of such evidence in Britain is the British Social Attitudes (BSA) survey, which has enabled us since 1983 to chart the changing attitudes of the British population to social welfare provision, public spending, taxation and the private provision of public services (Jowell *et al* 1984; 1990; 1996 and see Taylor-Gooby 1994b). A selection of key findings from the BSA is presented in Table 4.1. The story which these statistics tell suggests:

- that there has been widespread and increasing popular support for such mainstay public services as health care, education and state pensions;
- some forms of welfare – such as benefits for unemployed people and lone parents – have been markedly less well supported and such support has even tended in recent years to decline;
- paradoxically, many people are also supportive of – or are at least content to tolerate – the availability of private alternatives to state provision (though, except in the case of private pensions, such support has declined since the mid 1980s);
- perhaps half the population are supportive of the idea of a redistributive welfare state, although a similar proportion recognise that some stigma may attach to receiving social security benefits;
- support or sympathy for 'the poor' may have increased during the sharp recession of the late 1980s and early '90s, but there is a substantial minority (perhaps a third of the population) who hold hostile attitudes towards the payment of welfare benefits and/or the people who receive them.

Drawing upon such evidence, on other public opinion surveys, the British Election Studies and limited qualitative interview data, John Rentoul (1989) has sought to determine whether in the 1980s Britain had witnessed a shift from collectivist to individualist values and morality. Explaining her programme of monetarism, tax cuts and privatisation, the then Prime Minister, Margaret Thatcher,

Table 4.1 Data from the British Social Attitudes survey

	1983 %	1989 %	1995 %
Percentage agreeing that:			
1. If the government had to choose, it should			
(a) reduce taxes and spend less on health, education and social benefits;	9	3	5
(b) keep taxes and spending on these services at the same level as now;	54	37	31
(c) increase taxes and spend more on health education and social benefits.	32	56	61
2. [Of people agreeing with 1(c)] priority for extra government spending should be given to			
(a) health;	63	84	77
(b) education;	50	55	66
(c) social security.	12	14	11
3. [Of people agreeing with 2(c)] priority for extra social security spending should be given to			
(a) retirement pensions;	64	67	68
(b) benefits for disabled people;	57	60	58
(c) benefits for unemployed people;	33	25	25
(d) child benefit;	21	30	33
(e) benefits for lone-parents.	21	17	11
4. The government should redistribute income from the better off to those who are less well off.	N/A	50	47
5. The government should spend more money on welfare benefits for the poor even if it leads to higher taxes.	N/A	61	50
6. If welfare benefits weren't so generous, people would learn to stand on their own two feet.	N/A	32	33
7. The welfare state encourages people to stop helping each other.	37	33	32
8. Many people who get social security don't really deserve any help.	N/A	28	30
9. People receiving social security are made to feel like second class citizens.	48	53	48

	1986 %	1993 %
10. People who can afford it should be able to pay for better provision in respect of		
(a) health;	53	43
(b) education;	52	41
(c) pensions.	61	62

announced 'Economics are the method; the object is to change the soul' (*Sunday Times*, 3 May 1981). Rentoul's interpretation of the evidence is that, in the latter respect, the Thatcherite experiment failed: 'Rising living standards can make some people vote Tory once or twice. But they do not change people's basic values from co-operation to competition' (1989: 122). Rentoul's analysis is pre-occupied with voting behaviour, rather than popular conceptions of citizenship, but his analysis is useful because, like Marshall *et al* (1988) (whose work we discussed in Chapter 1), he is able to show that people's attachment to collectivism is not by and large altruistic, but rational and rooted in class interest. Rentoul (1989: 132) concludes that 'class antagonisms are alive and well'. People are inclined to support egalitarian principles on pragmatic not moral grounds. He also shows that when people are opposed to welfare state provision this is not because they are anti-egalitarian, but because of condemnatory moral-authoritarian attitudes towards welfare recipients: morality is something applied to other people. This appears to mean, for example, that people become less censorious and more supportive of help for unemployed people as the risk and immediacy of unemployment increases. With the rise in living standards in the 1980s, as we have seen, there was also an increase in the extent of inequality and greater insecurity of employment. Rentoul concludes that there is some evidence that this experience occasioned a shift from authoritarianism to liberalism as people became more preoccupied with the freedoms, choices and risks of an increasingly deregulated world, but there was no evidence of a wholesale shift from collectivism to individualism and the rejection of solidaristic guarantees. The implication is that most people draw on more than one moral repertoire.

Other recent research findings have suggested ways in which, as social rights of citizenship became increasingly restricted or conditional during the course of the 1980s, people's commitment to citizenship itself may have been eroded. For example, attention has been drawn to attempts by British governments to manipulate social security policy so as to increase incentives for labour market participation, family unity and the avoidance of state dependency. In the context of the casualisation of labour markets and changing household patterns it has been demonstrated that such attempts rub against the grain of popular aspirations and, in certain circumstances, can undermine people's sense of obligation as citizens (Dean and Taylor-Gooby 1992). The consequences for some may be a greater willingness to participate in fraudulent behaviour and/or illegal forms of economic activity; for others it may be a greater reluctance to acknowledge the nature of reciprocal rights and obligations (Dean and Melrose 1996; 1997). However, a consistent finding in this research has been that people have not necessarily rejected the idea of citizenship based on social rights and may feel betrayed by the extent to which conditionality and means-testing have been replacing contributory and universal principles of entitlement. People's commitment to welfarism and their expectations of the welfare state tend to lag behind or resist the desire of policy makers to modify the rights of citizenship (see also, for example, Baldock and Ungerson 1994). Although the nature of citizenship and, in particular, the substantive content of our social rights change over time, the moral repertoires on which people draw to apprehend the meaning of belonging to a democratic-welfare-capitalist society are likely to evolve more gradually.

CONCLUSION

There has been extensive intellectual debate towards the end of the twentieth century concerning the extent to which citizenship might yet be championed in ways that would give greater effect to the cause of human welfare, or even in ways which are inimical to capitalism (Hall and Held 1989; Turner 1991; Wood 1995; Offe 1996). These are important arguments to which we shall return in the concluding chapter of this book. Our purpose here, however, has been to pave the way for further discussion of the existing status and role of citizenship discourses in everyday life.

This chapter has been concerned with the past and the present, rather than the future; with the extent to which the notion of citizenship has so far succeeded or failed to provide a means of ensuring the welfare of individuals within human society, and to furnish an alternative to struggles between competing social classes. We have traced competing philosophical traditions of citizenship, distinguishing between those which posit an abstract contract between the free individual and the state and those which envision a common solidaristic basis for society; between those which would tolerate and those which would limit the nature and the degree of social inequality. We have pointed to the problematic features of such traditions in relation to gender and the position of women in society, and in relation to territoriality, 'race', and nation. However, the chapter has also introduced the concept of 'social' citizenship, to which the modern welfare state has given expression. We have discussed a range of arguments about the validity of a citizenship that affords rights which are substantive and which transcend economic and political relations of domination. We have also sought to outline a taxonomy of the different moral repertoires upon which an understanding of a 'social' component of citizenship might draw. That taxonomy distinguishes between repertoires which are preoccupied with individual liberty or behaviour and those which are preoccupied with collective well-being or cohesion; between those which are preoccupied with order and control and those which are preoccupied with entitlement and obligation.

Finally, in this chapter we have begun to discuss the ways in which people do in fact relate to issues of citizenship and welfare, issues which we shall tackle in greater detail in the chapters which follow. What we have sought to demonstrate here, however, are two things: first, that citizenship does not necessarily obscure social class as a factor in people's understanding of their interests and welfare; second, that people's understandings may be complex and seem to draw on a variety of traditions, repertoires or discourses. We may not all aspire to be gentlemen or gentlewomen and our concerns for our own and others' welfare are subtly and variously shaped.

5 Security Versus Freedom

.... a welfare state is people working together for a better community, for a better standard of life for everybody. I think that, to me, that's what welfare says. It doesn't mean go to the bottom, it means bring everybody up to a decent level.

[Male, middle-aged marketing manager]

The right to social security or healthcare isn't a right, it's a privilege.... I work hard for my money, I pay my taxes, I pay a lot of tax. What right does a 16 year old have to come along, get pregnant and then be looked after for the rest of their life when they've never worked? That's not a right of citizenship.

[Thirty-something, middle-income, self-employed woman]

Our previous chapter distinguished two competing traditions of citizenship, the social-solidaristic and the social-contractual. In this chapter we shall examine how these different traditions are reflected in contemporary popular discourse. The above quotations (taken from interviews conducted in the course of a recent investigation by the authors) each illustrate contemporary applications of these respective traditions. In practice, the traditions are not so easily separated. People seldom self-consciously choose which tradition they will adopt, rather they seek, according to their circumstances, to reconcile competing desires; the desire for security through citizenship with the desire for freedom of choice. In the process, we may – perhaps any of us on occasions – draw upon not one but several, even mutually contradictory, discursive traditions or moral repertoires.

In the last chapter we also examined how, depending on the socio-political context, each of the different traditions could be inflected towards different ideological interpretations. In this chapter we shall firstly, therefore, discuss the current socio-political context in Britain, before devoting the remainder of the chapter to an account of findings from research which has explored the meaning which people attach to the concept of citizenship, their expectations and experiences of the welfare state, and the way in which competing traditions and themes are negotiated and resolved within popular discourse.

BRITAIN'S SCHUMPETERIAN WORKFARE STATE

During the period of time in which this book was written, the British electorate returned a Labour government under the premiership of Tony Blair. The 'new' Labour Party which, after 18 years in opposition, finally succeeded in wresting power from the Conservatives is conspicuously different from the 'old' Labour Party that had presided over the creation of the modern welfare state in the post-Second World War period and which had developed it during later terms of office in the 1960s and '70s. The Labour manifesto (Labour Party 1997) to which the electorate gave its endorsement contains a subtle mixture of discourses. In his introduction to the manifesto, Blair draws on social-solidaristic discourses when he speaks of wanting 'a Britain that is one nation, with shared values and purpose. . . . run for the many not the few'. However, he also draws very explicitly on social-contractual discourse, not least in his final flourish, which claims 'This is our contract with the people'. The 'bond of trust' which Labour seeks to forge is with 'the broad majority of people who work hard, play by the rules [and] pay their dues'. In substance, the manifesto promises not to increase income tax, but to keep public spending within the stringent limits set by the preceding Conservative government. It proposes to implement welfare reform 'based on rights and duties going together', including a 'welfare-to-work programme' for unemployed people, and a 'proactive' Employment Service for lone parents. Blair had previously argued that, on the one hand, 'social justice is a necessity not a luxury', but that on the other, 'the most meaningful stake anyone can have in society is the ability to earn a living and support a family' (1996). The kind of 'stakeholder capitalism' envisaged by Blair (see Hutton 1996: ch. 12; Deacon, 1996) is ambiguously conceived. It is a concept which vacates the ground conventionally occupied by social democrats by calling upon elements of conservative communitarianism in the Christian democratic tradition *and* upon more individualistic moral repertoires: the stakeholding ideal hints at a potentially more radical, egalitarian communitarianism (of the sort which we suggested in Chapter 4 was prefigured by Rousseau) although it seems in practice to confound itself by borrowing simultaneously from authoritarian and utilitarian conventions in a manner redolent of the Reaganite/Thatcherite orthodoxy which it purports to displace. It has been observed that it is the particular brand of communitarian thinking made fashionable by Etzioni (1994) which has been influential on the centre-left and which has lately had an audience both within the American Democratic Party under Clinton and the British Labour Party under Blair (Gray 1995; Campbell 1995). However, Gray (1995) has observed that this kind of communitarianism tends, not only to be morally authoritarian in outlook, but to neglect the pressing reality that 'globalisation is bound to *undermine* communities and to endanger the cohesion of society as a whole' [emphasis added].

Bob Jessop (1994) has argued that in the latter part of the twentieth century we are witnessing a global process of transition from the norms of a Keynesian Welfare State (KWS) to the norms of a Schumpeterian Workfare State (SWS). The KWS was characterised by a commitment to full employment, social welfare and the management of aggregate demand. The SWS is characterised by a commitment to market opportunity, popular capitalism and supply-side management. This describes the contrast between the policies of British governments in the 1940s with those pursued in the 1980s. As Whiteside puts it, 'Whereas the former aimed to shape the international economy in accordance with broader social and political objectives, the latter accepted international economic forces as given and aimed to create a labour market that conformed to them' (1995: 69). The result is a more highly heterogeneous but unequal society, and a more highly centralised but technocratically pervasive form of political regulation.

For example, British governments have sought since the late 1970s to moderate social security spending and to tighten control over benefits administration. The former was achieved, in part at least, by a shift in favour of more means-testing and discretionary benefits; the latter by a more managerialist approach and an increase in centralised control (see Dean 1993). Such policies have contributed to the growing gap between rich and poor which we have documented in Chapter 1 and have been described as part of a deliberate 'strategy of inequality' (Walker 1997). The tendency to tie training and employment initiatives increasingly closely to social security and unemployment relief has been taken as evidence of a shift towards 'workfare' on the United States model (see, for example, Ainley 1993). However, as Whiteside (1995) points out, the origins of the 'workfare' principle may be traced, not to the USA, but to the Elizabethan Poor Laws: in its harshest form it may do no more than require unproductive forced labour or valueless 'training' in return for the payment of unemployment relief.

Workfare in this 'pure' form has in fact rarely been implemented in the USA and the experimental work-welfare measures developed during the Reagan era sometimes involved high quality training initiatives, child care provision for lone parents, and resource-intensive case management (Walker 1991); precedents which the Conservative government in Britain had been slow to emulate. Though it rejects the pejorative term 'workfare', Labour Party policy at the time of writing is informed by the recommendations of the Commission on Social Justice (Borrie 1994: 172–82) and the example of the Australian Jobs, Education and Training (JET) scheme. This proposal envisages, not a job guarantee or direct investment in employment creation, but 'active' re-employment services, training to improve 'employability', encouragement of self-employment; after-school childcare initiatives, and selective short-term employer subsidies.

Clearly, therefore, the advent of a Labour government in Britain does not necessarily signal a reversal in the process of transition to a SWS. The SWS can as easily be presided over by a government of the centre-left as it can by a government of the right. The former may emphasise the values of social justice and community in ways which are not ostensibly 'Schumpeterian' and the workfare it espouses may be gentler in intent, but the logic of the SWS can remain in place. The ideal of the KWS is predicated on a concept of citizenship in which, as we saw in Chapter 4, a balance is struck between political freedoms, civil obligations and social rights. This requires a trade-off between collective expectations instigated through the development of a universal welfare state and the correlative obligations which constrain the individual citizen – to pay such taxes and contributions as may be due, and/or to observe certain rules attaching to the receipt of state services or benefits. In the SWS the space between citizen and state is 'hollowed out' (Jessop 1994: 24) as the balance shifts in favour of global market imperatives. Expectations are subordinated to economic forces and what remains of the social trade-off can indeed be defined – in Tony Blair's terms – as an individualised 'stake'. It is a stake which centre-left governments may claim to underwrite, but which also constitutes a wider set of strictly individual obligations, such as to earn a living and support one's self and family; obligations that are ultimately enforceable by the government through the conditions which attach to the receipt of state services and benefits.

Concepts such as 'social citizenship' or 'stakeholding' are for many people rhetorically vague or wholly unfamiliar. None the less it is possible to explore conceptions of citizenship through the ways in which people talk about rights and responsibilities (cf. Dean and Melrose 1996; 1997). Their discourse and their values will be informed by the ways in which the competing traditions of which we have spoken are mediated through current political debate and by the fundamental socio-economic shifts which drive that debate. The transition from KWS to SWS represents the immediate context in which competing assumptions about the basis of social belonging and governance are being negotiated within popular discourse. The values which underpinned the ideals of social democratic welfare citizenship are under threat, but they remain as an oppositional element within the currency of debate. The tension between the authoritarian and utilitarian moral agendas of the radical right may have been submerged by the ascendancy of the essentially conservative communitarianism lately espoused by the centre-left, but it remains close to the surface. All the moral repertoires which we outlined in Chapter 4 remain available in some guise and effective within contemporary discourse.

THE MEANING OF CITIZENSHIP

We turn therefore to evidence from the authors' own research which has investigated people's perceptions of citizenship through interviews conducted within the year that preceded the 1997 British General Election with 76 people with widely differing income levels (see Appendix). Some of the key findings to be discussed in the following section are summarised in Table A.4c.

Articulating Meaning

The first finding to record is that, when asked, almost a third of our respondents said they didn't know what being a citizen means or that, so far as they were concerned, being a citizen did not mean anything very much. Indeed, the terms in which many respondents replied underlined the extent to which most citizens are untouched by the animated debate in political and academic circles about the nature of citizenship. Citizenship is not a term that is current in everyday popular discourse.

This was also evident from the newspaper monitoring exercise that was conducted contemporaneously with our interviews. This is not to say that newspapers do not contain coverage of issues relevant to citizenship. In fact, within the necessarily fairly arbitrary categories applied for monitoring purposes, Britain's daily and Sunday newspapers in the course of 1996 carried more home news items relevant to citizenship than were relevant to poverty, but slightly fewer than were relevant to riches (see Table A.5c). The broadsheets carried twice as many such items as did the tabloids. Just over a third of such items related to tax and taxation, just over a quarter to social security benefits and pensions, and just over one eighth to public spending issues and/or the costs of the welfare state. Other issues having bearing on the rights and obligations, the nature and functions, or the limits and context of citizenship received fairly marginal coverage and tended to surface only in the context of specific and usually shortlived public debates, such as that which followed a proposal by the Home Secretary for national identity cards, and a call given prominence by the widow of a murdered headteacher for the explicit teaching of moral values and good citizenship in schools. Other writers (such as Gordon and Rosenburg 1989) have illustrated, for example, the ways that racialised concepts of citizenship are sustained through the jingoism of the tabloid press and the 'reasoned xenophobia' of the broadsheets. Concentrating on explicitly citizen-related discourses, however, our study showed that it is primarily as a tax-payer or benefit recipient that the citizen is made visible through the press. To talk about citizenship in any wider sense, the respondents in our interview sample had to draw on discursive repertoires other than those regularly or openly sustained through the news media.

Getting on for a quarter of our sample indicated that they thought about citizenship only in the restricted sense that it relates to nationality; to place of birth or residence. However, a similar proportion voiced a social-solidaristic conception of citizenship, saying that being a citizen means belonging to a community. A much smaller proportion at this point in the interview voiced a social-contractual conception of citizenship, saying *either* that citizenship means having certain rights, *or* that it means having certain duties.

In their direct responses, men and respondents from 'lower' occupational groups were rather more likely than others to have no conception of citizenship, while women and respondents from 'higher' occupational groups were rather more likely to equate citizenship with narrow concepts based on nationality. This reflects the extent to which the former groups could be quite cavalier or even con-temptuous in their refusal to engage with what seemed to them an irrelevant concept; and to which the latter groups could be rather more guarded, but minimalistic, in their responses. Respondents whom we had identified as drawing particularly on survivalist and conformist (that is, less reflexive) discourses predominated among those who said they didn't know what citizenship meant or that it meant nothing much. Respondents whom we had identified as draw-ing particularly on entrepreneurial or reformist (that is, more re-flexive discourses) – and those who read broadsheet newspapers – predominated among those who said that citizenship meant belonging to a community. To conceive of oneself as socially situated in rela-tion to others as a citizen requires a degree of reflexivity and it is important to observe that, when directly asked, the more ostensi-bly reflexive respondents tended to give expression to a social-solidaristic definition in preference to a social-contractual one. It will be seen in a moment, however, that a closer analysis of people's underlying conceptions and ideas discloses a rather different picture.

What also emerged was a complex pattern of responses in rela-tion to disposable income, the detail of which is diagrammatically presented in Figure 5.1. It may be seen that respondents in the band with disposable incomes below half the national average ('the poor' – see Table A.3, p. 176) were especially likely to adopt either a nihilistic or nationalistic approach to the idea of citizenship, as indeed were respondents from the 'Middle England' income band. These groups stood out from others – including those from the 'nearly poor' and 'nearly rich' income bands – who seemed to be rather more inclined to engage with the concept of citizenship. We already know from the evidence presented in Chapter 2 that 'the poor' do not necessarily acknowledge poverty or exclusion and it can now be seen that 'the poor' perhaps have more in common in their attitudes to citizenship with those who are comfortably off than with those who are 'nearly poor'. The 'nearly poor', on the other hand, have more in common with the 'nearly rich' than with comfortably-off Middle England and, following our discussions in previous chapters, we would tentatively suggest that the idea of citizenship may have the greatest purchase for those who approach the boundaries of either poverty or riches. In this instance, how-ever, the evidence indicates that it was respondents with over twice average disposable incomes ('the rich') – and, incidentally, those with the highest savings – who were the most likely explicitly to

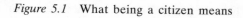

Figure 5.1   What being a citizen means

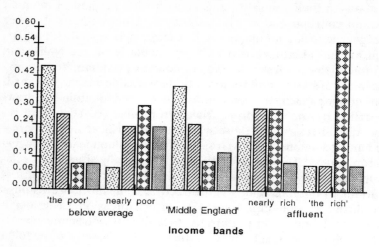

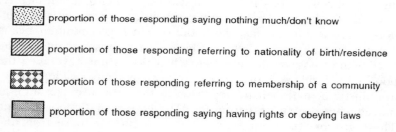

proportion of those responding saying nothing much/don't know

proportion of those responding referring to nationality of birth/residence

proportion of those responding referring to membership of a community

proportion of those responding saying having rights or obeying laws

prefer a social-solidaristic definition of citizenship and to think of citizenship in terms of belonging to a community. The rich, of course, stand to benefit from the security of a socially cohesive society: to put it crudely, they have the most to fear from the poor!

Pressed to say whether they thought of themselves as citizens, over two-thirds of the sample – including, perversely, ten respondents who had said that they didn't know what citizenship was or didn't think it meant very much – said that they did, or that they sometimes did. This seems to demonstrate that, for some people, citizenship is a *de facto*, but essentially unremarkable, or even meaningless, status: it is synonymous with being 'just an ordinary person'. Of the respondents whom we had identified as drawing on entrepreneurial and survivalist (that is, more autonomistic discourses), the latter – the *less* ostensibly reflexive group – were more likely than the former to say that they were citizens: they even seemed to be more likely – perhaps unthinkingly – to say they were citizens than were respondents favouring less autonomistic discourses, whose attachment to group or social membership might understandably make them more critical or ambivalent about whether they had themselves attained a *de jure* or procedurally effective citizenship status. It was also noticeable that respondents from 'the rich' income band, who had been most likely to offer social-solidaristic definitions of citizenship, were, if anything, the least likely to regard themselves as citizens: 'the rich', though they valued the ideal of social cohesion and inclusive citizenship, did not necessarily feel socially included themselves.

A closer but more holistic analysis of the underlying formulations, concepts and ideas represented within the discourses of our respondents (see Figure A.2 and pp. 177–8) revealed a deeper dimension. Paying attention, not to the answers respondents gave to our questions, but to the discourses on which they drew throughout the course of their interviews, it could be seen that the use of discourses which embodied or implied a social-contractual notion of citizenship status predominated over the use of discourses which embodied or implied a social-solidaristic discourse of citizenship status. Instances of the former might include references to the importance of choice, freedom or independence on the one hand, or reciprocal rights and duties on the other. Instances of the latter might include references to such ideas as social cohesion and the common good on the one hand, or to principles of altrusim and sharing on the other. Social-contractual discourse was ascendant even in the case of those respondents whom we had identified as drawing more generally on reformist and conformist (that is, less autonomistic) discourses. Respondents whom we had identified as drawing generally on entrepreneurial and reformist (that is, more reflexive) discourses were more likely than others to draw specifically on social-solidaristic citizenship discourse, but it was still social-contractual discourse which predominated in their interview transcripts. The profile illustrated in Figure 5.2 demonstrates that, although more affluent income groups tended to be more discursive (that is, they talked more) than others, and below average income groups tended to resort more than others to narrow nation-based discourses of citizenship, the overall pattern is quite consistent. Social-contractual discourse currently dominates the way in which people articulate and apprehend the nature of citizenship status.

Poverty, Riches and Social Citizenship

Figure 5.2 Profile of citizenship discourses

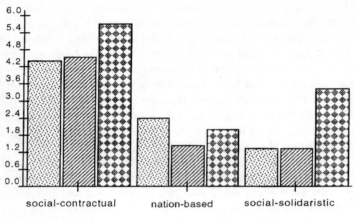

Type of discourse

Average number of instances in transcripts of respondents with below average disposable household income

Average number of instances in transcripts of respondents with average to one and a half average disposable incomes

Average number of instances in transcripts of respondents with above one and a half average disposable incomes

Good and Bad Citizens

In our study, some of the clearest expressions of the meaning which people attach to the idea of citizenship were obtained when respondents were asked first, what is a good citizen; and second, what might a bad citizen be? In response to the first of these questions three principal kinds of reply were forthcoming, either on their own or in combination with others. Some respondents believed that a good citizen is someone who looks after other people, some that it is someone who contributes to the community, and others that it is someone who obeys the law and/or pays their taxes. Superficially, these replies imply that the good citizen is seen as being either altruistic, solidaristic or obedient – or as combining two or more of these qualities. It was these kinds of reply which predominated, although other replies included such statements as 'someone who takes pride in their country' and 'someone who works hard at what he or she does'.

Women were rather more likely than men to think the good citizen is someone who looks after others or who is obedient. However, it was respondents whom we had identified as drawing particularly on survivalist discourse who predominated among those who subscribed to the idea that the good citizen looks after others. For several of these respondents, their answer was not so much about altruism in the sense celebrated by Fabian defenders of the welfare state settlement (see Page 1996) as about the pragmatic acceptance of mutual interdependence and the kind of 'do-it-yourself' welfare increasingly demanded by the SWS. Respondents whom we had identified as drawing particularly on entrepreneurial discourse tended to feature among those who subscribed to the idea that the good citizen contributes to the community. For several of these respondents, their answer clearly did not imply an egalitarian idea of solidarity so much as the kind of conservative 'active citizenship' favoured on the political right (see Hurd 1989 and Chapter 4 above). Respondents whom we had identified as drawing on reformist or conformist (that is, less autonomistic) discourses figured prominently among those who subscribed to the idea that the good citizen obeys the law and pays her/his taxes. For several of these respondents, their answer was not about blind obedience to the dictates of a Hobbesian social contract, so much as a sense that citizenship entails reciprocal rights and duties.

Taking this more subtle interpretation into account, the pattern of replies in relation to disposable incomes casts further light on the findings already reported (see Figure 5.3). Respondents from 'the poor' income band were more likely than other groups to subscribe to the value of helping each other, arguably because increasingly they have to. Respondents from the boundary income groups (the 'nearly poor' and the 'nearly rich') were more likely than other groups to favour reciprocal compliance within a legal framework. Respondents from 'the rich' income band were more likely to favour the kind of 'active citizenship' which we might in part associate with latterday principles of *noblesse oblige*, or which we might also conclude reflects some sensibility to their increasing and perhaps precarious distance from the lifestyles of other citizens.

In response to the question, what is a bad citizen, there were two principal kinds of answer, sometimes given in conjunction with

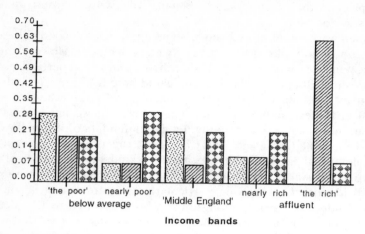

Figure 5.3   Qualities of a good citizen

Income bands

proportion of those responding saying someone who looks after others

proportion of those responding saying someone who contributes to community

proportion of those responding saying someone who obeys law/pays taxes

each other. The first referred to people who break the law; the second to people who act in self-interested ways. Superficially, these replies imply that the bad citizen is either disobedient or selfish, reflecting an ostensibly authoritarian view of citizenship on the one hand and a selfless view on the other. It was these kinds of reply which predominated, but a range of other replies was given, including references by some respondents to 'people who don't respect others'.

In general, respondents were more likely to equate bad citizenship with disobedience than with selfishness, reflecting the extent to which the base-line for their conception of citizenship was submission to the rule of law, rather than commitment to social collaboration. Men were rather more likely than women to equate being a bad citizen with selfishness, reflecting no more, we suggest, than a certain tendency to rhetorical radicalism. Respondents whom we had identified as drawing primarily on survivalist and conformist (that is, less reflexive) discourses predominated among those

Figure 5.4 Qualities of a bad citizen

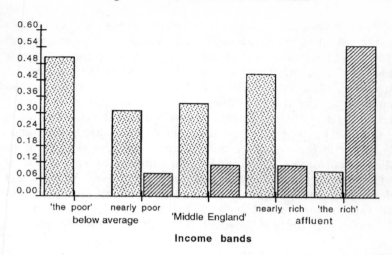

Income bands

proportion of those responding saying someone who disobeys law

proportion of those responding saying someone who acts self-interestedly

who equated bad citizenship with disobedience and those drawing primarily on entrepreneurial and reformist (that is, more reflexive) discourses were more likely to equate it with selfishness. The detailed pattern of responses by respondents from different income bands is presented in Figure 5.4. This might be interpreted as suggesting that many people, and especially 'the poor', are authoritarian in their attitudes to citizenship (cf. Rentoul 1989 and see discussion on pp. 37–8 above), but that, curiously, 'the rich' appear uniquely selfless. In the light of our previous discussion, however, we suggest that many people, including and perhaps especially 'the poor', are pragmatic in their acceptance of the reciprocal rights and obligations of citizenship, but that 'the rich' are not so much selfless as mindful of the precarious nature of the advantages they have over other citizens.

EXPECTATIONS OF THE STATE

Our concern now shifts specifically to the question of social citizenship and the extent to which people accept that welfare provision and rights to welfare are a part of citizenship. The respondents in our study were asked whether they thought that rights to health care, education and social security are the same sort of rights as the right to vote, the right to free speech or the right to enforce a legal contract. A clear majority of the sample agreed that they were the same sort of rights or said that they ought to be. Understandably, those in lower income and occupational groups were more inclined than others to agree. Respondents whom we had identified as drawing particularly on entrepreneurial discourse were less inclined than others to agree. None the less, our sample demonstrated clear support for a social dimension to the rights of citizenship.

More detailed probing, however, reveals a more complex picture.

Sceptical Support for Welfare

We have already discussed in Chapter 4 evidence from the British Social Attitudes survey which demonstrates that most people will say that they support the idea that taxes should rise and that more should be spent on welfare provision. Such findings have been consistently supported in similar large scale opinion polls (see, for example, the ICM poll reported in *The Guardian*, 4 February 1997). In the 1995 BSA survey additional questions were introduced to establish first, whether people support additional public spending because it is perceived to be in their own interest, or because it is in the national interest; and secondly, whether people are prepared personally to pay extra taxes or whether they wish that the costs of additional public spending should fall on other tax payers (Brook *et al* 1996). The findings indicate that support for public spending was highest in relation to those spending programmes which were perceived to be both personally and nationally beneficial. However, the popularity of certain spending increases declined when the tax consequences for individual responents were made explicit. None the less, support for spending on such services as health and education and for the universal state pension remain high and, even among the better off, there is a willingness to finance these through progressive taxation. The conclusion is 'that people are neither wholly individualistic not wholly altruistic in their attitudes to welfare' (*ibid*: 200).

This picture of what might be called instrumental altruism was replicated in our own study. Although ours was a small-scale qualitative study, selected questions from the BSA were included in our interview schedule, partly to enable us to 'bench-mark' the attitudes of our sample against those of the much bigger BSA sample, and partly to enable us to explore such questions more discursively. Respondents were asked whether they agreed or disagreed that:

1. The government should spend more money on welfare benefits for the poor, even if it leads to higher taxes.
2. If welfare benefits weren't so generous, people would learn to stand on their own two feet.
3. The welfare state encourages people to stop helping each other.
4. Many people who get social security don't really deserve any help.
5. People receiving social security benefits are made to feel like second class citizens.

In each instance responses were broadly consistent with recent BSA findings, although our respondents were able to qualify their answers and to discuss related questions in ways which BSA respondents were not (see Table A.4d on p. 186). For example, in response to the first of these propositions – with which half of BSA respondents agreed in 1995 – an even higher proportion of our respondents agreed to some extent, once allowance was made for the various reservations they wished to express. As in the BSA, men were more likely to agree than women, and younger age groups were slightly more inclined to agree than older age groups, reflecting a common pattern of difference upon which we have now remarked several times. Respondents whom we had identified as drawing on survivalist discourse were prominent within the minority who disagreed. Those respondents who agreed were also asked whether they personally would be prepared to pay additional tax in order to improve welfare provision. Fully two thirds said they were; a third saying they would pay up to 5 per cent more and a further third saying they would pay up to 10 per cent more. Understandably, those from 'the poor' income band were less inclined to pay more tax than respondents from other income groups and, perhaps reassuringly, those in the highest income bands ('the rich' and the 'nearly rich') were the most willing to pay more tax. Respondents from the 'Middle England' income band seemed less inclined than those from the 'nearly poor' income band to pay more tax, possibly because they believed they were too highly taxed already.

The second of the BSA propositions turned respondents' attention to the question, not of taxes, but the relative generosity of social security benefits. Only a third of BSA respondents agreed with this proposition in 1995 and, although a rather smaller proportion of our respondents agreed, when allowance is made for the kind of qualifications which respondents attached to their replies, almost a half of our respondents felt that there are individuals or groups for whom social security benefits are too generous. None the less, a majority of respondents still disagreed and those whom we had identified as drawing on conformist and especially reformist (that is, less autonomistic) discourses figured prominently among those who disagreed. Respondents who disagreed or equivocated were specifically asked whether welfare benefits could be made more generous and over half said they should. Curiously, although more affluent respondents had been relatively the most supportive of paying more tax, they were the least supportive of more generous benefits. Once again, although richer people may be supportive of citizenship principles, they are not necessarily sympathetic to the needs of the poor.

Turning to the third of the BSA propositions, the proportion of our respondents who agreed – about a third – was directly comparable with that of BSA respondents in 1995. Men were once again more likely to agree than women, reflecting an apparent contradiction between men's relatively liberal attitudes on taxes and their relatively illiberal attitudes towards the recipients of state largesse. Respondents whom we had identified as drawing on entrepreneurial and survivalist (that is, more autonomistic) discourses figured prominently among those who agreed. None the less, about half the sample (a slightly larger proportion than in the BSA sample) actively disagreed with the proposition. Following from this question, we asked respondents whether charity (rather than the welfare state) was a good way of helping people. Only a third of those responding agreed, a response which found most favour among those respondents from the 'Middle England' income band, but none at all from among those in 'the rich' income band.

The fourth of the above-mentioned BSA propositions turned respondents' attention, not to the desirability of state largesse, but to whether its recipients are deserving. Just under a third of BSA respondents agreed with this proposition in 1995, as did a similar proportion of our respondents. None the less, a very substantial proportion of our respondents (almost half), while not agreeing with the proposition, indicated that they believed there were at least a few social security recipients who were not deserving of help. Women were slightly more inclined to this rather measured response than men. In general, however, it was respondents whom we had identified as drawing on survivalist discourse who featured among those who agreed. To see just how judgemental or authoritarian respondents were prepared to be, we also asked whether those claimants who don't deserve any help should be denied their other rights as citizens. Only six respondents agreed with this draconian suggestion.

The last of the BSA propositions was used as the focus for a more extended discussion with respondents about the nature of citizenship. Whereas about half the BSA sample agreed with the proposition in 1995, a higher proportion – around two thirds – of our sample agreed. It should firstly be said that support for this proposition by the BSA sample was lower in 1995 than it had been in several previous years. Additionally, the context in which the proposition is put will undoubtedly influence replies: our respondents usually considered this question after they had already spent up to an hour talking and thinking about poverty and citizenship. Even among respondents who disagreed with the proposition, some explained that they might in the past have agreed, but that they now felt that redundancy and unemployment were so commonplace it had lessened the stigma attaching to the receipt of benefits. The proposition was most frequently supported by respondents whom we had identified as drawing on reformist discourse and supported, for example, more frequently by respondents from the 'nearly poor' income band than those from 'the poor'.

Respondents were also asked what they thought a 'first class citizen' might be; whether they thought of themselves as a 'first class citizen'; and whether rich people and poor people were equally able to be 'first class citizens'. Several respondents shrank from addressing the first of these questions, refusing to recognise the propriety of a distinction between first and second class citizens. However, among the diverse answers offered, the most frequent (given by two fifths of those responding) was one which drew upon the discourse of the earlier BSA proposition by suggesting that a first class citizen is someone 'who stands on his or her own two feet and has a job'.

Some respondents, it must be said, maintained a certain ironic distance and were clearly offering this definition with 'tongue in cheek'.

More revealing was the fact that, of those responding, barely half acknowledged that they themselves were first class citizens. Respondents from the 'nearly poor' income band, who had been the most likely to believe that social security claimants are made to feel like second class citizens, were the least likely to regard themselves as first class citizens. Those from 'the rich' income band were more diffident about regarding themselves as first class citizens than the 'nearly rich'. A bare majority of respondents acknowledged that it was not only rich people that could be first class citizens and that poor people could also be first class citizens. These responses signal a deep ambivalence in popular beliefs and a considerable measure, not just of uncertainty, but of scepticism about the realities of welfare state citizenship: a scepticism consistent with the hollowness of social citizenship under a highly privatised, consumer oriented SWS.

Addressing the Gap between Rich and Poor

This emerges most clearly when we consider the answers our respondents gave to a series of questions about the gap between the rich and the poor. Most respondents were asked (not necessarily in this order) whether they were conscious of the gap between the rich and poor; whether that gap is a problem; why it might be a problem; and whether the state should be doing anything about it.

A majority of the sample claimed that they were aware of the gap between rich and poor, or that they were aware of it at least sometimes – such as when they were reminded of it by news media stories or the sight of homeless people on the street. Respondents whom we had identified as drawing particularly on reformist discourses seemed rather more likely than others to claim awareness, but women were more likely than men to deny awareness (possibly, because they were being more honest with the interviewer, or else because they are less concerned with issues which are perceived as lying in the realm of 'the public'). An even larger majority agreed that the gap between the rich and poor was a problem, or acknowledged that it might become a problem. Respondents whom we had identified as drawing on entrepreneurial and particularly reformist (that is, more reflexive) discourses featured prominently among those acknowledging the gap to be a problem.

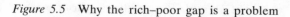

Figure 5.5 Why the rich–poor gap is a problem

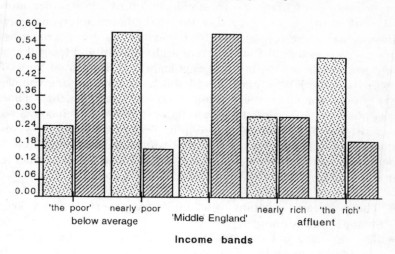

As to why the gap should be a problem, two principal kinds of answer were given. Some respondents (particularly men) were concerned about the potential threat to social cohesion. Others (particularly women) made reference to the unpleasantness of poverty and/or to the injustice of such disparities of income and wealth. Understandably, respondents with below half average incomes ('the poor') were more likely to be concerned about the unpleasantness or injustice of poverty than about the threat to social cohesion, but so too were respondents from the Middle England income band (see Figure 5.5). Curiously, it seemed that it was respondents from the 'nearly poor' income band and those with more than twice average incomes ('the rich') who were more concerned about the risk to social cohesion than unpleasantness or injustice. This is to some extent consistent with the findings reported in Chapter 2 that those who are close to and those who are most distant from poverty may fear poverty and its consequences the most.

When asked whether the state should intervene to deal with the gap between rich and poor, it was once again a majority of the sample who said it should. Respondents whom we had identified as drawing particularly on reformist discourse were rather more likely than others to agree that the state should intervene, as in this instance were respondents from younger age groups: older age groups can on some issues be more authoritarian and less tolerant of poverty than others, but it is significant that, in spite of the shift away from the KWS, there should still be support among younger age groups for state intervention to ameliorate inequality. There was none the less a predictable relationship between income and support for redistributive state action. That relationship, however, stands in interesting contrast to that which applied in relation to our other questions about the gap between rich and poor and whether it is a problem. It would seem that, from Figure 5.6:

- 'The poor' are reluctant to acknowledge poverty, but are keen on state intervention.
- 'The rich' are not only inclined to acknowledge the rich-poor gap, but are more likely than others to think it is a problem. In spite of this, however, and in spite of the ostensibly solidaristic and selfless sentiments which they expressed about citizenship in the interviews for our study, they are hardly more likely than other groups to support state intervention to remedy the rich-poor gap. Their apparent concern about the risks of social equality does not necessarily translate into a corresponding level of approval for redistributive social policy.
- The 'nearly poor' demonstrate high levels of awareness of and concern about the gap between rich and poor, but more muted support for state intervention. We might speculate that this could stem, in part at least, from scepticism about the efficacy of current welfare state arrangements.

EXPERIENCES OF TRANSITION

The thesis emphasised in this chapter is that the last quarter of the twentieth century was a time of transition from a universal KWS to a more selective SWS. The conviction of radical right-wing ideologues (Schumpeter 1942, Friedman 1962, Seldon 1990) was that maximum freedom in the market place and the strict control of state welfare provision would not only allow every member of society to have an equal opportunity of success, but also ensure that

Figure 5.6 Awareness of and attitudes towards the rich–poor gap

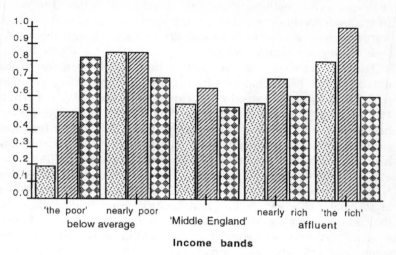

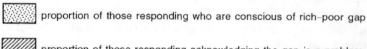

proportion of those responding who are conscious of rich–poor gap

proportion of those responding acknowledging the gap is a problem

proportion of those responding supporting state intervention

the wealth created by those who did well could 'trickle down' and indirectly benefit those who did less well. The economic success, which it was held would inevitably follow, should compensate for any passing social dislocation and generate a 'feel good factor', if not for all, then for most. This was the premise of the Thatcher and Major governments in Britain in the 1980s and early '90s. Political debate in 1996, when the fieldwork for our study was being carried out, focused on the continuing absence of the elusive 'feel good factor'. Britain survived global recession during this period, but at the expense of increasing economic inequality and insecurity. People had begun to lose faith in the KWS but, far from embracing the SWS, had lapsed into a kind of pragmatic and suspicious fatalism. Though people may of necessity have reappraised their attitudes to the choices and risks which they had personally to confront (Rentoul 1989), they remained by and large censorious of the perceived injustice both of the benefits still believed to accrue to the undeserving poor through the state *and* of the excessive rewards seen to accrue to the undeserving rich through the market (see Chapters 2 and 3 above).

The research on relative deprivation which Runciman conducted in the 1960s had also been set in the context of an analysis of transition: a transition 'between 1918 and 1962 – between Lloyd George's "homes fit for heroes" and Harold Macmillan's "never had it so good"' (1966: 55). We might now call this the transition from imperialist capitalism to the KWS. Runciman contends that it was a period which witnessed the decline of class militancy and a trend towards 'egoistic' as opposed to 'fraternalistic' relative deprivations (see discussion on pp. 12–13 above). He did not crudely argue that the working-class had become more middle-class, but that 'more manual workers and their families came to feel heightened aspirations of status [which] tended to detach them from those whose more "traditional" working-class attitudes involved a relative deprivation of status – if any – only on behalf of all manual workers as such' (*ibid*: 228). Though Runciman does not make the point, there is an implicit parallel with T.H. Marshall's (1950) contention that the KWS would ameliorate social class through the creation of social citizenship.

For comparative purposes, certain of the questions used in Runciman's study were replicated in ours. Five key questions which, though not identical, are very similar to those used by Runciman were discussed with respondents in our sample (see Table A.4e on p. 188):

1. Is there anything the state could be doing at the moment to help you that it isn't doing?
2. Are you satisfied with your current income?
3. What income do you think is necessary for someone like you to have a proper standard of living?
4. What kind of people do you think are doing better than you financially?
5. Who do you think of when you think of 'people like you'?

A little over a third of Runciman's sample believed that Macmillan's Conservative government of 1962 was doing enough for them (manual workers being rather less inclined to say so than non-manual workers);

and, of those who replied, most (58 per cent) responded in terms of some specific personal need. Only a quarter of our (much smaller) sample said that there was nothing that John Major's Conservative government of 1996 could do for them but, bearing in mind that higher income and occupational groups were statistically speaking over-represented in our sample, this would seem rather strongly to suggest that the level of satisfaction with state provision was less in 1996 than it had been 34 years before. Of those respondents in our sample who said the state could do more, getting on for half spoke, not directly about some personal need, but about a general need for improvement in state services, with reference to health, education, pensions or help for the homeless. Other respondents mentioned more specific problems which the government might address, such as homeowner's negative equity, low wages and the difficulties of small businesses. On this finding expectations of the welfare state have not fallen, but have risen in the last three decades. In our sample this seemed to apply particularly to the younger rather than older age groups. Only a few respondents (a smaller proportion than in Runciman's study) said they would like to pay lower taxes.

Turning to the second of the Runciman questions, Runciman himself found that 55 per cent of respondents in his sample were satisfied with their present incomes. His key finding, however – expressed in terms which reflect the assumptions of the 1960s about women's dependency on their husbands – was that 'their retention of working-class standards of comparison means that manual workers and their wives are consistently less likely to feel relatively deprived than are non-manual workers and their wives who are earning the same (or at the top level probably a great deal more). Only among the poorest does this conclusion need to be qualified at all' (1966: 207). In our study, a very similar proportion of respondents (44 out of 75) said they were happy with their present incomes. Women and younger people were more likely than men and older people to say they were not happy with their incomes, reflecting we might assume the lower independent incomes which women and younger people attract. Respondents whom we had identified as drawing on more reflexive discourses were less inclined than others to be dissatisfied, demonstrating that reflexivity in the late modern age does not necessarily give rise to discontent. When respondents were also asked whether they felt they were better off financially than they were a year ago, half of them agreed and almost another quarter said they were neither better nor worse off. If respondents were not 'feeling good' about their present incomes, for most this had not resulted from any recent change in personal circumstances. The discontent expressed by those who were not happy with their present incomes stemmed from longer term factors.

Respondents from 'the poor' income band were – with good cause – more likely than other groups to be dissatisfied with their present income, while respondents from 'the rich' and 'nearly rich' income bands were least likely to express dissatisfaction. Respondents from the 'nearly poor' and 'Middle England' income bands were *equally* likely to express dissatisfaction. To the extent that the 'nearly poor' might have been expected to be *more* dissatisfied than 'Middle England' group, this finding does provide an important measure of support for Runciman's general argument. However, over half the respondents from manual, service, routine clerical and other occupations expressed dissatisfaction with their present income compared to just a quarter of those from professional and managerial occupations; to the extent that in the 1990s this reflects a comparable distinction to that which applied in the 1960s between manual and non-manual workers, it suggests that 'lower' occupational classes are now less acquiescent about income inequality than 'higher' occupational classes and that the position of the 1960s may even have been reversed. The issue, however, is by no means clear cut.

The third of the Runciman questions explored the extent to which respondents felt they needed higher incomes. Runciman found that over a quarter of his sample (28 per cent) felt that a 'proper' income was a sum less than, equal to or not more than 10 per cent higher than their present income. Non-manual workers with relatively low incomes were more likely than manual workers with relatively low incomes to feel they needed a higher income. In our sample, a somewhat larger proportion (almost half) said that a necessary income was either less than or the same as their present incomes. A part of this difference may relate to the different way in which the question was introduced, and it must be remembered that our sample had a higher proportion of higher income earners than Runciman's. Among our respondents, lower income groups were much more likely than higher income groups to feel they needed higher incomes. Similarly, those from manual, service, routine clerical and other occupations were more likely than those from professional and managerial occupations to feel they needed higher incomes. It does appear that the disparities of expectation with regard to living standards which arise from differences in occupational status are more in step with those which arise from differences in income than they were 30 years ago. To test this statistically, however, it would be necessary to replicate Runciman's study with a larger and a more rigorously representative sample.

What is more important for present purposes is to establish whether there have been changes in the basis on which people compare their lot with that of others. When Runciman's respondents were asked in 1962 what sort of people were doing better than they were, nearly half (48 per cent) referred to people in other jobs or occupational classes and just over a third (36 per cent) referred to people with higher incomes or fewer financial commitments. Very few (3 per cent) referred to people who were better educated. Runciman's findings supported his contention that 'reference groups tend to be chosen from close to people's own situation' (1966: 196). In our study a very similar proportion of our respondents (34 out of the 70 responding) referred to people in other occupational groups (and specifically, in a third of these cases, to managers or 'bosses'): reference was often made to people working in financial institutions or the City of London. Consistent (in this instance) with Runciman's findings, respondents from 'lower' occupational groups were less likely to respond in these terms than were those from 'higher' occupational groups. Where our sample did differ from Runciman's was in the number of respondents (9) who, while not necessarily mentioning education, referred to people who were more intelligent, more competent, better motivated or more ambitious than were the respondents themselves: although this represented only a small proportion of our sample, it suggests that – at the margins – the expression of meritocratic beliefs has become more pronounced with the transition to a SWS. Respondents who identified others who were doing better than themselves were asked whether they felt envious. Of those asked, around three-quarters said they did not. There was, however, a minority (mostly respondents whom we had identified as drawing particularly on survivalist discourse) who admitted they sometimes felt envious. Also at the margins, therefore, is a largely autonomistically minded but relatively unreflexive minority for whom increasing inequality fuels feelings of envy.

Of the Runciman questions which we used, the last was the one which most directly addressed the issue of the social reference group or class with which respondents identified. The majority (61 per cent) of Runciman's sample, when asked who they thought of as 'people like them', replied either in terms of the class or the specific occupational status of the people with whom they identified. It was a slightly smaller majority of our sample who replied in these terms, but a majority none the less. Of the remainder, most gave situationally oriented replies, referring to people in similar family circumstances or of a similar age to themselves. Others talked for example of people of similar income or financial standing. Whereas Runciman found that non-manual workers were more likely to reply in terms of class or occupational status than were manual workers, we similarly found that those from professional and managerial occupational groups were more likely than those from manual, service, routine clerical and other occupations to reply in such terms. Men, whose identity continues in spite of labour market restructuring to be fashioned more in relation to labour market status than that of women, were more likely than women to reply in class terms and, notwithstanding the supposed erosion of the cultural salience of class, younger age groups were actually more likely to do so than older age groups.

When asked to what class respondents assigned themselves, although our respondents were more likely to assign themselves to the middle class and less to the working class than were Runciman's, this is almost certainly a function both of social change and sample composition: our sample undoubtedly did contain proportionately more respondents in occupations traditionally defined as 'middle class' than would Runciman's. What was striking was that members of our sample were certainly no less willing than those in Runciman's to assign themselves to a social class. If the KWS was supposed to have ameliorated class consciousness, the coming of the SWS has certainly not extinguished it. Asked to say why they would assign themselves to a particular class, a few of those who claimed to be working class responded by saying it was because they had to work for their living, but almost two thirds of those responding gave replies which referred either to considerations of social background, or to considerations of occupation, income and/ or education, or to a combination of such factors. People are able to engage with the complex but familiar issue of class, sometimes in a quite sophisticated manner.

People are much better able to comment on their class location than they are to situate themselves in relation to the distribution of incomes. Asked to say where they would place themselves on a notional scale on which being 'poor' was represented as 0 and being 'rich' was represented as 100, 48 of our respondents situated

Figure 5.7   Self-location on a notional 0–100/poor–rich scale

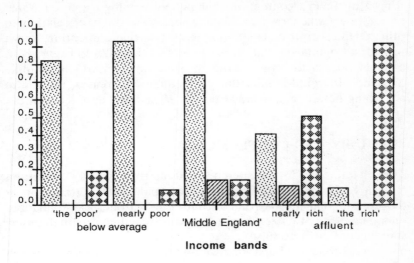

proportion of respondents locating themselves below 50

proportion of respondents saying 'in the middle'

proportion of respondents locating themselves above 50

themselves below the 50 mark (the mid-mark on the scale), five situated themselves 'somewhere in the middle', and 22 situated themselves above the 50 mark. Had the respondents located themselves accurately in relation, for example, to their disposable household incomes only 25 of them would have been below the 50 mark, and 51 of them would have been above the 50 mark. The exercise was obviously and quite deliberately oversimplistic. While some respondents may have been attempting to respond intuitively in relation to an imagined unilinear distribution of incomes or wealth, others may have been taking into account their own assumptions about the distribution of the population between different income bands. None the less, the finding is instructive (see Figure 5.7). Although a few of our respondents bizarrely overestimated their relative position within the overall income distribution, it is clear that, by and large, people tend to underestimate their relative position, and may do so by a substantial margin. The finding confirms Runciman's contention that people employ a limited frame of reference when they consider where they stand in relation to others. However, it casts additional light on that contention, and it provides a significant clue to the failure of the SWS to bring about a 'feel good factor' among the denizens of comfortable 'Middle England'. It would appear that as inequality increases, those who are doing better than average do not necessarily appreciate it.

SUMMARY AND CONCLUSIONS

This chapter has investigated the extent to which the transition from a KWS to a SWS has been accompanied by a transition at the level of popular values and discourses away from social-solidaristic understandings of citizenship in favour of social-contractual understandings of citizenship.

We have concluded first, that within the SWS, the meanings which attach to citizenship tend to be shallow or, for many people, non-existent. In spite of this, discourses which embody or imply a social-contractual understanding of citizenship are strongly in evidence within popular discourse. Social-solidaristic discourses have by no means been eclipsed and people who draw more strongly on relexive discourses and people who are relatively affluent may give explicit emphasis to them. However, popular values exhibit a distinctly autonomistic social-contractual undercurrent.

Within this general pattern, there are important variations. People on poverty level incomes are inclined to a view that combines pragmatic self-interest with practical altruism: it is a view that is in some ways resigned to the contraction of the KWS. People at the highest wealth and income levels are inclined to a largely rhetorical concern for social cohesion: a concern arising at best from a sense of paternalistic obligation and at worst from the pressures of private worries about their personal security. For people who are nearly poor or nearly rich, we suggest, ideas of citizenship do seem to have a particular salience, reflecting a particular apprehension of risk and the perceived role of the state in ameliorating or excacerbating such risk. For comfortable 'Middle England', citizenship under the SWS appears to have become a rather incoherent if largely submerged issue.

With regard to the social rights of citizenship, people as is well established are supportive of such bedrock services as the National Health Service, the education system and the state pension. This reflects an instrumental rather than an altrusitic commitment to state collectivism. The moral concerns which people express regarding the gap between the rich and the poor do not necessarily translate into support for redistributive intervention to redress that gap. None the less, it would seem that, in spite of the ideological shift entailed by the transition to a SWS, people's expectations of the state are greater now than in the days of the KWS. If people are more inclined than in the recent past to autonomistic social-contractual conceptions of citizenship, these may be inflected towards more highly focused and instrumentally specific demands upon the state; towards a contract that is quite full and substantive, not rather empty and minimalist. Essential in this context is the finding that people seem to be as dissatisfied with their own incomes as they were under the KWS and to be at least as conscious of class differences. In spite of this, however, they are not conscious of the sheer scale of social inequality that is associated with the SWS. Though the spectre of poverty haunts even those who are materially comfortable, the reality of inequality remains unseen.

To summarise:

- On pragmatic grounds, people still by and large value the social-solidaristic principles of the KWS and they are still mindful of the class differences which it was believed by some that the KWS could ameliorate.
- They are, however, strongly predisposed to the kind of social-contractual principles that are consistent with the SWS and, at the margins, commitment to the pragmatic egalitarianism of the KWS is eroding.
- Socially constructed horizons do not by and large permit people the kind of overview that is necessary for a developed understanding of citizenship. Not only is it difficult for them to situate themselves in relation to the overall social distribution of resources, but there is a sense in which the inherent tensions between the need for security and the desire for freedom which the SWS exasperates is paralysing people's capacity to negotiate a coherent understanding of their relationship as individuals to the social collectivity.

It is to this last point that we shall return in our final chapter.

6 Citizenship and Social Difference

[Citizenship] means belonging to a country, town, area, whatever; belonging to something or somebody. Somebody's acknowledged your existence. That's about it really. . . . I'm probably one of those statistics that make up the citizens of Great Britain, but apart from that. . . .

[Middle-aged woman, divorcee, with well paid full-time employment]

You're only a citizen really if you play sport or you're doing something really constructive for the country. Otherwise, you're not. You're just one of those West Indian chaps who's on the dole an' stealing our money and taking our jobs an' stuff. . . . Other people don't think of me as a citizen. I personally do. . . . I'm quite proud of being British, even if they're not proud to have me. Well you're stuck with me an' I'm not going nowhere.

[Thirty-something British-born African-Caribbean man in low paid part-time employment]

In Chapter 4 we prefigured certain of the essential arguments which are to be developed in this chapter when we explained that the dominant traditions of citizenship discourse leave out of account social differences based on gender and ethnicity. Citizenship is a 'totalising' concept which, though it may purport to be gender neutral, constructs the citizen as essentially universal, ahistorical and masculine. The development of citizenship, what is more, has been associated with the development of exclusive territorial administration and the nation-state: in the process, concepts of citizenship may become more or less explicitly racialised.

In any discussion of citizenship it is important to distinguish between normative and material accounts (see Harrison 1991). In this book we have sought to advance a distinctive account of the different traditions and moral repertoires from which normative accounts of citizenship are constructed. However, citizenship and the processes by which individuals are constituted or incorporated

130

as members of a society is also a material phenomenon and this book is concerned with the ways in which people experience as well as understand that process. Malcolm Harrison has urged that we should 'stress the differential nature of citizenship experiences in general: men and women, black and white, groups within the working class, are all demarcated and differentiated by the institutions which encourage or regulate activities, secure or confer status, and grant material benefits' (*ibid*: 210). To Harrison's list we might add the differences which result from disability, age, sexuality, religion and other dimensions. None the less, the objectives of this chapter are necessarily modest and extend to looking at differential experiences relating first to gender, and second to 'race' or ethnicity.

The two sections of this chapter share, however, a common approach: they are concerned with the gap between the normative and the material dimensions of citizenship – between public discourses and values and private experiences and identities – and the particular bearing which this gap has on women on the one hand and the members of minority ethnic groups on the other.

WELFARE AND SISTERHOOD

Whether we conceptualise citizenship as emancipation through civil, political and social rights (Marshall 1950) or in terms of the 'normal range of lifestyles' which lie between the extremes of deprivation and privilege (Scott 1994: 173) the citizen, if he is not male by default, is androgynous or undifferentiated. Marshall, though he does comment on the legal disadvantages to which women had historically been subject (1950: 12), apparently assumes that the subsequent development of rights has redressed inequalities between men and women. He is conspicuously silent on the question of women's economic dependency and the profound implications which this has for their citizenship (Lister 1990a: 56). Those who are assumed safely to occupy the sphere within the 'catastrophic boundaries' that exclude the rich and poor from citizenship are acknowledged by Scott (1994: 173) to have unequal access to resources and to power. He contributes none the less to a status-based conception of citizenship which, without actually ignoring sexual difference, tends to obscure its full consequences, particularly the significance for women – within their 'normal range of lifestyles' –

of the emotional dependency that arises from the burden of caring work; of the extent to which they may not necessarily be able to distinguish an identity and 'voice' as citizens in their own right (see, for example, S. James 1992).

In this section we shall discuss the issue of gender and citizenship; we shall review the recent debate about the 'feminisation' of poverty; we shall consider the distinction between the public and the private spheres of citizenship that has been central to feminist analyses; and we shall draw on our own evidence in order to illustrate the significance of that distinction.

Gender and citizenship

Women's accession to civil, political and social rights has lagged behind that of men. We have already observed (p. 73) that in ancient Greece women were entirely excluded from citizenship and that even post-Enlightenment theorists of citizenship supposed that 'natural' differences between men and women rendered the latter less suited to the full rights and responsibilities of citizenship. With the end of feudalism, women ceased to be the chattels of their fathers or husbands, but the laws of marriage and inheritance continued to subordinate women to the interests of men. In Britain, this was challenged – with little effect at the time – by early feminists such as Mary Wollstonecraft, who declared that 'If the abstract rights of men will bear discussion and explanation, those of women, by a parity of reasoning, will not shrink from the same test' (1792: 87, and see discussion in Held 1987: 79–85). Wollstonecraft and later John Stuart Mill were to demand for women civil freedoms within marriage, enfranchisement and education.

In the event, significant change did not come about until the late nineteenth century when the Married Women's Property Act of 1882 gave married women the independent right to own property, to enter contracts and to sue (see Gittins 1993). However, it is only as recently as 1990 that married women have gained the right of independent taxation of their incomes, rather than having their incomes treated as an extension of those of their husbands. In spite of a vociferous campaign for women's suffrage, it was not until the end of the First World War that women over 30 were grudgingly afforded the vote and it was not until 1928 that they were politically enfranchised on the same terms as men. Though the Education Act of 1870 introduced elementary education for boys and girls alike, and such education was to become compulsory in 1880 and free in 1891 (Thane 1982), the Act was intended, in the words of its architect, Forster, to underwrite 'the safe working of our constitutional system' (1870: 105). To this end, the nature of the education to which boys and girls were entitled was qualitatively different: 'The idea was to provide a more skilled and docile male workforce as well as a more domesticated group of future mothers, wives and domestic servants' (Gittins 1993: 144). The consequences of the gender-specific nature of school curricula, including its subtler manifestations, have remained a matter of enduring concern (see, for example, Spender 1981).

Marshall himself was astute to observe that social rights do not necessarily confer the status of citizenship, especially in the case of women. The early nineteenth century Factory Acts, for example, provided for improvements in working conditions and a reduction in working hours for women and children, but 'they meticulously refrained from giving this protection to the adult male – the citizen *par excellence*. And they did so out of respect for his status as a citizen' (Marshall 1950: 15). Such discrimination was opposed by the Women's Protective and Provident League (Humm 1992: 5) and the extension of factories' legislation by the end of the nineteenth century to protect women and men on equal terms was taken by Marshall to signal the proper realisation of such protection as a right of citizenship.

It might similarly be argued that the special provision for widows introduced under the Widows, Orphans and Old Age Contributory Pensions Act of 1925 (Lewis and Piachaud 1992) amounted to a negation rather than an affirmation of women's citizenship. Until quite recently, widows' benefits, though never generous, remained relatively resistant to erosion when compared with other elements of the post-Second World War social security system. This privileging of the needs of widows represented, in one sense, the posthumous compensation of citizen-husbands through the protection of women as surviving dependants.

The most comprehensive stage in the development of social rights was achieved with the implementation of the Beveridge Report following the Second World War, but the recognition which this gave to women as citizens was qualified. Through the creation of family allowances it gave effect, in part, to the 'endowment of motherhood' for which Eleanor Rathbone and others had campaigned (Land 1975; Thane 1982). Though this bestowed a particular form of citizenship status on women, it simultaneously promoted a racialised ideology of motherhood and of women's role in the perpetuation of an imperial race (see Williams 1989). What is more, the Beveridge Plan reaffirmed the male breadwinner family model and established paid employment as the key to citizenship within the welfare state (Oakley 1981; Pascall 1986; Pateman 1989). Beveridge claimed that he was giving women 'an equal footing in social provision' (Thane 1982: 249). He proposed that single women should have equivalent social insurance status to men and that working married women should have an option to choose such status. Housewives, however, because of the 'other duties' which they were supposed to owe to their families and to the nation were to rely for benefits upon their husbands' social insurance. In this, Beveridge insisted, women were to be regarded 'not as dependants of their husbands, but as partners sharing benefits and pension when there are no earnings to share' (1942: para. 117; and see discussion in Lister 1994).

Though this formulation found wide acceptance, there were critics even at the time (Abbott and Bompas 1943) who protested that it did not give all women full and equal status as citizens. Certainly, the long term consequence has been that while men have been the principal recipients of social insurance benefits to which entitlement is obtained through contributions from wages, women have tended to be the principal recipients of means-tested safety-net benefits. The former, it has been suggested, represent a 'badge of citizenship', the latter a 'badge of poverty' (Lister 1990b: 453). Referring to a broadly similar distinction between insurance based and social assistance schemes in the USA, Fraser has suggested that the former are 'masculine sub-systems' which constitute recipients as rights-bearers, while the latter are 'feminine sub-systems' which constitute recipients as clients (1989: 111–12).

The feminisation of poverty

The expression, 'the feminisation of poverty', seems first to have been coined by Hilda Scott (1984). The term is capable of being applied in different ways. It may refer to the increased risk of poverty for women, the increased visibility of women's poverty, or the reconstitution of the concept of poverty from a woman's perspective. Certainly, it is true that, globally, women suffer more poverty than men because their labour – both paid and unpaid – is undervalued.

It is also true that structural changes in the labour market and demographic changes affecting patterns of household composition have brought the poverty of unemployed women, female lone-parents and older single women more sharply into focus. However, when applied in the first and narrowest meaning, the feminisation of poverty thesis is suspect. Women have perhaps *always* been poorer than men. Lewis and Piachaud (1992) have argued that the feminisation of poverty cannot be a recent phenomenon since the proportion of women amongst adults in receipt of some form of poor relief at the turn of the twentieth century, at around 60 per cent, was much the same as (if not a little higher than) the proportion amongst adults in households that are in receipt of means-tested social assistance today.

Whether or not women as a whole are at greater risk of poverty than in the past, it is the case that in Britain:

- In 1991 within the poorest 10 per cent of the population, around two thirds of the adults were women, and those women had about half as much independent income as men (Webb 1993).
- In 1992 approximately 5.4 million women and 4.2 million men had incomes no higher than the prevailing level of means-tested social assistance (Oppenheim and Harker 1996).
- It has been calculated that around half of all married women have insufficient independent income to keep them out of poverty (Davies and Joshi 1994).
- In 1994, average gross full-time weekly pay for women was 72 per cent of men's, and of all those on low pay (that is, with wages below the Council of Europe 'decency threshold') 64 per cent were women (Oppenheim and Harker 1996).

There are three principal reasons for women's poverty. First, women do not have equal access to income and resources. In particular they do not have equal access to the 'core' of the labour market (or to the social insurance rights which flow from permanent paid employment with earnings above the required minimum level). Although the proportion of women who work has increased dramatically from just 43 per cent in 1951 to 71 per cent in 1993 (Hakim 1993), women still made up only 35 per cent of the full-time labour force, but 88 per cent of the part-time labour force (Callendar 1996). The jobs which women do are less likely to be full-time and more likely to be low-paid and/or temporary.

Second, women undertake a disproportionate share of the tasks involved in social reproduction; that is, in unpaid care work and domestic labour. Women, regardless of whether they also undertake paid employment, still undertake the bulk of unpaid domestic work (Kiernan 1992). Mothers, it is calculated, contribute around 70 per cent of all domestic labour, which, valued on a substitute wage basis, represents a contribution to the economy of around £130 billion per annum (Thomas 1997). The personal cost to a woman, in earnings forgone, of a career break to have two children can typically amount to twenty times the value of her annual salary when she stopped work (Joshi 1992). As H.G. Wells' Miss Miniver put it – 'While we were minding the children they stole our rights and liberties. The children made us slaves and the men took advantage of it' (from *Ann Veronica*, quoted in Oakley 1981: 17). The particular contribution which women also make in caring for elderly or disabled parents, spouses or other relatives can have similar consequences (Glendinning 1992).

Third, the distribution of income and resources within households does not necessarily work to the advantage of women. There is a growing body of research (including Pahl 1989; Bradshaw and Holmes 1989; Kempson *et al* 1994) which shows that men tend generally to command a disproportionate share of household resources and to retain control over the distribution of money within households. In low income households, however, it is usually women who have the responsibility for managing money and who will characteristically make personal sacrifices in order to sustain the living standards of other household members.

The public and the private

It is in the privacy of the home that many women's poverty may arise. A 'feminised' definition of poverty, therefore, might be construed as the breach of 'the individual right to a minimum degree of potential economic independence' (Jenkins 1991: 464): independence, that is, from or within the private sphere of the family. We have drawn before on John Scott's important insight that 'deprivation' and 'privilege' share a common etymological root with the word 'private'. It is precisely because citizenship is defined with reference to the sphere of public, not private life that the rights of citizenship have not generally extended to homemakers (women) in the way they have to breadwinners (men). This is the context *in* which individual women may experience relative deprivation (and in which individual men may experience relative privilege). It is also the context *from* which women must to some extent distance themselves in order to enter the labour market and the sphere of public participation.

While mainstream or 'malestream' theories of citizenship have concentrated on analysing the relationship between the state and the market, feminist theorists have insisted on the importance of understanding the state-market-family nexus (Sainsbury 1994). The private sphere of the ideologically constructed family is 'part of civil society and yet is separated from the public world of freedom and equality, rights, contract, interest and citizenship' (Pateman 1989: 5).

It is important, none the less, not to overstate the failures of the welfare state. The development of social rights has had beneficial consequences for women and, though welfare states exhibit a form of 'public patriarchy', this has in some respects been preferable to the system of private patriarchy that applied before (Fraser 1989). The British welfare state has not only afforded social rights to citizen-workers, both male and female, it has also redistributed money from men to women to a quite significant extent (Pascall 1986). However parsimoniously, through family allowance and subsequently child benefit it has given status indirectly to citizen-mothers (although these were/are benefits for children, they have usually been paid to mothers); and through invalid care allowance (see McLaughlin 1991) it has given status directly to citizen-carers. Social assistance benefits, though arguably conferring client rather than citizen status, have afforded many women an independent existence and, in some instances, a means of escape from violent or abusive men (Graham 1987).

With this in mind, the changes which the welfare state is currently undergoing have particular consequences for women. In Chapter 5 (see pp. 103–5), following Jessop (1994), we characterised those changes as a transition from a Keynesian Welfare State (KWS) to a Schumpererian Workfare State (SWS). The value of benefits like child benefit have been seriously eroded: the level of child benefit, which had never been intended to cover the full costs of bringing up children (let alone the opportunity costs incurred in caring for them) was frozen between 1987 and 1991 and has not since recovered. Since the 1980s, rights to maternity benefits under the National Insurance scheme have been whittled away.

The child support scheme introduced in the 1990s is explicitly intended to enable 'parents with care' (mainly women) to claim support from 'absent parents' (mainly men) rather than the state. At the same time, the recognition given to the special needs of lone-parents (90 per cent of whom are women), both through one-parent benefit and within the income support scheme has been curtailed and, at the time of writing, the new Labour government is contemplating new proposals to 'encourage' lone-parents into the labour market. The general direction in which the welfare state is changing is one which will curtail the rights of citizen-mothers to an independent income from the state and oblige them to either accept greater dependency on men, or to become citizen-workers. The development of community care policies is adding significantly to the responsibilities of citizen-carers (who are predominantly women) without any commensurate increase in provision for their economic independence.

The dilemma this poses directly reflects what Pateman (1989) has characterised as 'Wollstonecraft's dilemma'; the long-standing tension which exists between liberal feminist and welfare feminist perspectives (see also Williams 1989). Wollstonecraft, as we have seen, demanded that the rights of citizenship should be extended to women on equal terms, but at the same time she insisted that women had different concerns and capacities than men: their work as mothers and carers should be as central to their citizenship as remunerative labour was central to men's citizenship. Men and women, in short, are equal but different. In practice, however, it is the male standard of the citizen-worker which remains dominant. Individual women must choose between equality with men on men's terms, which requires the jettisoning of family responsibilities, or recognition of their different status as mothers and homemakers. The choice in terms of social policy is between a feminisation of the KWS through the introduction of a citizenship income for full-time mothers, and continued progress towards a SWS which encourages all women to provide for their own livelihood. The problem with the former, as Ruth Lister puts it, is that 'Mothers' work as citizens in the "private" sphere would receive greater recognition, but at the expense of locking them out of the "public" sphere economically and politically'; while the problem with the latter is that 'So long as mothers continue to do the bulk of caring work, without fathers and the wider community sharing the responsibility, a social security policy which treats them as unfettered individuals in the labour market will simply increase the burdens on them' (1994: 42–3).

A third policy option, which would unlock the dilemma, would involve a renegotiation of the basis upon which the rights and responsibilities of citizenship are understood. Pateman argues that 'the opposition between men's independence and women's dependence has to be broken down, and a new understanding and practice of citizenship developed' (1989: 204). Though the feasibility of social rights which embrace the mutual interdependency of men and women is often theorised (for example, Dean and Taylor-Gooby 1992; Twine 1994), it is not an issue that has come to the surface in practical political debate. In the meantime, women face increasingly difficult choices. They may choose actively to embrace dependency (and dependability) in the private sphere or to compete for 'success' in the public sphere. In fact, the actual lives of many women involve a demanding but unsatisfactory compromise in which they combine part-time or inferior jobs with motherhood and domestic labour. If women as citizens cannot transcend Wollstonecraft's dilemma, how do they in practice contend with it?

Poor Mothers and Comfortable Workers

In previous chapters (2, 3 and 5, and see Appendix) we have recounted findings from research conducted by the authors and have remarked upon the differences between women and men in their perceptions of poverty, riches and citizenship. We have already cautioned that certain differences may be attributable to the macho flamboyance with which some men can treat interview questions (especially when put by a female interviewer – see Melrose 1996). It must be borne in mind that the differences between women and men in our study were not great (and no claims can be made for their significance in the strict statistical sense) and, in many ways, the similarities were as important as the differences. The images which women had of poverty and riches tended to be as distant and almost as likely to be masculine or androgynous in their connotations as those of men. Women were as likely as the men to draw more intensively on prevailing social-contractual discourses of citizenship than upon social-solidaristic discourses. Though poverty, riches and citizenship are all consequences or hegemonic constructions of a man-made social order, women are inclined to see them much as men do. None the less, there are we believe a number of observations which can be made. On certain issues women do seem to be rather more conservative than men, not in any political sense, but in the sense that they are, perhaps necessarily, more pragmatic (see also Dean and Melrose 1996):

- Women were more inclined than men towards 'hard-nosed' definitions of poverty, and to equate riches with freedom from constraint. This is intelligible in as much that women are more likely than men to *experience* financial constraint and, perhaps, to set the standards by which they judge others accordingly. Women were similarly slightly more likely than men to think that some recipients of state benefits are undeserving. On the other hand, they were more inclined than men to say they were not conscious of the gap between the rich and the poor, which might reflect the extent to which they were (or considered themselves to be) relatively isolated from knowledge of 'public affairs' and the lives of distant others.
- Women were more inclined than men to think about the loss of respect and the unpleasantness which poverty entails; and, though they were less inclined to say that they would themselves like to be rich, they were more inclined than men to say they would like to be 'comfortable' rather than rich. This too is intelligible when one remembers that the roles imposed on women as household managers within the sphere of the 'private' might render them vulnerable to the daily pressures of coping and to censure should they fail, while their inferior command over resources in the sphere of the 'public' can render them chronically dependent and insecure. Women were also more likely than men to declare themselves dissatisfied with their present incomes and they engaged slightly more intensively than men with what we have described as the discourses of worry and comfort (see Figure A.2).
- Women were more inclined than men to think that poverty is inevitable and that becoming rich is a matter of luck. This possibly reflects the extent to which women experience less control over their lives than men.
- Women were more inclined than men to apply narrow, nationalistic conceptions of citizenship. To the extent that women, as has been argued, have less of a stake in citizenship, it would not be surprising if their conceptions of citizenship were narrower than men's (in spite of which the women in our sample were *less* likely than the men to say they didn't know what citizenship meant!).

- Women were rather more likely to say that a 'good' citizen is someone who looks after others, reflecting feminine values on the one hand, but also perhaps a greater awareness of the extent to which it is increasingly necessary for families and communities to provide care for their own members. In this context, women were more likely than men to *disagree* with the suggestion that the welfare state stops people helping each other.
- When asked what sort of people they had in mind when thinking of 'people like you', women were rather more likely than men to locate themselves in relation to people in similar family or personal circumstances, rather than in relation to people in similar occupations. This would be consistent with the contention that women are primarily citizen-mothers (or citizen-carers) rather than citizen-workers. It also chimes with recent findings from the British Household Panel Survey which found that, when asked to identify the most important thing to happen to them in the past year, women were more likely than men to refer to a family related event, while men were more likely than women to refer to a work related event (cited in Pahl 1995).

Women from households falling within what we have characterised as the 'Middle England' income band seemed to stand out as being particularly severe in their definitions of poverty, particularly opposed to state intervention to redress the gap between rich and poor, yet particularly worried by the prospect of poverty: as one said, 'who knows?'. However, it must be emphasised that it is not possible simply to read off women's attitudes from their income or occupational status. There was, for example, one 'poor mother' in our sample – a lone parent in a low paid part-time job – who insisted that she didn't think 'anyone's got a right to rooves over their head or money from the state'; and, conversely, there was a minority of 'comfortable workers' – women with well paid full-time jobs – who agreed they might be prepared to pay more tax to finance increased welfare spending.

It must also be admitted that none of our female respondents made explicit or even implicit reference to gender when they talked about citizenship or welfare. There clearly is a potential community of interest between poor mothers and comfortable women workers so far as the funding of welfare goes. An enlarged or renegotiated concept of citizenship which compensated for the needs of women during motherhood and the particular vulnerabilities of women in the labour market might embody (or engender?) a certain sense of sisterhood. This possibility, however, is largely obscured and would certainly be inhibited by the gender neutral terms in which citizenship continues to be countenanced within popular discourse.

ETHNICITY AND BELONGING

If concepts of citizenship tend to construe the abstract citizen as male, they tend also to construe citizens in general as ethnically homogeneous. Within the principal conceptual traditions of citizenship, citizenship is not necessarily synonymous with nationality any more than nationality is necessarily dependent on ethnicity. None the less, discourses of citizenship can in practice be inflected towards, or expressed in terms of, discourses of nation or 'race'. In Britain this tendency has been fuelled – particularly since the 1960s – by the development of immigration law, culminating in the Nationality Act of 1981, by which the 'ancient right of birth on British soil (*jus soli*)' has been superseded as the basis of citizenship by the principle of 'descent and patriality (*jus sanguinis*)' (Sivanandan 1989: 86). Nor is it a tendency unique to Britain as First World nations become increasingly concerned to shore up their borders against economic migrants from the Third World.

Although the concept of 'race' has no biological justification or valid scientific basis and the concept of ethnicity, with its somewhat elastic connotations, is itself contested, discussion of racism and ethnic identity have become increasingly prevalent at both a political and academic level. The reasons for this stem in part from recent critical appraisal of anti-racist policies and social movements (Barker 1981; CCCS 1982; Miles 1989; 1993), and in part from reactions to the impact of global economic restructuring, the collapse of communism in Eastern Europe, the resulting labour migrations, and re-emerging ethnic and nationalist conflicts in various parts of the world (Simpson 1993; Mitchell and Russell 1994). It is not possible here to revisit the detailed controversies over terminology and concepts (but see Law 1996 for an excellent introduction). None the less, we shall discuss controversies about racism and the nature of modern citizenship; about racial exclusion and what might be called 'the racialisation of poverty'; and about new concepts of 'cultural citizenship'. Our purpose is to set the scene for an examination of the hierarchies of identity which people apply when thinking about citizenship and ethnicity in relation to poverty and riches.

Racism and Citizenship

In Chapter 4 we observed that in ancient Greece slaves were explicitly excluded from citizenship status. Slaves were, and continued throughout history to be, if not in fact ethnically distinct from the ruling elites which exploited their labour, then in effect a 'racialised' social sub-stratum. In so far that notions of citizenship endured into the mediaeval period, they merely denoted the exclusive privileges of a feudal nobility, whose right to rule was founded on the presumption of 'natural' superiority by birth. To this extent, it may be argued, citizenship was always a potentially racist contrivance, at least until the modern era when formal civil and political rights were conceded by stages to classes other than ruling aristocracies and, eventually, injunctions against slavery were incorporated into bills of rights and international conventions. There is a view, however, that even modern law and cititizenship is inherently racist. Fitzpatrick (1992), drawing on Foucault and Derrida, argues that the very basis of modern law (and the juridical status of the citizen) is an ideological construction of white Europeans. In place of the myth that men are descended from god(s), the new mythology of the Enlightenment contended that modern subjects are risen from savages. The mythical sovereignty of law was the corner-stone of civilised citizenship by which imperialist and Eurocentric notions of progress were sustained in opposition to the 'Other'; against the imagined barbarism and disorder of the uncivilised non-Western world (cf. Miles 1989).

Against this kind of analysis, Marxists like Callinicos (1993) argue that modern racism is something more than mere 'heterophobia'. Callinicos even questions the assertion that the slave societies of classical Greece and Rome had necessarily 'relied on racism to justify the use of chattell slaves to provide the ruling class with its surplus product' (*ibid*: 19). To define modern racism he points to historically specific processes of conflict set in train as a result of colonialism, imperialism and global labour migration patterns that accompanied the rise and development of capitalism. The social divisions that racism generated weakened the working class and therefore, it is claimed, had specific functionality for capital accumulation. Though less explicitly functionalist, writers like Hall similarly insist that racism is not a universal or timeless phenomenon, rather there are and have been many 'historically-specific racisms' (1980, cited in Miles 1993: 85).

If we accept that racism can encompass several different ideologies and practices, we can begin to detect the sense in which different traditions of citizenship can have different racialising effects. Miles (1993) has forged an extensive definition of racism in which he associates the concept with the ideological construction of real or imagined 'natural' differences; differences which are construed as being genetically or culturally transmitted and reproduced, and which are contrived specifically to marginalise a social collectivity that may be defined, not only with reference to that which is supposed to lie *exterior* to a nation, but with reference to *interior* differences as well. Thus the process of 'civilisation' (Elias 1978), during which modern European conceptions of citizenship were forged, also entailed a process which Miles calls 'the racialisation of the interior':

... an ideology of 'breeding' justified political and economic privilege by representing class differences in terms of somatic or genetic characteristics. For a certain period, this *'racisme de classe'* justified the exclusion of the peasantry and working class from full or equal participation in the political system. Later in the nineteenth century, the nation was constructed and reproduced, was imagined in some way as a homogeneous collectivity with common interests. In this process of nationalisation, the dominant class sought to represent certain of its characteristics as collective characteristics of the nation. (*ibid*: 103)

In Britain in the Victorian era there is evidence that the poor were in this sense 'racialised': they were regarded as backward, uncivilised and genetically inferior (Lorimer 1978 and see discussion in Law 1996: 10). At the other end of the scale, the old aristocracy, were believed – by radical bourgeois and popular opinion alike – to be increasingly enfeebled through inter-breeding, and to be corrupt and parasitic. The ethnic identity of the British nation was therefore fashioned on the mythical virtues of the Victorian middle class.

There is a parallel here with Scott's model of citizenship, wherein the deprived and the privileged are excluded from citizenship. Within the social-contractual tradition of citizenship, we can see that the poor and the rich alike are each in their way a burden on the contract: the latter if they are regarded as congenital (and therefore irredeemable) failures, or if they are looked upon as freeloaders and cheats; the former if they are regarded as congenital (and therefore unmerited) 'successes', or if they are looked upon as dilettantes and spivs. Within the social-solidaristic tradition of citizenship, we can see that the poor and the rich alike are each in their way a burden on the community; the former if they are regarded as congenitally barbaric and uncivilised, or if they are looked upon as being disruptive of social cohesion; the latter if they are regarded as congenitally parasitic, or if they are looked upon as aloof and socially elitist.

We do not wish to argue that it is especially helpful to regard the poor and the rich as 'racialised' minorities in this sense. We do, however, wish to draw attention to mechanisms of exclusion from citizenship; to the ways in which exclusion from belonging within the social mainstream may be signified and apprehended. There is a clear parallel between the ways in which the poor and even the rich can be excluded and the ways in which minority ethnic groups are excluded.

The Racialisation of Poverty

In the section above reference was made to the feminisation of poverty thesis. It is possible in the same way to speak of the racialisation of poverty. Not only are minority ethnic groups in Western countries especially vulnerable to poverty, but they can be especially stigmatised by welfare provision: there is an association between poverty and minority ethnic status. Arguably, it is possible to reconceptualise poverty from a 'Black' political perspective, both in the context of the impoverishment of the Third World and in terms of the experiences of diasporic communities in the First World.

In Britain, though there are significant differences between minority ethnic groups (and controversy about the basis of their definition), statistical sources demonstrate that African-Caribbean, Pakistani and Bangladeshi minorities, who together make up almost half the minority ethnic population (which itself constitutes almost six per cent of the total population), are particularly prone to unemployment, to low pay, to benefit dependency and to poverty

Table 6.1 Poverty measures by ethnic group

	White	Black (African-Caribbean)	Indian	Pakistani/ Bangladeshi
Average hourly pay of those in employment[1]	£7.73	£6.88	£7.12	£6.43
Unemployment rate[2]	8%	24%	12%	27%
Proportion of households in receipt of income support (social assistance benefit)[3]	15%	35%	20%	44%
Proportion within lowest household income quintile (after housing costs)[4]	19%	35%	30%	63%

Notes: 1 1994/5, Labour Force Survey (ONS 1996)
      2 Spring 1995, Labour Force Survey (ONS 1996)
      3 1994/5, Family Resources Survey (DSS 1996b)
      4 1994/5, HBAI data (DSS 1996a)

(see Table 6.1). In particular, while over two-thirds of white women were active in the labour force in the mid-1990s, less than half of women from minority ethnic communities were active and, for example, young Black men (16–24 year old African-Caribbeans) were three times as likely to be unemployed as their white counterparts (Bloch 1996: 112–13). People from minority ethnic groups who are in employment are more likely to be found in low paying industries and occupations (Amin and Oppenheim 1992).

Inevitably, therefore, certain minority ethnic groups are more likely than white British people to be not only numbered among the poorest in society but to be in receipt of social security benefits. For minority ethnic groups in Britain, the receipt of public funds has a very particular salience. Since the turn of the twentieth century British immigration legislation has sought to deny or restrict access by aliens or those of immigrant status to state welfare provision. It is a restriction which has applied with increasing severity as the automatic right of residence in Britain granted to citizens of former British colonies was eroded by immigration and nationality legislation between the 1960s and the 1980s (Solomos 1989). In the mid 1990s severe legal restrictions were placed on the social entitlements of refugees and asylum seekers (Carter 1996). The association, both in the minds of officials and administrators and in the popular imagination, between ethnic minority status and the policy objective of restricting the rights of immigrants has inevitable consequences for all members of minority ethnic groups, even those who are legally settled in Britain or who were born in Britain and have established full rights of citizenship. One consequence is that people from minority ethnic groups may be subject to unwarranted checks and suspicion when claiming the benefits to which they are entitled (Gordon 1989; NACAB 1991; Law 1996). The wider implication is that the value and meaning of their citizenship are compromised. James, for example, points out that '[t]he majority of Afro-Caribbeans [in Britain] possess formal citizenship but nevertheless suffer discrimination at the hands of employers, landlords, public officials and the police' (W. James 1992: 39). The experience of minority ethnic groups is that they are on the one hand especially prone to exclusion through poverty, and on the other the basis of their social rights as citizens is suspect.

Cultural Racism and Cultural Citizenship

For minority ethnic groups, therefore there are other modes of exclusion. Not all members of minority ethnic groups are poor by any means. Some groups in Britain, particularly Indians, African Asians and Chinese, may fare relatively well in economic terms (Jones 1993; Modood *et al* 1997). Ethnic difference should not be equated with disadvantage, but racism remains a central factor in the lives of minority ethnic groups. Recent research by the Policy Studies Institute noted that British Black and Asian people believed they were more unfairly treated by employers than 10 years ago. It also found that 13 per cent of people from minority ethnic groups reported they had been subject to racial harassment (Modood *et al* 1997).

The same research confirmed earlier findings (for example, Young 1992) that white people's prejudices against minority ethnic groups are influenced by more than just skin colour. Prejudice against South Asian groups has been reported to be greater than that against African-Caribbeans, reflecting the extent to which it is aspects of the culture of the latter rather than the former that have been accommodated within white popular culture (especially in relation to music, sport and fashion). However, there is no simple hierarchy of oppression. Racism affects different groups in different ways at different points in time. Components of a variety of ethnic cultures may pass elusively in and out of 'mainstream' fashionability or acceptability (W. James 1992), while such factors as religious difference may inform deep and abiding prejudices and persecution. Writers like Modood (1994) have therefore advocated a concept of cultural racism which would specifically account for cultural and religious diversity and the different experiences of racism to which different minority ethnic groups are subject. Of particular concern to Modood, for example, was the case of Muslim minorities.

At the same time, some writers on citizenship have urged a concept of cultural citizenship. Since the adoption of the Universal Declaration of Human Rights in 1948, international law has purported to recognise civil and political rights on the one hand, but also the notion of economic, social and *cultural* rights (see Eide 1997 for a commentary). As we have seen T.H. Marshall (1950, and see discussion in Chapter 4 above) sought, at least so far as Western welfare states are concerned, to assert the status of economic and social rights in parallel with civil and political rights, but debate about the cultural rights of citizenship has remained marginal. Bryan Turner has sought to develop a theory of citizenship which takes account of 'aboriginality, ethnicity and nationalism in the formation of modern citizenship' (1990: 197) and which looks beyond the question of citizens' access to economic resources to the issue of 'cultural resources such as education, knowledge, religion and language' (Turner 1997: 6). Pakulski goes further and would give primacy to the right to maintain and propogate cultural identities and lifestyles: he regards citizenship primarily as 'not a matter of legal, political and socio-economic location, but as a matter of symbolic representation, cultural-status recognition and cultural promotion' (1997: 80).

This is a controversial stance. It takes to its logical extreme an observation which has been made by Modood:

> Minority ethnicity, albeit white ethnicity like that of the Jewish community, has traditionally been regarded in Britain as acceptable if confined to the privacy of family and community, and it did not make any political demands. However, in association with other socio-political movements (feminism, gay rights, etc.) which challenge the public-private distinction or demand a share of the public space, claims are increasingly made today that ethnic difference is not just something which needs 'mere' toleration but needs to be publicly acknowledged, resourced and represented. (1994: 7)

Once again, as in the case of the feminist critique (see above), the fulcrum of the debate is the distinction between a citizenship located in the public domain of economic life, politics and national identity, and the subordinate status that may derive from the private domain of family, community and personal identity. The charge that liberal multiculturalism achieves no more than 'a narcissistic celebration of culture and identity' (Gilroy 1992: 56) stems from the failure of such an approach to make ethnicity anything other than a private matter. The promotion of uncritical religious tolerance, for example, can racialise minority religions and even create space within minority ethnic communities for reactive fundamentalism, zealotry and oppressive forms of religious observance (Yuval-Davis 1992). On the other hand, more proactive forms of resistance within minority ethnic communities to what Hall has termed 'cultural *diaspora-isation*' (1992: 258) can lead to radical 'new ethnicities' which mobilise the resources of a group or community in ways which challenge dominant public discourses and values.

Rex (1991; and see discussion in Anthias 1995) has sounded a certain note of caution about the 'two domains thesis'. The public and the private cultural domains are both fluid and interactive. There is no all-inclusive, publicly sanctioned, traditional, British national culture. For example, in spite of the anachronistic constitutional status of the Church of England and recent political attempts to privilege Christianity within religious education in schools, the place of white Protestantism has been conspicuously displaced from the public to the private domain. Conversely, though individualistic, conservative and patriarchal ideologies concerning rights and duties may continue to dominate the discourse of the public domain, these have been demonstrably modified through the insinuation of collectivist discourses associated with class pressures and the development of the welfare state, and libertarian equal-opportunities discourses informed – at least in part – by feminist and anti-racist movements. In this context, Rex argues, there are three kinds of future for Britain's minority ethnic groups: groups and their descendants will become less concerned to maintain their 'private' cultural identity; there will be continued conflict between the public and private cultural domains; or there will over time be a dialogue and a renegotiation of the public domain.

To the extent that this can be translated into an empirically testable proposition, the immediate question is that of how do minority ethnic groups currently apprehend and 'negotiate' the basis of their citizenship?

Hierarchies of Identity

In the authors' own study (see Appendix), our opportunity to pursue this question was quite limited. Our sample included only six Black respondents (five British-born African-Caribbeans and one African) and no respondents from any of the Asian communities. The latter deficiency partly reflects the fact that a large part of the sample was drawn from the labour force of a brewing company and partly the difficulties which are inherent for white researchers' when accessing Asian communities. On the basis of such a small and particularly constituted sub-sample, considerable caution is required in the interpretation of results. None the less, all five of the British-born African-Caribbean respondents made some reference to their experience of racism as a factor in the way they thought about citizenship. It is important, incidentally, to record that one of the white Irish respondents to whom we spoke made a similar remark: the consequences of ethnic difference, of course, are not restricted to people of colour.

Although they shared experiences of racism, the Black respondents fell into three distinct groups. The first consisted of two men in their forties with disposable household incomes in what we have termed the 'Middle England' band (see Table A.3, p. 176). Both these men drew predominantly on what we have characterised as survivalist discourse: that is they tended not to be highly reflexive, but did tend towards autonomistic kinds of explanation. Both assigned restrictive or 'hard-nosed' meanings to the term 'poverty' and insisted that they were making statements about poverty 'in this country': one of the two was African-born and explicitly contrasted evidence of poverty in the Third World with 'what's happening here': 'If I'm speaking in that frame of mind, there's nobody poor in Britain'. Both respondents were dismissive of citizenship rights in general. Neither valued the right to vote. Both emphasised the responsibilities of the individual over any concept of rights. In particular, neither of these respondents spoke in favour of the social rights of citizenship. The British-born respondent recalled the experiences of racism with which he grew up, as a result of which, he said, 'I've never considered myself English or British and I've never been proud of – well, this country or this government or whatever'. Though both respondents were clearly mindful of their ethnicity, neither when asked what sort of people they had in mind when thinking of 'people like you' replied in terms of ethnic identity: each was mindful of his occupational class.

The second group consisted of two men in their thirties with disposable household incomes below half the national average ('the poor' income band). These younger men both drew predominantly on what we have characterised as conformist discourse: that is they tended neither to be highly reflexive, nor autonomistic in the way they discussed and explained the issues we put to them. Though they were themselves poorer than the men described above, they shared very similar restrictive or 'hard-nosed' definitions of 'poverty' and made clear that they were talking about poverty in Britain:

> what everybody would class as poor here [in England] would probably be your down-and-outs, erm, your homeless, stuff like that. Now personally, as a black person now, any white person out there that's, erm, down-and-out or poor an' that, it's basically their own fault, as far as I'm concerned – well 99 per cent of them, 'cause like you're white in this country an' that, over a black person, you've got a head start.... When you go to ... the West Indies ... that's what I call poor over there. Now if you're poor there, you *are* poor.

What distinguished these younger men, however, was that they were much more supportive of the rights of citizenship. For them, nationality was the immediate issue when asked about the meaning of citizenship. One responded immediately by reference to the fact that he was born in England, the other to what it says in his passport. Although one then said it didn't really mean a lot to him 'being a citizen of England', he spoke at other times about Britain as 'our country', signalling a certain sense of belonging; the other respondent even declared himself proud to be a British citizen (see the second of the quotations which provide the epigram to this chapter). In particular, both respondents were strongly supportive of the social rights of citizenship, reflecting a strong sense of solidarity with 'the poor' (even if they tended to contradict themselves as to who should count as 'poor' or whether they were themselves 'poor'). Though both respondents were clearly mindful of their ethnicity, neither when asked what sort of people they had in mind when thinking of 'people like you' replied explicitly in terms of ethnic identity: each could be said to be mindful of his poverty. One referred to all his friends – 'we're all struggling'; the other to 'everybody I know that's not well off'.

The third group among the Black respondents consisted of two women – one in her thirties who in fact had a disposable household income in the 'nearly rich' income band, the other aged 17, a student with a part-time job who, on the basis of her income, would count as being at least temporarily 'poor'. In spite of their different circumstances, both these women drew predominantly on what we have defined as reformist discourse: that is they tended to be more reflexive than any of the men described above, and to favour deterministic rather than autonomistic explanations and/or collectivist in preference to individualist sentiments. Unlike their male counterparts, these respondents did not feel it necessary to distinguish the poverty that is experienced in this country from that in the countries where their ethnic origins lay. However, unlike the men, both women also had clear images of who 'the rich' might be: the younger woman was clear that rich people are white, her initial response being – 'old white men with grey hair, tailored suits, you know'. In fact her views of First World poverty and riches were informed, not by comparisons with the Third World, but by her recent stay with a relative in Brooklyn and a visit to the Bronx, where she was shocked by the state of virtual ethnic and economic apartheid which applies.

Asked what being a citizen means, the younger woman replied in terms similar to the younger men – 'its my home, and a burgundy passport' – while the older woman gave a considered social-contractual definition. However, when asked whether they thought of themselves as citizens, the younger woman intimated that England, while 'not exactly fitting perfectly or anything ... is home', while the older woman expressed herself in terms quite similar to those of the man quoted in this chapter's epigraph:

> When its to their advantage, you know, when its Linford Christie winning the Olympic Games ... all black people are nice and everybody's – 'we're all one big happy family'. Erm, when its that mugger out on the street, all black people are, you know, – 'send them back home and they're not really British, etcetera, etcetera.'

The older woman recounted an experience of racial harassment and it was within this context that she included within her formal social-contractual discourse of citizenship the prospect of having 'the right to walk down the road without being called names'. Though neither woman directly identified with the needs of 'the poor', both were almost as supportive as the younger men of the social rights of citizenship and the need for welfare provision. However, the women differed from all the men in that, when asked what sort of people they had in mind when thinking of 'people like you', each replied explicitly in terms of her ethnic identity: the older woman, whose income, when combined with that of her partner, was substantial, added 'I never equate myself with white people of the same income, age, that sort of thing, 'cause I think blacks have a different lifestyle to whites'.

Rejecting essentialist notions of ethnicity, Ian Law has made the point that 'We are all ethnically located in that our subjectivity and identity are contextualised by history, language and culture' (1996: 44). The evidence outlined above confirms this, by illustrating not only the importance of ethnicity to the way that people engage with issues of poverty, riches and citizenship, but the diverse and complex ways in which ethnicity may be expressed. For some within minority ethnic groups, and it may well be those who are more reflexive, ethnicity is the primary or defining dimension. For others, and it may well be those that *are* poor, it is poverty. For others, and it may well be those that have achieved comfortable incomes in reasonably secure jobs, it is occupational class.

CONCLUSION

This chapter has been concerned with the problems which the abstract concepts and public practices associated with citizenship can pose in relation to issues of social difference. We have been specifically concerned with differences based on gender and 'race' or ethnicity. Identities forged in the public domain through citizenship are not necessarily commensurate with the private concerns and lived experiences of women and minority ethnic groups and there are clear parallels between the arguments developed in the two main sections of this chapter. It has been shown that concepts of citizenship may do more than simply leave social differences out of account, they may actively reinforce the position of men over women and of majority over minority ethnic groups. At the level of policy and practice, this may mean that women and minority and ethnic groups are excluded from the rights of citizenship. Alternatively, it will mean that particular conditions, qualifications or impediments may attach to their rights of citizenship. A direct consequence of this is that women and minority ethnic groups are especially vulnerable to poverty, both in terms of their access to material resources, and in terms of their exclusion from a range of life-chances, opportunities and experiences. In this, women and minority groups may in some instances confront a very particular contradiction between their formal or notional equality of status as citizens and the substantive or practical inequality or subordination against which their citizenship does not protect them.

There are none the less differences in the way that women on the one hand and minority ethnic groups on the other negotiate their citizenship. In Britain, women have achieved formal rights of citizenship in most spheres, but it is especially in relation to their roles within the private sphere that their rights can in practice still be compromised. It would seem that popular discourses of citizenship tend not to admit a gender dimension and do not provide much of a basis on which women might pursue their common welfare interests. The citizenship rights of minority ethnic groups in Britain have been significantly compromised by the consequences of immigration policy and by the failure of the state effectively to ensure against discrimination or to secure cultural freedoms. It would seem, none the less, that popular discourses of citizenship allow members of minority ethnic groups to draw on a variety of alternative sources of identity, depending upon their specific circumstances.

Developing aspects of the suggestions advanced by Pateman and Rex (see above, p. 138 and 149 respectively), it might be argued that women and minority ethnic groups alike face three options: they may *assimilate* within the public domain and allow their rights to be defined with reference to dominant white masculine paradigms; they may *remain ghettoised* in the private domain by confining cultural practices and feminine/caring values to the privacy of home or community; or they may seek to *renegotiate* the basis of their citizenship by insisting on changes in publicly defined assumptions and universal values. It is through the third option that the nature and scope of social citizenship could be developed. This would require that social citizenship itself is accepted and recognised as an appropriate and intelligible terrain upon which to struggle.

7 Popular Paradigms and Welfare Values

The making of the working class is a fact of political and cultural, as much as economic, history. It was not the spontaneous generation of the factory system. Nor should we think of an external force – the 'industrial revolution' – working upon some nondescript undifferentiated raw material of humanity, and turning it out at the other end as a 'fresh race of beings'. The changing productive relations and working conditions of the Industrial Revolution were imposed, not upon raw material, but upon the free-born Englishman – and the free-born Englishman as Paine had left him or as the Methodists had moulded him. The factory hand or stockinger was also the inheritor of Bunyan, of remembered village rights, of notions of equality before the law, of craft traditions. He was the object of massive religious indoctrination and the creator of political traditions. The working class made itself as much as it was made.

> [E.P. Thompson, *The Making of the English Working Class* (1968), p. 213]

The above epigraph has been chosen for the way in which it contrasts with those for Chapter 1 (which reminded us of a deeply conservative nineteenth century view that riches and poverty were ordained by God) and Chapter 4 (which reminded us of a reformist nineteenth century view that modernity itself portended the amelioration of class inequality). E.P. Thompson seeks to remind us, first, that the awareness of the nineteenth century working class was forged from an amalgam of conflicting factors and influences and, second, that we are in spite of this the creators of our own history (albeit not in circumstances of our own choosing). As we approach the close of the twentieth century, the object of this book has been to examine the factors and influences which shape popular awareness of poverty and riches, but also to discuss the prospects for social citizenship as a strategy or vehicle by which to challenge or resist the persistence of poverty and riches in the present era.

The purposes of this final chapter are therefore twofold. First, we shall draw together and clarify the threads of the main arguments presented in the preceding chapters. Second, we shall present a discussion about the relationship between class, citizenship and identity and will contend that the basis still exists for a social citizenship project that is both redistributive and inclusive.

REPRISE: THE ARGUMENT SO FAR

To achieve a synthesis of the discussion up to this point, it would be helpful initially to draw out two conceptual insights. In Chapter 2 we made mention of Williams and Pillinger's (1996) helpful account of the relationship between inequality, social exclusion and poverty and in Chapter 6 we drew on feminist theory and the concept of cultural citizenship to outline the relationship between the public sphere of civil and political citizenship and the private sphere of family dependency and ethnic identity. In the summary which follows, we shall make use of both these insights by discussing each key argument at three different levels (see Figure 7.1). At the macro-level we shall be concerned with issues of inequality, class and the economic sphere; with social structure, civil society and the world of the citizen-worker. At the intermediate level we shall be concerned with issues of social exclusion, public participation and the social construction of 'ordinary' lifestyle: this is both an intermediate *and* a mediating level in which political discourse is fashioned and the social rights of citizenship may be defined, realised or denied. At the micro-level we shall be concerned with the sphere of private experience and personal identity in which poverty and riches have their effect; with the world in which excluded citizens, citizen-mothers, citizen-carers and minority citizens contend with the limitations of such rights as are bestowed by the public sphere.

It is within this framework that we shall revisit the arguments from our previous chapters.

Social Polarisation and Exclusion

Our starting point, which draws on recent evidence and the well-established theories of several commentators, is that unprecedented social polarisation in Britain and other liberal democracies in the last quarter of the twentieth century now constitute poverty and riches as socially constructed forms of exclusion from the realm of

Figure 7.1 Framework for summary of arguments

	social/welfare issues	sphere of life
macro-level (structure)	inequality	public/civil society and labour market
intermediate level	social exclusion	lifestyle and participation
micro-level (culture and agency)	poverty	personal identity and private experience

'ordinary' citizenship. At the macro-level the argument is concerned with the gap between the richest and the poorest in society. Regardless of how one defines poverty or riches or how one regards their social consequences, the fact remains that structural inequality worsened during the period from the 1970s to the mid-1990s – in the world in general and in Britain in particular. Not only did the distribution of material resources within society became more unequal, but the structural or class basis of inequality became qualitatively more complex.

At the intermediate level it may be argued that poverty and riches, though they may be defined with reference to more or less arbitrary thresholds of deprivation and privilege, are ultimately best understood as forms of exclusion from ordinary lifestyles. This observation goes beyond the conventional distinction between absolute and relative poverty. It acknowledges that there are ways in which 'the poor' and 'the rich' may be objectively excluded from customary patterns of economic activity, political participation and social intercourse: from community membership, or 'citizenship' in its most general sense. At the micro-level, however, the argument focuses, not on objective processes of exclusion, but on the intersubjective meanings of deprivation and privilege. People's horizons are so constructed that they often cannot easily locate themselves in relation to the social distribution of income and wealth. They do not necessarily 'feel' themselves to be relatively deprived or privileged and they tend by and large to perceive poverty and riches as distant phenomena with which they do not personally identify.

There is evidence that people are inclined, by and large, to locate themselves more in terms of class or occupational grouping than in terms of poverty, riches or citizenship. However, attitudes, for example towards the importance of formal citizenship guarantees, may be affected when people's circumstances come close to the boundaries which separate ordinary or acceptable lifestyles and consumption patterns on the one hand and those which might tenuously be associated with either poverty or riches on the other.

Worry, Comfort and Fun in a Risk Society

The second main strand of our argument has been that, as the capitalist welfare state gives way to what some have characterised as the 'risk society', poverty and wealth as symbolic spectres now bear upon the quotidian desires and anxieties of virtually all citizens – whether they be poor, rich or 'comfortable'. At the macro-level it is argued that the economic priorities which characterised the Keynesian Welfare State have changed. The objectives of full employment and the management of aggregate demand have given way to dual labour markets, structural unemployment (or underemployment), and supply-side management. Mass consumption in domestic markets has given way to the segmentation of consumption sectors and the globalisation of markets. Welfare provision itself is being reshaped in accordance with the dictates of the changing global economic order.

At the intermediate level, the argument relates to the changing basis on which individuals must therefore relate to the social order. The greater institutional complexities and material uncertainties of the world we inhabit have the capacity to demand greater reflexivity on the one hand, and to generate greater anxiety on the other. Vulnerability, opportunity and risk do more than increase the range of lifestyle choices with which people are confronted; they challenge the security of citizenship, while increasing the objective likelihood of poverty or riches. At the micro-level, however, the argument relates to the symbolic significance of poverty and riches. Poverty and riches are intelligible, not only as real risks, but as socially constructed spectres: poverty can present itself as 'an object of wholesome horror', not only to those struggling on low incomes, but particularly to those with higher incomes; riches can present themselves as 'an object of prurient fascination', not only to those whose wealth falls short of riches, but particularly to those with little or no wealth at all. None the less, people are driven more by worry and the fear of poverty than they are drawn by the allure of riches or the prospect of fun. The Contemporary sociological accounts which characterise the prevailing mood of welfare capitalism in terms of either comfortable complacency or chronic anxiety fail to account for the complexity of people's fears and aspirations.

There is evidence that people may be more resentful of class inequalities than in the recent past. However, while people do make class comparisons, it would seem that it is ontological security or 'comfort' that is the standard by which everyday lifestyles are judged and sustained. The resentments people express would seem, by and large, to be outweighed by a sense of powerlessness or absence of control; by the prospect for many people that either the worry or the fun that surround their quest for comfort might accelerate out of control and spiral into the excess of either poverty or riches.

Citizenship and Moral Repertoires

The third strand of our argument has been that discourses of citizenship and popular values tend to draw on conflicting sets of traditions and moral repertoires; an insight which helps explain the ambiguity of political debate and social attitudes concerning the welfare state. At the macro-level it is argued that the dominant traditions of citizenship which we have identified – the solidaristic and the contractarian – may be related to different views of social structure. The former is concerned with social integration and the resolution of conflict; the latter with the promotion of individual freedom within a social framework. Secondly, when interpreted at the intermediate level of the political process, each of the principal traditions is capable of drawing upon either a conservative/authoritarian or a radical/constitutionalist approach. As a consequence there are, broadly speaking, at least four traditions or repertoires which may inform discourses of citizenship: the liberal-individual; the moral-universalist; the moral-authoritarian; and the conservative-communitarian. All four are current within contemporary political discourse.

At the micro-level it is argued that, in terms of everyday individual morality, people draw upon a sometimes incoherent mixture of instrumentalist, pragmatic and altruistic justifications for the basis of their citizenship. Closely articulated with the traditions or repertoires outlined above are four corresponding discourses by which people might contend with the hazards of poverty and wealth, depending on the extent to which they may be autonomistic and/or reflexive: the entrepreneurial; the reformist; the survivalist; and the conformist. As a result, there are fundamental tensions within popular discourse between beliefs in meritocratic principles; concerns for social justice; fatalistic individual compliance; and commitment to social cohesion.

There is evidence that people still value certain of the assumptions on which the Keynesian Welfare State was based and may in some respects have even higher expectations of the state than in the recent past. However, though popular discourse lags behind prevailing political discourse, autonomistic discourses appropriate to the values of a Schumpeterian Workfare State are strongly in evidence. All citizens in countries like Britain are subject to certain confusions and tensions with regard to the shifting boundaries of class location, the conflation of contradictory political discourses, and the social and moral dilemmas which economic uncertainty and welfare retrenchment can exacerbate.

CLASS, CITIZENSHIP AND IDENTITY

Popular discourse, therefore, does not exhibit any clear transition from the politics of class to a politics of identity, while popular discourses of citizenship remain both poorly articulated and are stranded, as it were, between the two. In this final section we shall offer a normative rather than an empirical argument which falls into four parts. We wish to suggest, first, that we need to reassess the importance of class; second, that social redistribution is a central concern of any meaningful concept of citizenship; third, that it is possible to recapture the notion of political struggle within the democratic process; finally, that there is scope to reformulate our understanding of social citizenship as a strategic terrain on which to mediate both class and identity.

The 'Re-Retreat' to Class

The context in which this book has been written is one in which, as Peter Taylor-Gooby puts it, '[t]he "old sociology" of nation, nuclear family, capital and class has been supplanted by a "new sociology" of globalisation, individualism and diversity' (1997: 172). The trend, however, has not gone unquestioned. Taylor-Gooby himself defensively argues that there remains much mileage 'in the "second-best" theories of state, capital and class', not least because it is the supremacy of market forces that fuels inequality in ordinary life chances and '[i]f the working class is fragmented, the ruling class is organised, well aware of its own interests and increasingly able to use the institutional structure of government to express them' (*ibid*: 190). Similar calls have been heard from disparate quarters, including scholars adhering to both Marxist and Weberian traditions who, for different reasons, deny that the shifts in class structure (which we discussed in Chapter 1) signal the so called 'death of class' (Pakulski and Waters 1996) as a concept.

Of late the most vigorous defender of Marxist class analysis has perhaps been Ellen Meiksins Wood (1986; 1995). Wood condemns the genre of revisionist neo-Marxist theorists exemplified by Laclau and Mouffe (1985) for their 'retreat from class' and for their attempts to autonomize ideology and politics from any class foundation. The problem for revisionist Marxists – scornfully characterised by Wood as the 'new "true" socialists' – is how, in the face of the decline of the 'traditional' manual working class, to understand the contradictory position of the growing intermediate social and occupational strata whose members may indeed 'be torn between their exploitation by capital and the benefits they derive from their service to it' (1986: 178); and how an apparently diminished (and ostensibly reactionary) proletariat could ever fulfil its historic mission of overthrowing capitalism. The revisionist project has sought to understand social divisions in terms of ideologically derived categories (distinctions between 'productive' *vs.* 'non-productive' work, manual *vs.* mental labour, private *vs.* public sector employment and consumption), while advocating a politics of discourse which transcends material interests and bypasses class struggle. For Wood, the basis for understanding class remains the substantive exploitative character of the wage relation and she sides, for example, with theorists like Braverman (1974) who describe the 'proletarianisation' of the middle class through the control, routinisation and deskilling of much white collar work. She argues that, in spite of political, social and welfare reforms and the decline of class militancy, there is 'no convincing evidence to suggest that the conditions of modern capitalism have pre-empted the ground of class politics or rendered class unnecessary or unavailable as a political force' (Wood 1986: 175).

Finally, while acknowledging the moral force of the various new social movements espoused as vehicles for political struggle by the 'new "true" socialists', Wood insists that the apparent unity and popular appeal of such movements depends on the extent to which they are abstracted or detached from the conflicting social interests which constitute the existing social order. The emancipatory language of 'universal human goods' may well constitute 'the language of translation from working-class consciousness to socialist consciousness' (*ibid*: 178). However, to achieve freedom from exploitation (in all its forms), peace, security, ecological sustainability and a decent quality of life it is necessary to mobilise against the immediate and concrete structures of interest and power which stand in the way of their realisation. In this respect, Wood argues, the working class (broadly conceived) remains, not an inevitable revolutionary force, but the only class whose own interests 'cannot fully be served without the abolition of class and whose strategic position in the production of capital gives it a unique capability to destroy capitalism' (*ibid*: 187). Such an assertion leaves Wood open to the claim that she is 'privileging' class identity above other identities. In the event, she welcomes the extent to which the politics of identity can celebrate differences based on gender, ethnicity, culture or sexuality, but asks, 'in what sense would it be "democratic" to celebrate *class* differences?' (1995: 258). Class as an identity is by definition a relationship of inequality and domination which cannot be accommodated or made non-repressive without the overthrow of capitalism itself.

Against this view it must be remembered that, on the one hand, people who celebrate religion, nation or 'race' as a primary basis of identity may not regard class difference as oppressive or unacceptable, while on the other, the abolition of class can by no means guarantee an end to patriarchy, chauvinism or racism. In fact, although Laclau and Mouffe clearly do challenge the epistemological status of class, they do not deny its political importance. The issue here is the way in which class identity articulates with other aspects of identity. Rutherford, for example, puts it thus

> Identity . . . is constituted out of different elements of experience and subjective position, but in this articulation they become more than the sum of the original elements. Our class subjectivities do not simply co-exist outside [for example] our gender. Rather our class is gendered and our gender is classed. (1990: 19)

For Rutherford, class is not a last instance determinant, because it need not of itself determine final outcomes, but it is in fact a first instance determinant because it sets the conditions under which the elements of identity are articulated.

An entirely different set of arguments about the continuing salience of class is to be found in the 'middle-range' sociological theory of Gordon Marshall (1997). We called on the empirical findings of Marshall and his colleagues (Marshall *et al* 1988) in Chapter 1 when commenting on the extent to which society, in spite of the complexity of current trends, is still shaped by class; something our own evidence has helped to confirm. In a more recently published volume, which draws on a range of work of both national and international provenance, Marshall contends that much of the social mobility research conducted in the past throughout the industrialised world 'may have mistaken changes in the *shape* of the class structure for changes in social fluidity or the degree of *openness*' [original emphasis] (1997: 5). Acknowledging that class is a contested concept, Marshall pragmatically eschews notions based on relations of exploitation in favour of the neo-Weberian schema devised by Goldthorpe, which is based none the less on employment relations. Within this framework, it is clear that, although changes in the structure of the labour market have generated a shift from manual to white-collar occupations, the unequal distribution of opportunities between the different classes has remained the same; a finding which he acknowledges has 'profound implications for social policy'.

Marshall is dismissive of arguments about the recent fragmentation of the working class and of class consciousness, arguing that the working class has always been fragmented. Sectionalism and 'privatised instrumentalism' are not new: they were as evident in the working class organisations of the nineteenth century and among industrial workers of the 1960s as they are today. This, however, is something which works to the advantage of the capitalist classes and in no way implies the absence of distributional conflicts (*ibid*: 46–7). Marshall is similarly sceptical of the 'proletarianisation' thesis outlined above, arguing not only that 'there has been significant upward social mobility into skilled and routine non-manual work, with no counterbalancing downward movement' (*ibid*: 140), but that the evidence so far adduced concerning the deskilling of clerical work is in his view less than convincing when account is taken of the dynamics of individual career trajectories within the clerical labour force. None the less, on the basis of British data relating to social mobility outcomes and educational attainment, Marshall demonstrates unequivocally that it is class background rather than educational attainment which more decisively influences occupational opportunities. Class inequalities cannot therefore 'be justified as meritocratic or as consistent with opportunity for all' and 'the class structure of this country remains an obstacle along the path to distributive justice' (*ibid*: 178–9).

Citizenship and Redistribution

For the moment, we should perhaps leave aside the kind of arguments which would redress systemic inequality by the overthrow of capitalism and concentrate on the classic proposition that distributive justice and the amelioration of class inequality may be achieved through the development of social citizenship, as originally envisioned by T.H. Marshall (1950). It has been amply demonstrated in preceding chapters first, that this is a reformist project which so far has not succeeded, and second, that it is a project capable of different interpretations. Effective redistribution in the cause of social justice is not necessarily an axiom of citizenship.

The distinction which we have drawn between the contractual and solidaristic traditions of citizenship is reflected in fundamentally different interpretations of what might constitute the social rights of citizenship and whether, indeed, the realisation of such rights is dependent on redistribution. A social-contractual conception of citizenship might be broadly consistent with distributive arrangements which relieve poverty when it occurs by guaranteeing the citizen social assistance. A social-solidaristic conception of citizenship might be broadly consistent with distributive arrangements which prevent poverty from occurring in the first place by organising an inclusive system of social insurance. In the event, social security systems such as that which we have in Britain tend to be 'hybrid' systems that combine elements of relief and prevention (Dean 1996). What is more, depending on the circumstances, the redistribution achieved by either kind of system may not necessarily involve a redistribution of income from rich to poor, so much as 'horizontal' redistribution within the working class or over the life-time of the individual citizen. Comparative social policy analysts, like Esping-Andersen (1990), have demonstrated that it is possible to make certain generalisations about the different approaches which different countries take to the development of social rights. Esping-Andersen originally distinguished three 'types' of welfare regime: the typically Anglo-Saxon liberal regime, which was minimally redistributive; the typically continental European conservative regime, which was modestly redistributive; and the typically Nordic social democratic regime, which was highly redistributive.

None the less, it is difficult straightforwardly to read off the kind of social policy regime which might follow from any particular discourse of citizenship. Different approaches to social citizenship reflect different historical and political trajectories and may also be associated with quite different conceptualisations of poverty or social exclusion. We have already commented on the way in which in European social policy debates the term poverty has to some extent been superseded by the term social exclusion. Graham Room (1995) has attempted to articulate these different terms with the different traditions and regimes in which they have currency. Commenting on the difficulties encountered – by politicians and researchers – in developing a common approach within the EU, Room observed a particular tension between the essentially Anglo-Saxon notion of poverty and the essentially continental European notion of social exclusion:

This mutual incomprehension highlighted the very different theoretical paradigms that these traditions seem to involve for analysing poverty and social exclusion. The notion of poverty is primarily focused upon distributional issues: the lack of resources at the disposal of an individual or a household. In contrast, notions such as social exclusion focus primarily on relational issues, in other words, inadequate social participation, lack of social integration and lack of power. . . . If it is the liberal vision of society that inspires the Anglo-Saxon concern with poverty, it is the conservative vision of society . . . that inspires the continental concern with social exclusion. Or, insofar as the principal moral rights and obligations that shape social relations are those of an egalitarian citizenship, rather than traditional heirarchies, it is . . . the social democratic vision that shapes the debate on social exclusion. (1995: 5–6)

In the event, the accommodation reached when creating, for example, the European Commission's Observatory on social exclusion, was one which encompassed both distributional and relational concerns.

The conceptual distinction between distributional and relational

Figure 7.2   A taxonomy of welfare regimes

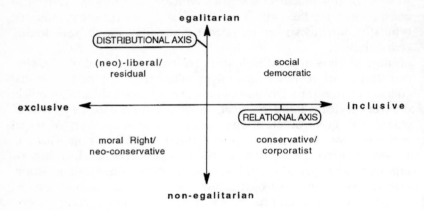

issues is important. Distributional issues are shaped by the political processes that distinguish constitutional (and therefore either formally or substantively egalitarian) approaches to the development of citizenship from more coercive or corporately brokered (and characteristically less egalitarian) approaches. Relational issues are shaped through ideological traditions that distinguish social-contractual (and potentially exclusive) from social-solidaristic (and implicitly inclusive) approaches to citizenship. In other words, the distinction draws us back to our discussion in Chapter 4 of the 'moral repertoires' which underpin political discourses of citizenship. By substituting the 'distributional' dimension – with its focus on equality *vs.* inequality – for the vertical axis in Figure 4.4 (see p. 95) and the 'relational' dimension – with its focus on inclusion *vs.* exclusion – for the horizontal axis, it is possible in Figure 7.2 to generate a somewhat simplified version of the same taxonomy.

This version can be related to Esping-Andersen's typology of welfare regimes, and serves at a conceptual level to develop it by the inclusion of a fourth 'ideal type' – the neo-conservative regime espoused by the moral Right. It may be seen in fact that the recent Anglo-Saxon orthodoxy of the Thatcher/Reagan era drew on both left-hand quadrants, while continental European orthodoxy to some extent drew on both right-hand quadrants. What arguably might now be happening across Europe (which is under pressure to achieve economic convergence in anticipation of monetary union), in Clinton's America, and certainly in Britain under New Labour is the emergence of a kind of welfare regime that is situated along a diagonal axis: which draws simultaneously from both the top left-hand quadrant and the bottom right-hand quadrant. There appears to be a certain tendency when articulating distributive with relational concerns to emphasise formal equality of opportunity (above substantive equality) and the duties (as much as the rights) associated with people's 'stake' in social membership.

The importance of articulating distributional with relational concerns in any normative conception of citizenship has also been underlined by Bryan Turner (1997). In an attempt to move conceptions of citizenship beyond the issues seminally identified by T.H. Marshall, Turner argues that citizenship does three things: it controls the allocation of resources (primarily economic, but also cultural); it confers identity; and it defines political communities. Underpinning this argument is the observation that:

> One can conceptualise all human societies as divided or organised along two contradictory principles, namely solidarity and scarcity. . . . All human societies must have some basis in solidarity in order to exist, but all human societies, precisely because they are human societies, are also characterised by scarcity. (1997: 10)

Solidarity, he argues, is required in a form which copes with problems of difference, diversity and conflict. Scarcity, he argues, is always relative to demand and, in affluent societies, it 'is a function as much of prosperity and wealth as it is of poverty'. The distributional or allocative functions of citizenship are – or ought to be – as critical as its relational or integrative functions. The tension between the need to moderate scarcity on the one hand and to maintain solidarity on the other represents 'the focal point of citizenship' (*ibid*: 11).

By itself this analysis reads as a recipe for a form of citizenship which, by integrating the contractual and solidaristic traditions, can manage or contain rather than challenge the structural inequalities of capitalist society.

Democratic Struggle and Individual Welfare

In fairness to Turner, however, he has also argued (1990; 1997) for a more dynamic theoretical framework which acknowledges the differing ways in which citizenship may entail active involvement in the public domain. Thus there are passive forms of citizenship in which citizens are subject to sovereign power or to a constitutional settlement imposed from above, and active forms of citizenship in which citizens can lay claim to some degree of individual sovereignty or may even seize power from below. Turner acknowledges the risk that attempts to establish more participative and more globally inclusive forms of citizenship may founder in the face of the new capitalist world order, but he points at least to the possibility of active political struggle to redress social injustice.

The issue to which this leads us is the question of the relationship between political democracy and welfare state capitalism. Claus Offe, developing themes from his earlier work concerning the contradictory potential of the welfare state under capitalism (1984), has recently pointed to particular ambiguities in the relationship between political democracy and the welfare state (1996). The development of the former supported the emergence of the latter at the point when the universal franchise empowered the working class to claim social rights of citizenship, but it became antagonistic to the latter at the point when class interests were fragmented and the legitimacy of the welfare state began to falter. The paradox, according to Offe, is that '[u]nless citizens consider the state's authority legitimate, they can obstruct mandatory cooperation through the ballot box. . . . [I]f a democratic state is a welfare state, this is not the case *because* of democracy, but *in spite* of democracy. It must be due to solidarities and modes of normative integration that underpin the continued production of collective goods and guarantee this production' (1996: 162–4). Offe goes on in an attempt to define the 'threshold' point at which collective-identity and trust give way to the rational calculation of individual self-interest – or vice versa; the point of the '*Gestalt*-switch' between normative support for collective distributive arrangements and individualistic anti-welfare backlash. Critical to the definition of this threshold are structural social changes that construct what Offe calls the 'parameters of sameness'. Here he develops a familiar treatise which probably somewhat overstates the extent to which the dominant axis of traditional class conflicts and solidarities have been undermined; in which the 'parameters of sameness' have been progressively narrowed. None the less, whether or not the point at which the welfare state is no longer politically sustainable has empirically been reached, Offe's threshold notion is, we believe, important.

What Offe appears to be describing is, perhaps, not so much a threshold as an equilibrium point between pragmatism and altruism. We have observed how people do in practice draw on conflicting moral and discursive repertoires; that they do not necessarily present a coherent account of their support for or opposition to the welfare state but hold contradictory values; that they are capable of combining autonomistic discourses consistent with a politics of identity with solidaristic discourses consistent with a politics of class. Individual citizens may tend to tip to one side or other of the equilibrium point, but this does not mean they have unequivocally crossed a threshold in the sense that Offe's model implies. What Offe describes as the parameters of sameness might in one sense relate to the intersubjectively constructed boundary which identifies the imagined community of 'ordinary' citizens. We have observed that though people are seldom able objectively to locate themselves in relation to the overall distribution of income and wealth, they quite consistently distance themselves from the states of poverty and riches that lie beyond commonly acceptable horizons. Without doubt the parameters of sameness are changing in quite complex ways, but the unacceptable extremities of social inequality continue, in a negative and symbolic sense, to provide a lowest common denominator by which to establish a tenuous unity for the political community.

For a rather different account of the relationship between political democracy and the capitalist welfare state we shall return briefly to the work of Ellen Meiksins Wood. We have already seen that Wood does not share the pessimism of Offe and others regarding the erosion of working class solidarity. Wood has drawn on the writings of E.P. Thompson to argue that class is a matter of process and relationship and not location and stratification. 'Where', she asks, 'is the dividing line between classes in a continuum of inequality?' (1995: 93). Classes are defined through relationships of power between classes and through the experiences shared between members of the same class. The significance of this for our argument is not that our evidence points to the survival of working class self-consciousness, but that popular discourse does reflect shared experiences of inequality (and, in Wood's or E.P. Thompson's terms, at least some scope for class formation). The thrust of Wood's own argument is that, with the collapse of Communism, the global ascendancy of capitalism within the new world order and, for example, the inexorable exploitative trends towards ever greater labour market flexibility, attempts to achieve human emancipation through a more equitable or humane form of capitalism would now be more un-realistically utopian than any attempt to achieve socialism. She contends that the form of democracy that is identified with liberalism and which has been specific to the social relations of capitalism is strictly limited and limiting. '[T]he greatest challenge to capitalism', therefore, 'would be an extension of democracy beyond its narrowly circumscribed limits. It is at this point', she says, 'that "democracy" arguably becomes synonymous with socialism' (*ibid*: 15).

Wood distances herself from the prescriptions of post-Marxist radical democrats, civil society socialists and social ecologists, but like them she is clearly grasping for a political project that would break free from the confines implied by the taxonomies we have modelled in this book and illustrated in Figures 1.6, 4.4 and 7.2. The scope that is evisaged for political struggle against substantive social inequality is implictly premised on the emergence or the creation of radical and entirely *new* popular discourses. There are other writers who premise other visions of a new politics of welfare quite explicitly on the invention of radical new discourse. Giddens (1994) seeks to define a 'generative' project that would transcend traditional discourses and conventional disitinctions between left and right through a form of dialogic democracy that would not be embedded within state-dominated relations of power, but somehow sustained by the power of individual reflexivity.

SOCIAL CITIZENSHIP AS A STRATEGIC TERRAIN

For our part, we wish to advance a speculative and more modest set of observations about the role of social policy but to suggest, none the less, that it is possible to engage with and synthesise from within the *existing* range of popular discourses. The institution of social citizenship does not supersede class conflict, nor need it on the other hand obscure identity and difference: it can, however, focus and mediate struggle in both spheres. In an attempt to conceptualise the future of the welfare state, Norman Ginsburg has summarised the two apparently contradictory ways in which the basis of the welfare state is shifting: '[o]n the one hand there is increasing economic injustice, particularly in class terms, and on the other, more effective organisation around cultural injustices' (1996: 12). He points, on the one hand, to the growth in inequality which we have discussed in Chapter 1 and, on the other, to the impact of 'new welfare activism' – welfare-oriented struggles around gender, age, disability, ethnicity and sexuality sustained in the postmodern age by the new politics of discourse and identity. Ginsburg draws on a suggestion by Nancy Fraser (1995: 89) that what is required is 'socialism in the economy *and* deconstruction in the culture' [our emphasis].

We read this, not as a call to relativism or compromise, but as a way of visualising social citizenship as an intermediate strategic resource which can at least partially advance different kinds of struggle towards human emancipation: struggles for social redistribution *and* struggles for cultural freedoms. In this book we have sought to show the way in which the practice of citizenship may call upon competing conceptual and political traditions, and in which popular discourse calls upon competing moral repertoires. There is no single or coherent hegemonic discourse, but many. No one discourse is ever pure or ascendant because it must exist in combination with others. One way of understanding the kind of future which Ginsburg and Fraser hold out is in terms of new strategic combinations. This probably comes close to what Gramsci meant by hegemonic struggle or 'war of position' (1971). We have been seeking to convey the sense in which poverty, in particular, is both a material and a discursive phenomenon, involving both objective exploitation and symbolic repression. Those who are oppressed by poverty may resist it both through the collective manipulation of diverse political strategies and policy instruments (cf. Thompson 1968) and through the individual exploitation of contradictory moral discourses (cf. Jordan 1993).

Social citizenship within a capitalist welfare state does not provide a medium through which to abolish class conflict, or for that matter to guarantee freedom of culture and identity. It can, however, furnish a terrain on which to mediate struggles both at the structural and at the discursive level. It is the public terrain on which claims for social justice and the recognition of individual difference are pursued; on which claims for redistribution can be fought and on which universal values can be continually renegotiated.

At first sight, it must be admitted, the basis for such a strategic project within prevailing popular paradigms and welfare values is not especially promising. What we believe we have shown, however, is that these paradigms and values are more complex than perhaps more pessimistic theorists would allow. Our particular concern has been with popular perceptions of poverty and riches and we have seen that images of poverty and riches are generated and sustained in such ways that the poor and the rich tend always to be the 'other'. To the extent that there is a common ideal of citizenship, its essence is an identification with the 'ordinary' rather than the 'other'. In their everyday lives people negotiate, for example, the risk of redundancy or the chance of winning the national lottery: the danger of poverty is feared and the prospect of wealth is revered, but each in its own way is constitutive of people's identity as 'ordinary' citizens.

In spite of this, people are by and large uncertain about what constitutes an ordinary or acceptable range of income and wealth and about what – if anything – the welfare state should do to moderate the threats and the opportunities which differentiate the rich, the poor and the imaginary community of those in between. The implication is that Schumpeterian workfare policies – even when they are dressed in the language of New Labour's stakeholder socialism – are not necessarily consistent with popular values and aspirations. Social redistribution is by no means politically impossible. The basis for solidarity in diversity is by no means wholly absent. What is urgent, however, is that social policy should find ways of imparting greater *certainty* to the meaning of citizenship. To this extent, we can agree with Giddens' (1994) contention that the welfare state is now primarily concerned with the management of risk. Risk, however, is to be comprehended, not only in terms of its impact at the level of individual experience, but also in terms of its relational and distributive context. Ontological security of personal autonomy (freedom from poverty) cannot be achieved without solidaristic security of collective organisation (protection from social exclusion) and the material security of redistributive state intervention (the reduction of inequality).

Appendix: The Poverty, Wealth and Citizenship Study

This exploratory study was conducted by the authors between November 1995 and June 1997 and funded by the Economic and Social Research Council under Grant reference R000236264. The aim of the project was to investigate prevailing beliefs and popular discourses relating to the nature, extent and 'risk' of poverty and wealth, and to see how such beliefs and discourses relate to people's understanding and experiences of citizenship.

Methods

The methods used involved in-depth interviews with a range of people at widely differing income levels. A stratified sample for the study was drawn with the generous assistance of a large national employer, Whitbread plc. Tranches of invitations to participate were dispatched to Whitbread employees at different locations in England in gross income bands ranging from more than £50 000 per annum to less than £7000 per annum. Additionally, as a result of direct approaches by the investigators, some informal contacts and assistance from Luton Borough Council, it was possible strategically to supplement the sample by interviewing some respondents not employed by Whitbread, including a small number on very high and very low incomes. Interviews were achieved with a total of 76 respondents.

A wide-ranging semi-structured interview schedule was used. Interviews were tape-recorded and fully transcribed. Respondents were interviewed at locations of their own choosing and were given strict undertakings as to confidentiality. During the fieldwork, a news-media monitoring exercise was undertaken in order to study the influences of media output on specific aspects of popular discourse.

Composition of the Interview Sample

Something over a third of the resulting sample was drawn from London and the South East and a similar proportion from the Luton area. The remainder was drawn from the South West, East Anglia and the North of England. In the event, such regional variations as were observable within the data were not consistent in their nature and could not easily be interpreted as an independent effect.

The composition of the sample with regard to gender, ethnicity and age is summarised in Table A.1 and with regard to occupational class and gross income in Table A.2.

Sixteen respondents were in part-time employment and five held more than one employment. Almost a quarter of the sample had no post-16 educational qualifications, while about a third were graduates.

Respondents were asked to volunteer information about the income of other members of the households in which they lived and about their savings. One fifth of the sample reported gross household incomes of less than £10 000 per annum and one fifth had gross household incomes of £50 000 per annum or more. However, the sample is and was not intended to be statistically representative of the population as a whole. The actual income distribution of the UK population is highly skewed with 63 per cent of all individuals having net incomes (adjusted for household size) below the national average (DSS 1996; and see the discussion in Chapter 1). The object of this research was to contrast the views of what might be called comfortable Britain (or, perhaps more specifically, 'Middle England') with those of people with lower incomes on the one hand and with those who are relatively affluent on the other. Because of the asymmetrical distribution of income within the population, a properly representative sample would not have allowed us satisfactorily to do this and it was necessary to attempt to construct a sample composed of broadly comparable numbers of people with below average/low incomes, middle range/higher incomes and (very) high incomes.

Because of differential response rates between these groups, this was not easy to contrive. What is more, the qualitative nature of the research had not of itself necessitated the collection of precise data relating to income and household composition, data which is in any event notoriously difficult to assemble reliably during face to face interviews (Runciman 1966: 189). For our purposes it was

Table A.1 Sample composition – gender and ethnicity by age

		Age group					
		under 25	26–35	36–45	46–55	over 55	totals
Gender	Ethnicity*						
Male	Black	–	3	–	1	–	4
	White	5	10	7	7	3	32
	sub-total	**5**	**13**	**7**	**8**	**3**	**36**
Female	Black	1	–	1	–	–	2
	White	10	9	7	8	4	38
	sub-total	**11**	**9**	**8**	**8**	**4**	**40**
totals		16	22	15	16	7	76

* 'Black' relates to Black British, African or African-Caribbean 'White' refers to White British, European or 'other' (including a Canadian and a South African)

Table A.2 Sample composition – occupational class and gross income

	Gross income				
	less than £12K p.a.	£12K to 24 999 p.a.	£25K to 49 999 p.a.	£50K p.a. or over	totals
Occupational class					
higher professional	–	–	–	3	3
employers & managers	1	5	10	6	22
lower professional	2	6	7	–	15
secretarial & clerical	6	7	1	–	14
shop & service workers	2	–	–	–	2
skilled manual	1	–	–	–	1
semi- and un-skilled	12	1	–	1	14
other	4	1	–	–	5
totals	28	20	18	10	76

necessary only to have a broadly accurate ordinal ranking of respondents' incomes. To achieve this, certain estimations and working assumptions had to be applied to the information which respondents had given and translating that information into equivalised net incomes for the purposes of ordinal ranking necessarily entailed approximate calculations. The approximate disposable incomes were then grouped as shown in Table A.3 into bands which are sufficiently broad at least to mitigate the inevitable margin of error entailed in the computations. Within the limitations of a small sample, drawn for the purposes of a qualitative investigation,

Table A.3 Sample composition – disposable income and savings

Disposable income*	Savings					grouping
	none	up to £10K	over £10K	undis-closed	totals	
less than half average	7	3	–	2	12 ⎫	
half to average	5	3	2	3	13 ⎭ 25	below average
average to one and a half average	8	14	5	3		30 'Middle England'
one and a half to twice average	2	2	5	1	10 ⎫	
over twice average	1	2	7	1	11 ⎭ 21	affluent
totals	23	24	19	10	76	

* Disposable income based on approximate calculation of equivalised household income (before housing costs)

the structure achieved has not only allowed us to compare the attitudes and experiences of the very poorest and the very richest, but it has also allowed us more broadly to contrast the attitudes and experiences of 'Middle England' with those of people with below average incomes and with those of people with incomes of more than one and a half times the average, who might reasonably be regarded as relatively affluent. The group of respondents with below average disposable incomes was almost equally divided between respondents with below half average income (who, by a widely accepted definition, would be termed 'the poor') and respondents with half to average incomes (arguably, 'the nearly poor'). The group of respondents with over one and a half times average disposable income was almost equally divided between respondents with more than twice average income (whom we might tentatively characterise as 'the rich') and respondents with one and a half to twice average income (arguably, 'the nearly rich').

In focusing on income differences, the investigators acknowledge that there are many other measures which bear upon the substantive quality of life which people experience. Income was taken as a proxy measure which, however imperfectly, tends to reflect the social distribution of life chances. It may, for example, be seen that there was a close association between income and savings levels. It must however be acknowledged that the accuracy of this self-reported data is dubious. The wealthiest member of the sample featured within the *Sunday Times* register of the top 200 wealth holders in Britain and was cited as having assets with a value well in excess of £150 million. However, the 'off the cuff' estimate he gave of his total wealth during our interview was just £10 million!

Of the respondents in the interview sample approximately one third (25) were regular tabloid newspaper readers, approximately one third (26) were regular broadsheet newspaper readers, and the remaining third (25) either did not regularly read a newspaper or read a selection of different papers.

News Media Monitoring

This exercise focused on home news coverage of all the ten principal national daily newspapers and the nine principal Sunday newspapers published in Britain between January and December 1996 (except on two days which were subject to local disruption of newspaper deliveries). The monitoring entailed the scanning of the newspapers, the extraction and filing of relevant news items, and the indexing of such items on a database. The newspapers which were monitored were:

Tabloids: Daily Express and Sunday Express; Daily Mail and Mail on Sunday; Daily Mirror and Sunday Mirror; Daily Star; Sun; News of the World; People.

Broadsheets: Financial Times; Guardian and Observer; Independent and Independent on Sunday; Times and Sunday Times; Telegraph and Sunday Telegraph.

Data Analysis

Transcripts from the interviews were analysed in three main steps. First, transcripts were coded for the substantive replies which respondents gave in the course of the interviews. Second, the transcripts were re-read and each respondent was assigned to one of four groupings on the basis of the discursive repertoires on which they appeared to the investigators predominantly to draw: the theoretical basis of the taxonomy of discourses is set out in Chapter 1 (Figure 1.6 and pp. 18–21) above and the resulting distribution of the sample is shown in Figure A.1. Third, the transcripts were coded again, using a computer aided discourse analysis software

Figure A.1 Sample composition – location of respondents in relation to taxonomy of discourses

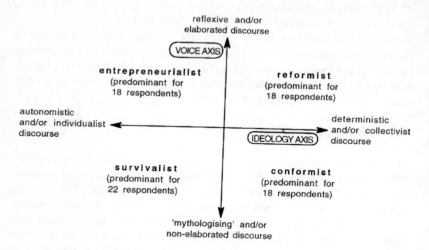

package (HyperResearch) in order to identify instances of ten principal discursive themes, as summarised in Figure A.2. Data from the newspaper monitoring exercise were subjected to a simple frequency analysis, although a more detailed analysis – including textual analysis of extracted news items – is still in progress at the time of writing.

Results

Findings from the study are discussed in detail in Chapters 2, 3, 5 and 6 of this volume. However, a selective summary of the principal results from the analysis of interview transcripts are set out in Tables A.4a to A.4e, inclusive.

The 'headline' conclusions from these data were:

• Fear of poverty extended up the income scale to respondents on middle and even high incomes. Poverty tended to be regarded, even by 'the poor', as a distant horror which usually happens to other people, but it manifested itself as a cause of everyday worry. It was a kind of worry that seemed to be felt less intensively by respondents who were nearly poor or nearly rich than it was either by the denizens of 'Middle England', who fell in between, or

Figure A.2 Discourse analysis codings

The discourses identified were not replies to the interview questions or quotations to illustrate a particular finding or argument, but instances within the transcripts of particular repertoires or uses of language around the following themes:

poverty-wealth discourses	**privation**	• discourse which speaks of the 'otherness' of poverty; the discomfort, hunger, misery, etc.; the loss of respect, self-esteem, cleanliness; the hopelessness, helplessness.
	worry	• discourse which incorporates the word 'worry', or which dwells on insecurity, uncertainty, anxiety and the risk of poverty.
	comfort	• discourse which incorporates the word 'comfort', or which dwells on security, certainty, happiness, contentment, fulfilment, having what one needs, or on the absence of worry.
	fun	• discourse which incorporates the word 'fun', or which dwells on luxury, entertainment, pleasure, escapism or on unfettered consumer choice/freedom.
	privilege	• discourse which speaks of the 'otherness' of wealth; the excesses, the indulgence, power or the abuse of power.
explanatory discourses	**individual desert**	• discourse which explains or apprehends wealth and/or poverty in terms of merit or lack of merit; individual success or failure; determination, weakness or state of mind; of just deserts.
	fate/injustice	• discourse which explains or apprehends wealth and/or poverty in terms of good or bad luck; naturally bestowed advantage or affliction; socially bestowed advantage or disadvantage, including references to systemic disparities of power, social or class structures; notions of injustice.
citizenship discourses	**social-contractual**	• discourse which embodies or implies a normative construct of citizenship as something which guarantees (or should but fails to guarantee) individual choice, freedom, independence, autonomy; or which emphasises reciprocal rights and obligations.
	nation/efficiency	• discourse which embodies or implies a construct of citizenship that either rests on Britishness/ Englishness; or which dwells on the pursuit of the national interest; or which is concerned to promote social/national efficiency.
	social-solidaristic	• discourse which embodies or implies a construct of citizenship that rests upon notions of social cohesion and the common good, or which emphasises the values of sharing/ altruism.

Table A.4a Summary of data on attitudes to poverty

	All respondents	Sex		Disposable income			Class		Predominant discourse grouping			
		male	female	below average	'Middle England'	affluent	profess-ional/ managerial	clerical and manual	'entrepre-neurial' group	'refor-mist' group	'survi-vor' group	'confor-mist' group
Totals	76	36	40	25	30	21	40	36	18	18	22	18
Being poor means												
0. no reply/not discussed	2	2	–	1	1	–	–	2	–	–	1	1
1. lacking means of subsistence	37	15	22	14	17	6	19	18	5	9	13	10
2. unable to do as others do	8	5	3	–	4	4	5	3	3	1	3	1
3. having no choice	4	1	3	–	2	2	3	1	3	–	–	1
4. multiple answers	7	4	3	2	3	2	4	3	1	4	2	–
5. other answers/don't know	18	9	9	8	3	7	9	9	5	3	2	5
Image of poverty												
0. no reply/not discussed	5	3	2	3	–	2	3	2	1	1	–	3
1. homelessness	16	7	9	4	6	6	6	10	5	5	3	5
2. council estates	7	3	4	4	3	–	2	5	–	2	3	2
3. welfare dependency	9	5	4	4	2	3	4	5	1	3	3	2
4. multiple images	24	12	12	7	10	7	17	7	8	9	4	3
5. other answers/don't know	15	6	9	3	9	3	8	7	3	–	9	3
Disadvantages of poverty												
0. no reply/question not put	5	3	2	2	1	2	3	2	2	1	1	1
1. opportunity constraints	47	25	22	15	17	15	28	19	12	12	11	12
2. shortcomings of the poor	6	3	3	1	2	3	4	2	2	2	2	–
3. lack of respect from others	9	3	6	2	6	1	1	8	–	1	6	2
4. other answers/don't know	9	2	7	5	4	–	4	5	3	1	2	3
The poor get less respect												
0. no reply/not discussed	8	6	2	3	2	3	4	4	1	4	–	3
1. agree	58	25	33	17	25	16	31	27	14	14	19	11
2. disagree	2	1	1	2	–	–	–	–	–	–	–	2
3. others answers/don't know	8	4	4	3	3	2	5	3	3	–	3	2

The poor have fewer rights												
0. no reply/not discussed	6	5	1	2	2	2	4	2	1	3	–	2
1. agree	44	23	21	14	18	12	27	17	13	9	9	13
2. disagree	20	6	14	7	8	5	5	15	3	4	11	2
3. other answers/don't know	6	2	4	2	2	2	4	2	1	2	2	1
Is respondent 'poor'?												
0. no reply/not discussed	5	3	2	2	1	2	3	2	2	1	1	1
1. yes	6	3	3	6	–	–	1	5	–	1	2	3
2. compared to some	2	1	1	2	–	–	1	1	–	–	–	2
3. no	62	29	33	15	28	19	35	27	16	16	19	11
4. other answers/don't know	1	–	1	–	1	–	–	1	–	–	–	1
Worry about being poor												
0. no reply/not discussed	8	5	3	3	4	1	4	4	2	1	2	3
1. does worry	49	24	25	13	22	14	26	23	11	15	13	10
2. doesn't worry	16	7	9	7	4	5	8	8	4	2	6	4
3. others answers/don't know	3	–	3	2	–	1	2	1	1	–	1	1
Why are some people poor?												
0. no reply/not discussed	1	–	1	1	–	–	–	1	–	–	–	1
1. external/structural factors	38	20	18	13	14	11	20	18	7	12	11	8
2. inevitability/fate	21	8	13	5	9	7	12	9	7	5	4	5
3. personal failings of the poor	6	4	2	2	4	–	3	3	–	1	3	2
4. multiple answers	7	2	5	3	2	2	3	4	3	–	3	2
5. others answers/don't know	3	2	1	1	1	1	2	1	1	–	1	1

Table A.4b Summary of data on attitudes to riches

	All respondents	Sex		Disposable income			Class		Predominant discourse grouping			
		male	female	below average	'Middle England'	affluent	professional/ managerial	clerical and manual	'entrepreneurial' group	'reformist' group	'survivor' group	'conformist' group
Totals	76	36	40	25	30	21	40	36	18	18	22	18
Being rich means												
0. no reply/not discussed	1	1	–	–	–	1	1	–	–	1	–	–
1. freedom from constraint	39	16	23	16	14	9	19	20	8	9	11	11
2. resources above a threshold	7	4	3	–	3	4	4	3	2	2	2	1
3. multiple answers	4	–	4	1	1	2	1	3	–	3	1	–
4. other answers/don't know	25	15	10	8	12	5	15	10	8	3	8	6
Images of riches												
0. no reply/not discussed	–	–	–	–	–	–	–	–	–	–	–	–
1. celebrity status	8	4	4	1	5	2	1	7	–	1	5	2
2. power status	12	6	6	3	5	4	6	6	2	4	2	4
3. conspicuous consumption	7	2	5	5	2	–	5	2	1	3	2	1
4. multiple images	25	13	12	9	10	6	13	12	5	7	5	8
5. no images	13	7	6	2	5	6	10	3	8	–	3	2
6. other answers/don't know	11	4	7	5	3	3	5	6	2	3	5	1
Advantages of being rich												
0. no reply/not discussed	–	–	–	–	–	–	–	–	–	–	–	–
1. privilege and power	37	17	20	11	15	11	19	18	8	7	9	13
2. unrestricted consumption	7	3	4	3	3	1	3	4	1	3	2	1
3. security	10	6	4	5	2	3	4	6	2	2	6	–
4. multiple answers	4	3	1	–	3	1	3	1	3	–	1	–
5. other answers/don't know	18	7	11	6	7	5	11	7	4	6	4	4
The rich get more respect												
0. no reply/not discussed	5	2	3	2	1	2	1	4	–	1	2	2
1. agree	27	12	15	8	12	7	15	12	8	8	7	4
2. depends on source of wealth	21	11	10	4	8	9	13	8	6	6	6	3
3. disagree	21	10	11	11	8	2	10	11	3	3	7	8
4. other answers/don't know	2	1	1	–	1	1	1	1	1	–	–	1

The rich have more rights												
0. no reply/not discussed	1	–	–	1	–	–	–	1	–	–	1	–
1. agree	40	25	15	11	17	12	23	17	7	14	9	10
2. disagree	31	11	20	11	12	8	15	16	10	3	11	7
3. other answers/don't know	4	–	4	2	1	1	2	2	1	1	1	1
Is respondent 'rich'?												
0. no reply/not discussed	6	2	4	2	4	–	2	4	1	–	4	1
1. yes	6	5	1	–	–	6	6	–	4	2	–	–
2. compared to some	5	3	2	–	2	3	3	2	2	1	1	1
3. not rich but comfortable	12	5	7	1	6	5	10	2	8	2	1	1
4. no	46	20	26	24	17	7	18	28	3	13	15	15
5. other answers/don't know	1	1	–	–	1	–	1	–	–	–	1	–
Desire to be rich												
0. no reply/not discussed	9	7	2	–	–	9	9	–	6	3	–	1
1. would like to	36	20	16	13	20	3	19	17	7	4	16	9
2. like to be 'comfortable'	13	3	10	6	4	3	3	10	1	6	2	4
3. wouldn't like to	11	4	7	2	5	4	5	6	3	4	3	1
4. other answers/don't know	7	2	5	4	1	2	4	3	1	1	1	4
Why are some people rich?												
0. no reply/not discussed	11	3	8	3	4	4	4	7	3	3	2	3
1. external/structural factors	18	13	5	5	8	5	13	5	4	9	4	1
2. inevitability/fate	22	10	12	6	8	8	14	8	6	4	4	8
3. personal attributes of the rich	5	2	3	1	3	1	2	3	1	1	4	1
4. multiple answers	16	5	11	9	5	2	4	12	3	2	8	5
5. other answers/don't know	4	3	1	1	2	1	3	1	3	–	–	1

Table A.4c Summary of data on attitudes to citizenship

	All respondents	Sex		Disposable income			Class		Predominant discourse grouping			
		male	female	below average	'Middle England'	affluent	professional/ managerial	clerical and manual	'entrepreneurial' group	'reformist' group	'survivor' group	'conformist' group
Totals	76	36	40	25	30	21	40	36	18	18	22	18
Being a citizen means												
0. no reply/not discussed	2	–	2	1	1	–	–	2	–	–	1	1
1. nothing/don't know	22	13	9	6	11	5	9	13	4	3	6	9
2. nationality of birth/residence	16	5	11	6	7	3	10	6	4	4	5	3
3. membership of a community	17	9	8	5	3	9	13	4	8	5	2	2
4. having rights/obeying laws	10	5	5	4	4	2	3	7	–	4	4	2
5. other answers	9	4	5	3	4	2	5	4	2	2	4	1
Feels like a citizen												
0. no reply/not discussed	3	2	1	1	–	2	1	2	–	2	–	1
1. yes/sometimes	54	27	27	18	23	13	29	25	11	13	18	12
2. no	17	7	10	5	6	6	10	7	7	3	3	4
3. other answers/don't know	2	–	2	1	1	–	–	2	–	–	1	1
Qualities of a good citizen												
0. no reply/not discussed	6	3	3	2	3	1	3	3	2	2	2	–
1. looking after others	11	3	8	4	6	1	2	9	1	1	8	1
2. contributing to community	13	8	5	3	2	8	11	2	6	3	2	2
3. obeying laws/paying taxes	15	6	9	6	6	3	9	6	1	5	4	5
4. multiple answers	15	7	8	5	4	6	7	8	6	2	3	5
5. other answers/don't know	16	9	7	5	9	2	8	8	2	5	5	4
Qualities of a bad citizen												
0. no reply/not discussed	6	3	3	2	3	1	3	3	2	2	–	2
1. disobeying laws/rules	23	10	13	9	9	5	8	15	2	4	9	8
2. acting self-interestedly	11	9	2	1	3	7	9	2	5	4	2	–
3. multiple answers	13	7	6	3	5	5	7	6	4	3	3	3
4. others answers/don't know	23	7	16	10	10	3	11	12	5	5	8	5

Social rights are or should be the same as other rights												
0. no reply/not discussed	3	–	3	1	1	1	2	1	1	–	–	2
1. agree	45	21	24	17	17	11	19	26	7	13	13	12
2. disagree	23	12	11	6	10	7	16	7	8	5	6	4
3. other answers/don't know	5	3	2	1	2	2	3	2	2	–	3	–
Conscious of rich-poor gap?												
0. no reply/not discussed	4	3	1	1	1	2	3	1	2	–	1	1
1. yes/sometimes	42	25	17	13	16	13	23	19	8	13	12	9
2. no	28	7	21	10	13	5	12	16	7	5	9	7
3. other answers/don't know	2	1	1	1	–	1	2	–	1	–	–	1
Is rich-poor gap a problem?												
0. no reply/not discussed	4	1	3	2	2	–	–	4	–	–	2	2
1. yes/could become so	53	27	26	17	18	18	31	22	14	17	10	12
2. no/not really	11	2	9	3	6	2	5	6	3	–	6	2
3. other answers/don't know	8	6	2	3	4	1	4	4	1	1	4	2
Why is it a problem?												
0. no reply/not discussed	20	7	13	5	11	4	7	13	5	1	10	4
1. threat to social cohesion	20	13	7	9	4	7	13	7	4	8	3	5
2. unpleasant/unjust for poor	21	6	15	6	11	4	11	10	4	7	5	5
3. other answers/don't know	15	10	5	5	4	6	9	6	5	2	4	4
Should the state intervene?												
0. no reply/not discussed	2	1	1	1	–	1	1	1	1	–	–	1
1. yes	46	23	23	18	16	12	23	23	9	14	12	11
2. no	4	4	–	–	2	2	4	–	1	2	1	–
3. other answers/don't know	24	8	16	6	12	6	12	12	7	2	9	6

Table A.4d Summary of data from questions drawn from BSA survey

	All respondents	Sex		Disposable income			Class		Predominant discourse grouping			
		male	female	below average	'Middle England'	affluent	profess-ional/ managerial	clerical and manual	'entrepre-neurial' group	'refor-mist' group	'survi-vor' group	'confor-mist' group
Totals	76	36	40	25	30	21	40	36	18	18	22	18
The government should spend more money on welfare benefits for the poor, even if it leads to higher taxes												
0. no reply/not discussed	1	–	1	1	–	–	–	1	–	–	–	1
1. agrees	32	20	12	9	11	12	19	13	5	13	5	9
2. agrees with qualifications	32	13	19	11	13	8	15	17	11	4	10	7
3. disagrees	10	3	7	3	6	1	6	4	2	1	6	1
4. don't know/not sure	1	–	1	1	–	–	–	1	–	–	1	–
If welfare benefits weren't so generous, people would learn to stand on their own two feet												
0. no reply/not discussed	1	–	1	1	–	–	–	1	–	–	–	1
1. agrees	17	7	10	7	7	3	9	8	4	–	9	4
2. agrees with qualifications	17	9	8	3	9	5	11	6	6	3	4	4
3. disagrees	36	17	19	13	12	11	18	18	7	14	8	7
4. disagrees with qualifications	4	3	1	1	2	1	2	2	1	–	1	2
5. don't know/not sure/other	1	–	1	–	1	–	–	1	–	1	–	–
The welfare state encourages people to stop helping each other												
0. no reply/not discussed	2	1	1	1	1	–	–	2	–	–	1	1
1. agrees	21	12	9	6	10	5	11	10	5	5	9	2
2. agrees with qualifications	6	2	4	–	4	2	3	3	3	–	1	2
3. disagrees	39	18	21	16	14	9	21	18	6	11	10	12
4. don't know/not sure/other	8	3	5	2	1	5	5	3	4	2	1	1

Many people who get social security don't really deserve any help

0. no reply/not discussed	2	–	2	2	–	–	–	2	–	–	1	1
1. agrees	11	4	7	6	4	1	2	9	1	1	5	4
2. agrees with qualifications	2	1	1	2	–	–	–	2	–	–	2	–
3. disagrees	21	12	9	7	6	8	13	8	5	7	4	5
4. disagrees with qualifications	34	17	17	6	19	9	23	11	10	9	9	6
5. don't know/not sure/other	6	2	4	2	1	3	2	4	2	1	1	2

People receiving social security benefits are made to feel like second-class citizens

0. no reply/not discussed	1	–	1	1	–	–	–	1	–	–	–	1
1. agrees	49	26	23	16	20	13	26	23	9	15	15	10
2. agrees with qualifications	6	3	3	2	2	2	5	1	2	2	–	2
3. disagrees	10	4	6	4	5	1	3	7	2	–	5	3
4. disagrees with qualifications	5	2	3	1	2	2	3	2	2	1	1	2
5. don't know/not sure/other	5	1	4	1	1	3	3	2	3	1	1	–

Table A.4e   Summary of data from questions drawn from Runciman's study

	All respondents	Sex		Disposable income			Class		Predominant discourse grouping			
		male	female	below average	'Middle England'	affluent	profess-ional/ managerial	clerical and manual	'entrepre-neurial' group	'refor-mist' group	'survi-vor' group	'confor-mist' group
Totals	76	36	40	25	30	21	40	36	18	18	22	18
Is there anything the state should be doing at the moment to help you that it isn't doing?												
0. no reply/not discussed	3	1	2	1	1	1	2	1	2	–	–	1
1. nothing	19	9	10	6	6	7	10	9	3	5	5	6
2. improve services/benefits	21	7	14	8	7	6	9	12	4	7	5	5
3. lower taxes	5	3	2	1	4	–	3	2	–	–	5	–
4. other replies	28	16	12	9	12	7	16	12	9	6	7	6
Are you satisfied with your present income?												
0. no reply/not discussed	1	–	1	1	–	–	–	1	–	–	–	1
1. yes	44	25	19	10	16	18	30	14	17	11	8	8
2. no	31	11	20	14	14	3	10	21	1	7	14	9
What income do you think is necessary for someone like you to have a proper standard of living?												
0. no reply/not discussed	1	–	1	1	–	–	–	1	–	–	–	1
1. more than I have	31	10	21	17	11	3	8	23	2	6	11	12
2. same as I have	13	7	6	3	9	1	9	4	–	4	7	2
3. less than I have	21	14	7	1	7	13	19	2	13	5	3	–
4. don't know/other reply	10	5	5	3	3	4	4	6	3	3	1	3

What kind of people do you think are doing better than you financially?

0. no reply/not discussed	6	2	4	3	1	2	2	4	2	1	1	2
1. class/occupation related	36	17	19	10	17	9	21	15	6	10	9	11
2. personal attribute related	9	7	2	–	2	7	6	3	4	3	1	1
3. don't know/other replies	25	10	15	12	10	3	11	14	6	4	7	8

Who do you think of when you think of 'people like you'?

0. no reply/not discussed	1	–	1	1	–	–	–	1	–	–	1	–
1. class/occupation related	47	27	20	15	17	15	29	18	12	10	13	12
2. situationally oriented	17	4	13	6	10	1	5	12	3	5	1	8
3. multiple answers	2	2	–	–	–	2	2	–	–	2	–	–
4. don't know/other replies	9	3	6	3	3	3	4	5	3	1	3	2

those who were rich. The former, though ostensibly comfortable, felt subjectively vulnerable, while the latter, arguably, had most to lose.

- The extent to which respondents feared poverty exceeded the extent to which they aspired to wealth. Wealth had a certain fascination – it would be fun to be free from everyday constraints – but many respondents made clear that they valued comfort above fun. Poverty was generally equated with low status, but the rich were not necessarily held in high esteem or thought to deserve their privileges. Comparatively few respondents blamed poverty on the failings of the poor or attributed wealth to the qualities of the rich, but the processes which result in poverty and wealth were differently understood. The dangers which can precipitate a descent into poverty are more transparent than the unfathomable good fortune that may lead to becoming rich.
- Respondents were seldom able to locate themselves within the social distribution of incomes. Asked to place themselves on a scale between rich and poor, few were able to do so with any accuracy. In particular, respondents with middle to higher incomes tended grossly to underestimate their relative standing, a finding which cast light, both on their underlying sense of insecurity (see above) and their ambivalence towards redistributive state welfare (see below).
- Though respondents frequently appeared indifferent or incoherent with regard to issues of citizenship, they could be seen none the less to be drawing on a diversity of often contradictory traditions and 'repertoires'. The important differences between respondents related partly to the moral and ideological substance of the explanations they used (which might rest on solidaristic, universalistic or collectivist values on the one hand, or contractarian, autonomistic or individualistic values on the other); and partly to the 'voice' or forms of expression upon which they would call (which might rest on reflexive or radical conventions on the one hand, or on received myths or established traditions on the other). It is possible to make sense of the depleted or ambiguous conceptions of citizenship that people exhibit when it is seen that popular discourse contains a complex mixture of competing explanations.
- In their attitudes to redistributive state welfare, respondents exhibited a similarly contradictory mixture of altruism and pragmatic instrumentalism. They generally valued key elements of

the solidaristic principles on which the welfare state was established, but were predisposed to ideological principles which would underpin more individualistic self-sufficiency. Expectations of the welfare state were high, but this was tempered in many instances by suspicion of it. Respondents who were poor were more strongly in favour of state redistribution than were respondents who were rich but, paradoxically, the poor were less inclined to indulge in solidaristic rhetoric than were the rich: the former, perhaps, have less occasion to believe that the state is going to help them; the latter have more occasion to fear the potentially disruptive consequences of growing social inequality.

A summary of the results from the newspaper monitoring exercise is set out in Tables A.5a to A.5c, inclusive.

The 'headline' conclusion from these data was that:

● Newspapers probably have a limited impact in shaping popular discourse, though they may help foster a general climate of insecurity and fatalism. In contrast to the preoccupations of respondents in the study, newspapers – especially tabloids – regarded wealth as far more newsworthy than poverty. News stories about poverty tended to feature such issues as homelessness and job losses, while coverage of issues relating to wealth was dominated by stories about national lottery winners and, for example, critical reports of extravagant remuneration packages awarded to 'fat

Table A.5a Summary of data from newspaper monitoring exercise (January to December 1996) – News items relating to poverty

Type/subject of item	Number of items relating to poverty in			as % age of all items on poverty
	All papers	Tabloids	Broad-sheets	
1. unemployment and/or redundancy	1145	381	764	55.8
2. welfare 'scrounging' or benefit fraud	218	115	103	10.6
3. low pay/poor wages	188	64	124	9.2
4. experiences and/or lifestyles of poor people (including critical comment)	169	61	108	8.2
5. homelessness or home repossessions	154	45	109	7.5
6. other items, including items with multiple themes	179	59	120	8.7
Totals	2053	725	1328	100.0

Table A.5b Summary of data from newspaper monitoring exercise (January to December 1996) – News items relating to riches

Type/subject of item	Number of items relating to riches in			as % age of all items on riches
	All papers	Tabloids	Broad-sheets	
1. extravagant pay deals/share-option schemes/'golden handshakes', etc.	1605	760	845	49.1
2. experiences and/or lifestyles of rich people (including critical comment and allegations of greed)	1129	796	333	34.6
3. sudden wealth and its effects/dangers	295	236	59	9.0
4. other items, including items with multiple themes	238	136	102	7.3
Totals	3267	1928	1339	100.0

Table A.5c Summary of data from newspaper monitoring exercise (January to December 1996) – News items relating to citizenship

Type/subject of item	Number of items relating to citizenship in			as % age of all items on citizenship
	All papers	Tabloids	Broad-sheets	
1. tax and taxation	1088	366	722	35.1
2. social security benefits/pensions	814	264	550	26.3
3. public spending and/or costs of the welfare state	405	123	282	13.1
4. rights and/or responsibilities	258	62	196	8.3
5. class distinctions or privileges	144	40	104	4.6
6. charity (giving to/receiving from)	116	44	72	3.7
7. other items, including items with multiple themes	275	87	188	8.9
Totals	3100	986	2114	100.0

cat' business chiefs: the impression conveyed was that people were becoming poor or rich in ways which were unmerited. Issues of citizenship tended to be discussed principally in relation to the burdens of taxation and the costs of welfare, contributing possibly to public scepticism about the welfare state. None the less, respondents clearly drew on a much wider range of experience and opinion than that presented through the news media.

References

Abbott, E. and Bompas, K. (1943) 'The woman citizen and social security', reproduced in J. Clarke, A. Cochrane and C. Smart (eds) (1987) *Ideologies of Welfare*, Hutchinson, London.

Abel-Smith, B. and Townsend, P. (1965) *The Poor and the Poorest*, Bell, London.

Ainley, P. (1993) 'The legacy of the Manpower Services Commission: Training in the 1980s', in P. Taylor-Gooby and R. Lawson (eds) *Markets and Managers: New issues in the delivery of welfare*, Open University Press, Buckingham.

Alcock, P. (1993) *Understanding Poverty*, Macmillan, Basingstoke.

Althusser, L. (1971) *Lenin and Philosophy and Other Essays*, New Left Books, London.

Amin, K. and Oppenheim, C. (1992) *Poverty in Black and White: Deprivation and ethnic minorities*, Child Poverty Action Group, London.

Anderson, B. (1983) *Imagined Communities*, Verso, London.

Anthias, F. (1995) 'Rex', in V. George and R. Page (eds) *Modern Thinkers on Welfare*, Prentice Hall/Harvester Wheatsheaf, Hemel Hempstead.

Aristotle (1981) *The Politics*, Penguin, Harmondsworth.

Baldock, J. and Ungerson, C. (1994) *Becoming Consumers of Community Care: Households within the mixed economy of care*, Community Care/Joseph Rowntree Foundation, York.

Balls, E. (1996) 'Tide is turning in attitudes to inequality', *The Guardian*, 29 July.

Barbalet, J. (1988) *Citizenship*, Open University Press, Milton Keynes.

Barclay, Sir Peter (1995) *Inquiry into Income and Wealth*, Vol. 1, Joseph Rowntree Foundation, York.

Barker, M. (1981) *The New Racism*, Junction Books, London.

Baudrillard, J. (1970) *Consumer Society* (*La Société de Consommation*), Gallimard, Paris.

Baudrillard, J. (1975) *The Mirror of Production*, Telos, St. Louis.

Bauman, Z. (1987) *Legislators and Interpreters: On modernity, postmodernity and intellectuals*, Polity Press, Cambridge.

Bauman, Z. (1988) *Freedom*, Open University Press, Buckingham.

Beck, U. (1992) *Risk Society: Towards a new modernity*, Sage, London.

Beck, U., Giddens, A. and Lash, S. (1994) *Reflexive Modernization*, Polity, Cambridge.

Becker, S. (1997) *Responding to Poverty: The politics of cash and care*, Longman, Harlow.

Berger, P. and Luckman, T. (1967) *The Social Construction of Reality*, Allen Lane, London.

Beveridge, W. (1942) *Social Insurance and Allied Services* ('The Beveridge Report'), Cmd. 6404, HMSO, London.

Blackwell, T. and Seabrook, J. (1985) *A World Still to Win: The reconstruction of the post-war working class*, Faber and Faber, London.

194   *References*

Blair, T. (1996) 'Battle for Britain', *The Guardian*, 29 January.
Bloch, A. (1996) 'Ethnic inequality and social security policy', in A. Walker and C. Walker (eds) *Britain Divided: The growth of social exclusion in the 1980s and 1990s*, Child Poverty Action Group, London.
Booth, C. (1902) *The Life and Labour of the People in London*, Macmillan, London.
Borrie, Sir Gordon (1994) *Social Justice: Strategies for national renewal* (The report of the Commission on Social Justice), IPPR/Vintage, London.
Bottomore, T. (1992) 'Citizenship and social class, forty years on', in T. H. Marshall and T. Bottomore, *Citizenship and Social Class*, Pluto, London.
Bottomore, T. and Rubel, M. (1963) *Karl Marx: Selected writings in sociology and social philosophy*, Penguin, Harmondsworth.
Bradshaw, J. and Chen, J. (1997) 'Poverty in the UK: A comparison with nineteen other countries', *Benefits*, Issue 18, January.
Bradshaw, J. and Holmes, H. (1989) *Living on the Edge: A study of the living standards of families on benefit in Tyne and Wear*, Tyneside Child Poverty Action Group, Newcastle.
Braverman, H. (1974) *Labour and Monopoly Capital*, Monthly Review Press, New York.
Brook, L., Hall, J. and Preston, I. (1996) 'Public spending and taxation', in R. Jowell, J. Curtice, A. Park, L. Brook and K. Thompson (eds) (1996) *British Social Attitudes, The 13th report*, Dartmouth, Aldershot.
Burrows, R. and Loader, B. (eds) (1994) *Towards a Post-Fordist Welfare State?*, Routledge, London.
Callender, C. (1996) 'Women and employment', in C. Hallett (ed.) *Women and Social Policy: An introduction*, Harvester Wheatsheaf, Hemel Hempstead.
Callinicos, A. (1993) *Race and Class*, Bookmarks, London.
Campbell, B. (1984) *Wigan Pier Revisited: Poverty and politics in the 1980s*, Virago, London.
Campbell, B. (1995) 'Old fogeys and angry young men', *Soundings*, Issue 1.
Campbell, T. (1983) *The Left and Rights: A conceptual analysis of the idea of socialist rights*, Routledge and Kegan Paul, London.
Carter, M. (1996) *Poverty and Prejudice*, Commission for Racial Equality and the Refugee Council, London.
Centre for Contemporary Cultural Studies (CCCS) (1982) *The Empire Strikes Back: Race and racism in '70s Britain*, Hutchinson, London.
Childs, M. (1936) *The Middle Way*, Yale University Press, New Haven.
Chiozza-Money, L. (1905) *Riches and Poverty*, Methuen, London.
Cohen, R., Coxall, J., Craig, G. and Sadiq-Sangster, A. (1992) *Hardship Britain: Being poor in the 1990s*, Child Poverty Action Group, London.
Culpitt, I. (1992) *Welfare and Citizenship: Beyond the crisis of the welfare state?*, Sage, London.
Dahrendorf, R. (1996) 'Citizenship and Social Class', in M. Bulmer and A. Rees (eds) *Citizenship Today: The contemporary relevance of T.H. Marshall*, UCL Press, London.
Davies, H. and Joshi, H. (1994) 'Sex, sharing and the distribution of income', *Journal of Social Policy*, Vol. 23, No. 3.
Davis, K. and Moore, W. (1945) 'Some principles of stratification', *American Sociological Review*, Vol. 10, No. 2.
Deacon, A. (ed.) (1996) *Stakeholder Welfare*, IEA, London.

Deakin, N. and Wright, A. (1995) 'Tawney', in V. George and R. Page (eds) *Modern Thinkers on Welfare*, Prentice Hall/Harvester Wheatsheaf, Hemel Hempstead.

Dean, H. (1991) *Social Security and Social Control*, Routledge, London.

Dean, H. (1992) 'Poverty discourse and the disempowerment of the poor', *Critical Social Policy*, Issue 35 (Vol. 12, No. 2).

Dean, H. (1993) 'Social security: The income maintenance business', in P. Taylor-Gooby and R. Lawson (eds) *Markets and Managers: New issues in the delivery of welfare*, Open University Press, Buckingham.

Dean, H. (1996) *Welfare, Law and Citizenship*, Prentice Hall/Harvester Wheatsheaf, Hemel Hempstead.

Dean, H. (forthcoming) 'Bodily metaphors and conceptions of social justice' in K. Ellis and H. Dean (eds) *Social Policy and the Body: Transitions in corporeal discourse*, Macmillan, Basingstoke.

Dean, H. and Melrose, M. (1996) 'Unravelling citizenship: The significance of social security benefit fraud', *Critical Social Policy*, Issue 48 (Vol. 16, No. 3).

Dean, H. and Melrose, M. (1997) 'Manageable Discord: Fraud and resistance in the social security system', *Social Policy and Administration*, Vol. 31, No. 2.

Dean, H. and Taylor-Gooby, P. (1992) *Dependency Culture: The explosion of a myth*, Harvester Wheatsheaf, Hemel Hempstead.

Department of Social Security (DSS) (1996a) *Households Below Average Income: A statistical analysis 1979–1993/94*, HMSO, London.

Department of Social Security (DSS) (1996b) *Family Resources Survey 1994/5*, HMSO, London.

Donzelot, J. (1980) *The Policing of Families*, Hutchinson, London.

Douglas, M. (1978) *Natural Symbols*, Penguin, Harmondsworth.

Doyal, L. and Gough, I. (1991) *A Theory of Human Need*, Macmillan, Basingstoke.

Dryzek, J. (1990) *Discursive Democracy: Politics, policy and political science*, Cambridge University Press, Cambridge.

Eide, A. (1997) 'Human rights and the elimination of poverty', in A. Kjønstad and J. Veit-Wilson (eds) *Law, Power and Poverty*, CROP/ISSL, Bergen.

Elias, N. (1978) *The Civilising Process: The history of manners*, Blackwell, Oxford.

Esping-Andersen, G. (1990) *The Three Worlds of Welfare Capitalism*, Polity, Cambridge.

Etzioni, A. (1994) *The Spirit of Community*, Touchstone, New York.

European Commission (EC) (1994a) *European Social Policy: A way forward for the Union*, European Commission, Luxembourg.

European Commission (EC) (1994b) *Growth, Competitiveness, Employment: The challenges and the ways forward into the 21st. Century*, European Commission, Luxembourg.

EUROSTAT (1977) *The Perception of Poverty in Europe*, European Commission, Luxembourg.

Featherstone, M. (1991) *Consumer Culture and Postmodernism*, Sage, London.

Field, F. (1996) *Making Welfare Work: Reconstructing welfare for the millennium*, Institute of Community Studies, London.

Fitzpatrick, P. (1992) *Mythology of Modern Law*, Routledge, London.

Forster, W. (1870) 'Speech introducing Elementary Education Bill, House of

Commons', in S. Maclure (ed.) (1986) *Educational Documents*, Methuen, London.

Foucault, M. (1977) *Discipline and Punish: The birth of the prison*, Penguin, Harmondsworth.

Foucault, M. (1981) *The History of Sexuality: An introduction*, Penguin, Harmondsworth.

Fraser, N. (1989) *Unruly Practices: Power, discourse and gender in contemporary social theory*, Polity, Cambridge.

Fraser, N. (1995) 'From redistribution to recognition: Dilemmas of justice in a 'post-modern age', *New Left Review*, No. 212.

Friedman, M. (1962) *Capitalism and Freedom*, University of Chicago Press, Chicago.

Funken, K. and Cooper, P. (eds) (1995) *Old and New Poverty: The challenge for reform*, Rivers Oram, London.

Galbraith, J.K. (1992) *The Culture of Contentment*, Penguin, Harmondsworth.

Gamble, A. (1988) *The Free Economy and the Strong State*, Macmillan, Basingstoke.

George, V. (1973) *Social Security and Society*, Routledge and Kegan Paul, London.

George, V. and Howards, I. (1991) *Poverty Amidst Affluence: Britain and the United States*, Edward Elgar, Aldershot.

George, V. and Wilding, P. (1985) *Ideology and Social Welfare*, Routledge and Kegan Paul, London.

George, V. and Wilding, P. (1994) *Welfare and Ideology*, Harvester Wheatsheaf, Hemel Hempstead.

Giddens, A. (1990) *The Consequences of Modernity*, Polity, Cambridge.

Giddens, A. (1991) *Modernity and Self-Identity: Self and society in the late modern age*, Polity, Cambridge.

Giddens, A. (1994) *Beyond Left and Right: The future of radical politics*, Polity, Cambridge.

Giddens, A. (1996) 'T. H. Marshall, the state and democracy', in M. Bulmer and A. Rees (eds) *Citizenship Today: The contemporary relevance of T. H. Marshall*, UCL Press, London.

Gilroy, P. (1992) 'The end of anti-racism', in J. Donald and A. Ratansi (eds) *'Race', Culture and Difference*, Sage, London.

Ginsburg, N. (1996) *The Future of the Welfare State*, professorial inaugural lecture, University of North London, 30 October.

Gittins, D. (1993) *The Family in Question: Changing households and familiar ideologies*, second edition, Macmillan, Basingstoke.

Glendinning, C. (1992) '"Community care": The financial consequences for women', in C. Glendinning and J. Millar (eds) *Women and Poverty in Britain: The 1990s*, Harvester Wheatsheaf, Hemel Hempstead.

Golding, P. (1985) 'Public attitudes to social exclusion: Some problems of measurement and analysis', in G. Room (ed.) *Beyond the Threshold: The measurement and analysis of social exclusion*, Policy Press, Bristol.

Golding, P. and Middleton, S. (1982) *Images of Welfare: Press and public attitudes to poverty*, Martin Robertson, Oxford.

Goldthorpe, J., Lockwood, D., Bechhofer, F. and Platt, J. (1969) *The Affluent Worker in the Class Structure*, Cambridge University Press, Cambridge.

Goldthorpe, J., Llewellyn, C. and Payne, C. (1980) and (1987) *Social Mobility and Class Structure in Modern Britain*, first and second editions, Oxford University Press, Oxford.

Goodman, A. and Webb, S. (1994) *For Richer, For Poorer: The changing distribution of income in the United Kingdom 1961–1991*, Institute of Fiscal Studies, London.

Goodwin, B. (1987) *Using Political Ideas*, second edition, Wiley, Chichester.

Gordon, D. and Pantazis, C. (eds) (1997) *Breadline Britain in the 1990s*, Ashgate, Aldershot.

Gordon, P. (1989) *Citizenship for Some? Race and government policy 1979–1989*, Runnymede Trust, London.

Gordon, P. and Rosenburg, D. (1989) *Daily Racism: The press and black people in Britain*, Runnymede Trust, London.

Gough, I. (1979) *The Political Economy of the Welfare State*, Macmillan, London and Basingstoke.

Gould, A. (1993) 'The end of the middle way? The Swedish welfare state in crisis' in C. Jones (ed.) *New Perspectives on the Welfare State in Europe*, Routledge, London.

Gould, A. (1996) 'Sweden: The last bastion of social democracy', in V. George and P. Taylor-Gooby (eds) *European Welfare Policy: Squaring the welfare circle*, Macmillan, Basingstoke.

Graham, H. (1987) 'Being poor: Perceptions of coping strategies of lone-mothers', in J. Brannen and G. Wilson (eds) *Give and Take in Families*, Allen and Unwin, London.

Gramsci, A. (1971) *Prison Notebooks*, Lawrence and Wishart, London.

Gray, J. (1995) 'Hollowing out the core', *The Guardian*, 8 March.

Habermas, J. (1976) 'Systematically distorted communication', in P. Connerton (ed.) *Critical Theory*, Penguin, Harmondsworth.

Habermas, J. (1986) *Autonomy and Solidarity: Interviews with Jürgen Habermas*, ed. P. Dews, Verso, London.

Hakim, C. (1993) 'The myth of rising female employment work', *Employment and Society*, Vol. 7, No. 1.

Hall, S. (1980) 'Race, articulation and societies structured in dominance', in UNESCO *Sociological Theories: Race and colonialism*, UNESCO, Paris.

Hall, S. (1992) 'New ethnicities', in J. Donald and A. Ratansi (eds) *'Race', Culture and Difference*, Sage, London.

Hall, S. and Held, D. (1989) 'Citizens and citizenship' in S. Hall and M. Jacques (eds) *New Times: The changing face of politics in the 1990s*, Lawrence and Wishart, London.

Hall, S. and Jacques, M. (eds) (1989) *New Times: The changing face of politics in the 1990s*, Lawrence and Wishart, London.

Hamnett, C. (1989) 'Consumption and class in contemporary Britain', in C. Hamnett, L. McDowell, P. Sarre (eds) *Restructuring Britain: The changing social structure*, Sage, London.

Haraway, D. (1991) *Simians, Cyborgs and Women: The reinvention of nature*, Routledge, London.

Harrington, M. (1962) *The Other America: Poverty in the United States*, Macmillan, New York.

Harrison, M. (1991) 'Citizenship, consumption and rights: A comment on B. S. Turner's theory of citizenship', *Sociology*, Vol. 25, No. 2.

Hartman, P. and Husband, C. (1974) *Racism and the Mass Media*, Davis Poynter, London.

Hayek, F. (1976) *Law, Legislation and Liberty, Vol. 2: The mirage of social justice*, Routledge and Kegan Paul, London.

Hegel, G. (1821) *Elements of the Philosophy of Rights*, 1991 edition, edited by A. Wood, Cambridge University Press, Cambridge.

Held, D. (1987) *Models of Democracy*, Polity, Cambridge.

Hewitt, M. (1992) *Welfare, Ideology and Need*, Harvester Wheatsheaf, Hemel Hempstead.

Hills, J. (1995) *Inquiry into Income and Wealth*, Vol. 2, Joseph Rowntree Foundation, York.

Hirsch, F. (1977) *Social Limits to Growth*, Routledge and Kegan Paul, London.

Hirst, P. (1994) *Associative Democracy: New forms of economic and social governance*, Blackwell, Oxford.

Hobbes, T. (1651) *Leviathan*, 1968 edition edited by C. MacPherson, Penguin, Harmondsworth.

Hobsbawm, E. (1962) *The Age of Revolution 1789–1848*, Mentor, New York.

Humm, M. (1992) *Feminisms: A reader*, Harvester Wheatsheaf, Hemel Hempstead.

Hurd, D. (1989) 'Freedom will flourish where citizens accept responsibilities', *Independent*, 13 September.

Hutton, W. (1996) *The State We're In*, revised edition, Vintage, London.

James, S. (1992) 'The good-enough citizen: Female citizenship and independence', in G. Bock and S. James (eds) *Beyond Equality and Difference*, Routledge, London.

James, W. (1992) 'Migration, racism and identity: The Caribbean experience in Britain', *New Left Review*, No. 193.

Jenkins, S. (1991) 'Poverty measurement and the within household distribution: Agenda for action', *Journal of Social Policy*, Vol. 20, No. 4.

Jessop, B. (1994) 'The transition to post-Fordism and the Schumpeterian workfare state', in R. Burrows and B. Loader (eds) *Towards a Post-Fordist Welfare State?*, Routledge, London.

Johnson, N. (1990) *Reconstructing the Welfare State: A decade of change, 1980–1990*, Harvester Wheatsheaf, Hemel Hempstead.

Jones, T. (1993) *Britain's Ethnic Minorities*, Policy Studies Institute, London.

Jordan, B. (1993) 'Framing claims and weapons of the weak', in G. Drover and P. Kerans (eds) *New Approaches to Welfare Theory*, Edward Elgar, Aldershot.

Jordan, B. (1996) *A Theory of Poverty and Social Exclusion*, Polity, Cambridge.

Joshi, H. (1992) 'The cost of caring', in C. Glendinning and J. Millar (eds) *Women and Poverty in Britain: The 1990s*, Harvester Wheatsheaf, Hemel Hempstead.

Jowell, R. and Airey, C. (1984) *British Social Attitudes: The 1984 report*, Gower, Aldershot.

Jowell, R., Witherspoon, S. and Brook, L. (eds) (1990) *British Social Attitudes: The 7th report*, Gower, Aldershot.

Jowell, R., Curtice, J., Park, A., Brook, L. and Thompson, K. (eds) (1996) *British Social Attitudes: The 13th report*, Dartmouth, Aldershot.

Keegan, V. (1996) 'Highway robbery by the super-rich', *The Guardian*, 22 July.

Kemp, P. and Wall, D. (1990) *A Green Manifesto for the 1990s*, Penguin, Harmondsworth.

Kempson, E. (1996) *Life on a Low Income*, Joseph Rowntree Foundation, York.

Kempson, E., Bryson, A. and Rowlingson, K. (1994) *Hard Times? How poor families make ends meet*, Policy Studies Institute, London.

Kiernan, K. (1992) 'Men and women at work and at home', in R. Jowell *et al* (eds) *British Social Attitudes: The 9th report*, SCPR/Gower, Aldershot.

Kincaid, J. (1975) *Poverty and Inequality in Britain: A study of social security and taxation*, revised edition, Penguin, Harmondsworth.

Klein, R. (1993) 'O'Goffe's tale', in C. Jones (ed.) *New Perspectives on the Welfare State in Europe*, Routledge, London.

Labour Party (1997) *New Labour: Because Britain deserves better*, General Election Manifesto, London.

Lacan, J. (1977) *Ecrits*, translated by Alan Sheridan, Tavistock, London.

Laclau, E. and Mouffe, C. (1985) *Hegemony and Socialist Strategy*, Verso, London.

Land, H. (1975) 'The introduction of family allowances: An act of historic justice?', in P. Hall, H. Land, R. Parker, A. Webb *Change, Choice and Conflict in Social Policy*, Heinemann, London.

Law, I. (1996) *Racism, Ethnicity and Social Policy*, Prentice Hall/Harvester Wheatsheaf, Hemel Hempstead.

LeGrand, J. (1982) *The Strategy of Equality*, Allen and Unwin, London.

LeGrand, J. (1990) 'The state of welfare', in J. Hills (ed.) *The State of Welfare: The welfare state in Britain since 1974*, Clarendon, Oxford.

Levitas, R. (1996) 'The concept of social exclusion and the new Durkheimian hegemony', *Critical Social Policy*, Issue 46 (Vol. 16, No. 2).

Lewis, J. and Piachaud, D. (1992) 'Women and poverty in the twentieth century', in C. Glendinning and J. Millar (eds) *Women and Poverty in Britain: The 1990s*, Harvester Wheatsheaf, Hemel-Hempstead.

Lilley, P. (1996) Letter to Paul Coggins, Chair of the UK International Year Against Poverty Coalition, 15 March.

Lis, C. and Soly, H. (1979) *Poverty and Capitalism in Pre-Industrial Europe*, Harvester, Brighton.

Lister, R. (1990a) *The Exclusive Society: Citizenship and the poor*, Child Poverty Action Group, London.

Lister, R. (1990b) 'Women, economic dependency and citizenship', *Journal of Social Policy*, Vol. 19, No. 4.

Lister, R. (1994) '"She has other duties": Women, citizenship and social security', in S. Baldwin and J. Falkingham (eds) *Social Security and Social Change*, Harvester Wheatsheaf, Hemel Hempstead.

Lister, R. (1997) *Citizenship: Feminist perspectives*, Macmillan, Basingstoke.

Lorimer, D. (1978) *Colour, Class and the Victorians: English attitudes to the negro in the mid-nineteenth century*, Leicester University Press, Leicester.

Mack, J. and Lansley, S. (1985) *Poor Britain*, Allen and Unwin, London.
Mann, K. (1994) 'Watching the defectives: Observers of the underclass in the USA, Britain and Australia', *Critical Social Policy*, Issue 41, (Vol. 14, No. 2).
Mann, M. (1987) 'Ruling class strategies and citizenship', *Sociology*, Vol. 21, No. 3.
Manning, N. (ed.) (1985) *Social Problems and Welfare Ideology*, Gower, Aldershot.
Marcuse, H. (1964) *One-Dimensional Man*, Routledge and Kegan Paul, London.
Marshall, G. (1997) *Repositioning Class: Social inequality in industrial societies*, Sage, London.
Marshall, G., Newby, H., Rose, D. and Vogler, C. (1988) *Social Class in Modern Britain*, Hutchinson, London.
Marshall, T.H. (1950) 'Citizenship and Social Class', in T.H. Marshall and T. Bottomore (1992) *Citizenship and Social Class*, Pluto, London.
Marshall, T.H. (1981) *The Right to Welfare and Other Essays*, Heinemann, London.
Marx, K. (1847) *Poverty of Philosophy*, reprinted in Marx, K. and Engels, F. (1976) *Collected Works*, V-VI, Lawrence and Wishart, London.
Marx, K. and Engels, F. (1848) *The Communist Manifesto*, 1970 Merit Pamphlet, New York.
Marx, K. (1867) *Capital, Volume I*, 1970 edition, Lawrence and Wishart, London.
Marx, K. (1894) *Capital, Volume III*, 1959 edition, Lawrence and Wishart, London.
Mayhew, H. (1861) *London Labour and the London Poor* (4 volumes), Charles Griffin and Co., London.
McLaughlin, E. (1991) *Social Security and Community Care: The case of invalid care allowance*, Department of Social Security, HMSO, London.
Mead, L. (1986) *Beyond Entitlement: The social obligations of citizenship*, Free Press, New York.
Melrose, M. (1996) 'Enticing subjects and disembodied objects', in H. Dean (ed.) *Ethics and Social Policy Research*, University of Luton Press/ Social Policy Association, Luton.
Merton, R. (1957) *Social Theory and Social Structure*, Glencoe Free Press, Illinois.
Miles, R. (1989) *Racism*, Routledge, London.
Miles, R. (1993) *Racism After 'Race Relations'*, Routledge, London.
Mishra, R. (1984) *The Welfare State in Crisis*, Harvester Wheatsheaf, Hemel Hempstead.
Mitchell, M. and Russell, D. (1994) 'Race, citizenship and "Fortress Europe"', in P. Brown and R. Crompton (eds) *Economic Restructuring and Social Exclusion*, University College of London Press, London.
Modood, T. (1994) *Racial Equality: Colour, culture and justice*, Commission on Social Justice Issue Paper No. 5, IPPR, London.
Modood, T., Berthoud, R., Lakey, J., Nazrun, J., Smith, P., Virdee, S. and Beishon, S. (1997) *Ethnic Minorities in Britain*, Policy Studies Institute, London.

Moore, J. (1989) 'The end of the line for poverty', speech to Greater London Conservative Party constituencies meeting, 11 May.

Murray, C. (1984) *Losing Ground: American social policy 1950–1980*, Basic Books, New York.

National Association of Citizens' Advice Bureaux (NACAB) (1991) *Barriers to Benefit*, NACAB, London.

Oakley, A. (1981) *Subject Women*, Penguin, Harmondsworth.

O'Connor, J. (1973) *Fiscal Crisis of the State*, St. Martins, New York.

Offe, C. (1982) 'Some contradictions of the modern welfare state', *Critical Social Policy*, Vol. 2, No. 2.

Offe, C. (1984) *Contradictions of the Welfare State*, MIT Press, Cambridge, Mass.

Offe, C. (1993) 'Interdependence, difference and limited state capacity', in G. Drover and P. Kerans (eds) *New Approaches to Welfare Theory*, Edward Elgar, Aldershot.

Offe, C. (1996) *Modernity and the State: East, West*, Polity, Cambridge.

Office for National Statistics (ONS) (1996) *Social Focus on Ethnic Minorities*, HMSO, London.

Oppenheim, C. and Harker, L. (1996) *Poverty: The facts*, third edition, Child Poverty Action Group, London.

Orshansky, M. (1969) 'How poverty is measured', *Monthly Labour Review*, Vol. 92, No. 2.

Orwell, G. (1937) *The Road to Wigan Pier*, 1962 edition, Penguin, Harmondsworth.

Page, R. (1996) *Altruism and the Welfare State*, Avebury, Aldershot.

Pahl, J. (1989) *Money and Marriage*, Macmillan, Basingstoke.

Pahl, R. (1995) *After Success:* Fin-de-siécle *anxiety and identity*, Polity, Cambridge.

Pakulski, J. (1997) 'Cultural citizenship', *Citizenship Studies*, Vol. 1, No. 1.

Pakulski, J. and Waters, M. (1996) *The Death of Class*, Sage, London.

Papadakis, E. and Taylor-Gooby, P. (1987) *The Private Provision of Public Welfare*, Wheatsheaf, Brighton.

Parkin, F. (1979) *Marxism and Class Theory: A bourgeois critique*, Tavistock, London.

Pascall, G. (1986) *Social Policy: A feminist analysis*, Tavistock, London.

Pashukanis, E. (1978) *General Theory of Law and Marxism*, Ink Links, London.

Pateman, C. (1989) *The Disorder of Women*, Polity, Cambridge.

Peden, G. (1991) *British Economic and Social Policy: Lloyd George to Margaret Thatcher*, second edition, Philip Allen, Hemel Hempstead.

Pen, J. (1971) 'A parade of dwarfs (and a few giants)', in T. Preston (ed.) *Income Distribution*, Penguin, Harmondsworth.

Piachaud, D. (1981) 'Peter Townsend and the Holy Grail', *New Society*, 9 September.

Plant, R., Lesser, H., Taylor-Gooby, P. (1980) *Political Philosophy and Social Welfare*, Routledge and Kegan Paul, London.

Powell, M. (1995) 'The struggle for equality revisited', *Journal of Social Policy*, Vol. 24, No. 2.

Rawls, J. (1972) *A Theory of Justice*, Oxford University Press, Oxford.

Rees, A. (1995) 'The other T.H. Marshall', *Journal of Social Policy*, Vol. 24, No. 3.

Rentoul, J. (1989) *Me and Mine: The triumph of the new individualism?*, Unwin Hyman, London.

Rex, J. (1991) 'The political sociology of a multicultural society', *Ghandian Perspectives*, Vol. 4, No. 1.

Roche, M. (1992) *Rethinking Citizenship: Welfare, ideology and change in modern society*, Polity, Cambridge.

Room, G. (ed.) (1995) *Beyond the Threshold: The measurement and analysis of social exclusion*, Policy Press, Bristol.

Rousseau, J. (1762) *The Social Contract*, 1968 edition, Penguin, Harmondsworth.

Rowntree, B. (1901) *Poverty: A study of town life*, Macmillan, London.

Runciman, W.B. (1966) *Relative Deprivation and Social Justice*, Routledge and Kegan Paul, London.

Rutherford, J. (1990) 'A place called home', in J. Rutherford (ed.) *Identity: Community, culture, difference*, Lawrence and Wishart, London.

Sainsbury, D. (1994) 'Introduction', in D. Sainsbury (ed.) *Gendering Welfare States*, Sage, London.

Sarre, P. (1989) 'Recomposition of the class structure' in Hamnett, C., McDowell, L. and Sarre, P. (eds) *The Changing Social Structure*, Sage, London.

Saunders, P. (1984) 'Beyond housing classes: The sociological significance of private property rights in means of consumption', *International Journal of Urban and Regional Research*, Vol. 8, No. 2.

Saunders, P. (1990) *A Nation of Homeowners*, Unwin Hyman, London.

Schumpeter, J. (1942) *Capitalism, Socialism and Democracy*, 1976 edition, Allen and Unwin, London.

Scott, H. (1984) *Working Your Way to the Bottom: The feminisation of poverty*, Pandora Press, London.

Scott, J. (1994) *Poverty and Wealth: Citizenship, deprivation and privilege*, Longman, Harlow.

Seabrook, J. (1985) *Landscapes of Poverty*, Blackwell, Oxford.

Seldon, A. (1990) *Capitalism*, Blackwell, Oxford.

Silburn, R. (1995) 'Beveridge', in V. George and R. Page (eds) *Modern Thinkers on Welfare*, Prentice Hall/Harvester Wheatsheaf, Hemel Hempstead.

Simpson, R. (1993) 'Fortress Europe?', in R. Simpson and R. Walker (eds) *Europe: For richer or poorer*, Child Poverty Action Group, London.

Sivanandan, A. (1989) 'New circuits of imperialism', *Race and Class*, Vol. 30, No. 4.

Smart, C. (1989) *Feminism and the Power of Law*, Routledge, London.

Solomos, J. (1989) *Race and Racism in Contemporary Britain*, Macmillan, Basingstoke.

Spencer, P. (1996) 'Reactions to a flexible labour market', in R. Jowell, et al (eds) *British Social Attitudes: The 13th report*, Dartmouth, Aldershot.

Spender, D. (ed.) (1981) *Men's Studies Modified*, Pergamon, Oxford.

Spicker, P. (1984) *Stigma and Social Welfare*, Croom Helm, Beckenham.

Spicker, P. (1988) *Principles of Social Welfare*, Routledge, London.

Spicker, P. (1991) 'Solidarity', in G. Room (ed.) *Towards a European Welfare State?* SAUS, Bristol.

Squires, P. (1990) *Anti-Social Policy: Welfare, ideology and the disciplinary state*, Harvester Wheatsheaf, Hemel Hempstead.

Sydie, R. (1987) *Natural Women, Cultured Men: A feminist critique of sociological theory*, Open University Press, Milton Keynes.

Tawney, R. (1913) 'Poverty as an industrial problem', inaugural lecture, in *Memoranda on the Problems of Poverty*, Vol. 2, William Morris Press, London.

Tawney, R. (1931) *Equality*, Allen and Unwin, London.

Taylor-Gooby, P. (1990) 'Social welfare: The unkindest cuts', in R. Jowell, S. Witherspoon and L. Brook, (eds) *British Social Attitudes: The 7th report*, Gower, Aldershot.

Taylor-Gooby, P. (1991) *Social Change, Social Welfare and Social Science*, Harvester Wheatsheaf, Hemel Hempstead.

Taylor-Gooby, P. (1994a) 'Postmodernism and social policy: A great leap backwards?', *Journal of Social Policy*, Vol. 23, No. 3.

Taylor-Gooby, P. (1994b) 'Welfare outside the state', in R. Jowell, J. Curtice, L. Brook, and D. Ahrendt (eds) *British Social Attitudes: The 11th report*, Dartmouth, Aldershot.

Taylor-Gooby, P. (1995) 'Comfortable, marginal and excluded', in R. Jowell, J. Curtice, A. Park, L. Brook and D. Ahrendt (eds) *British Social Attitudes: The 12th report*, Dartmouth, Aldershot.

Taylor-Gooby, P. (1997) 'In defence of second-best theory: State, class and capital in social policy', *Journal of Social Policy*, Vol. 26, No. 2.

Taylor-Gooby, P. and Dale, J. (1981) *Social Theory and Social Welfare*, Arnold, London.

Thane, P. (1982) *Foundations of the Welfare State*, Longman, Harlow.

Thomas, R. (1997) 'Wife and mother beyond price', *The Guardian*, 19 May.

Thompson, E.P. (1968) *The Making of the English Working Class*, Penguin, Harmondsworth.

Townsend, P. (1979) *Poverty in the United Kingdom*, Penguin, Harmondsworth.

Townsend, P. (1993) *The International Analysis of Poverty*, Harvester Wheatsheaf, Hemel Hempstead.

Turner, B. (1986) *Citizenship and Capitalism: The debate over reformism*, Allen and Unwin, London.

Turner, B. (1990) 'Outline of a theory of citizenship', *Sociology*, Vol. 24, No. 2.

Turner, B. (1991) 'Prolegomena to general theory of social order', position paper for ESRC workshop, *Citizenship, Civil Society and Social Cohesion*, London, 23 February.

Turner, B. (1997) 'Citizenship studies: A general theory', *Citizenship Studies*, Vol. 1, No. 1.

Twine, F. (1994) *Citizenship and Social Rights: The interdependence of self and society*, Sage, London.

United Nations (1996) *The Human Development Report*, Oxford University Press, Oxford.

Walker, A. (1997) 'Introduction: The strategy of inequality', in A. Walker and C. Walker (eds) *Britain Divided: The growth of social exclusion in the 1980s and 1990s*, Child Poverty Action Group, London.

Walker, R. (1991) *Thinking about Workfare: Evidence from the USA*, HMSO, London.

Walker, R. (1995) 'The dynamics of poverty and social exclusion', in G. Room (ed.) *Beyond the Threshold: The measurement and analysis of social exclusion*, Policy Press, Bristol.

Walter, J. A. (1979) *A Long Way from Home: A sociological exploration of contemporary idolatry*, Paternoster Press, Exeter.

Warde, A. (1994) 'Consumers, consumption and post-Fordism', in R. Burrows and B. Loader (eds) *Towards a Post-Fordist Welfare State*, Routledge, London.

Webb, B. and S. (1909) *Break Up the Poor Law!* (Part I of the Minority Report of the Royal Commission on the Poor Laws), Fabian Society, London.

Webb, S. (1993) 'Women's incomes: Past, present and prospects', *Fiscal Studies*, Vol. 14, No. 4.

Whiteside, N. (1995) 'Employment policy: A chronicle of decline?', in D. Gladstone (ed.) *British Social Welfare: Past, present and future*, UCL Press, London.

Williams, F. (1989) *Social Policy: A critical introduction*, Polity, Cambridge.

Williams, F. (1992) 'Somewhere over the rainbow: Universality and diversity in social policy' in Manning, N. and Page, R. (eds) *Social Policy Review 4*, Social Policy Association, Canterbury.

Williams, F. with Pillinger, J. (1996) *New Thinking on Social Policy Research into Inequality, Social Exclusion and Poverty* (an amended version of a paper presented to the ESRC seminar on Social Welfare Systems, London, February 1995 and at the annual conference of the Social Policy Association, Sheffield, July, 1995), Centre for the Analysis of Social Policy, Bath.

Wilson, W. (1987) *The Truly Disadvantaged: The underclass, the ghetto and public policy*, Chicago University Press, Chicago.

Wollstonecraft, M. (1792) *Vindication of the Rights of Women*, 1982 edition, Penguin, Harmondsworth.

Wood, E. Meiksins (1986) *The Retreat from Class: A new 'true' socialism*, Verso, London.

Wood, E. Meiksins (1995) *Democracy Against Capitalism: Renewing historical materialism*, Cambridge University Press, Cambridge.

Wright, E. (1985) *Classes*, Verso, London.

Young, K. (1992) 'Class, race and opportunity', in R. Jowell, *et al*, *British Social Attitudes: The 9th report*, SPCR/Gower, Aldershot.

Yuval-Davis, N. (1992) 'Fundamentalism, multiculturalism and women in Britain', in J. Donald and A. Ratansi (eds) *'Race', Culture and Difference*, Sage, London.

Name Index

Subject Index

Note: emboldened page numbers denote illustrations.

209